D0710659

The Unappropriated People

Jerome S. Handler

THE UNAPPROPRIATED PEOPLE: FREEDMEN IN THE SLAVE SOCIETY OF BARBADOS

The Johns Hopkins University Press
Baltimore and London

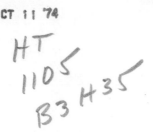
This book has been brought to publication with the generous assistance
of the Andrew W. Mellon Foundation.

The Johns Hopkins University Press, Baltimore, Maryland 21218
The Johns Hopkins University Press Ltd., London

Library of Congress Catalog Card Number 73-18489
ISBN 0-8018-1565-7

Library of Congress Cataloging in Publication data will be
found on the last printed page of this book.

For Henia

CONTENTS

Figures

ACKNOWLEDGMENTS

This book is a considerably expanded and modified version of a manuscript, "The Freedman in Barbados Slave Society," written in 1970, and a shorter published paper derived from that manuscript.[1] Both of these essays were co-authored with Arnold A. Sio, and a brief acknowledgment of this kind cannot do full justice to Sio for his role in the collaboration and the insights he contributed to my understanding of Barbadian slave society and its freedman population. In fact, it has sometimes been difficult to sort out my own views from his, but I, of course, must accept full responsibility for whatever shortcomings appear in the following pages.

In writing this book, I re-analyzed notes from primary sources used in the earlier essays, employed new sources of data, and acquired additional data that were not available at the time the essays were written. The re-examination of previously collected materials, as well as the addition of new data, sometimes required corrections of factual statements and statistics that appeared in the essays, as well as different interpretations of various events and social phenomena. In general, then, although the present work to some extent overlaps the earlier essays, it treats a variety of topics in much greater detail, discusses a number of issues and topics that were not considered in the essays, and, where the same topics and issues are discussed, reveals variation in factual detail and interpretation.

Most of the data for this book were collected between 1965 and 1970 (and some during the winter of 1971/72) in the course of a study of the social and cultural life of Barbados's slave population in the seventeenth, eighteenth, and nineteenth centuries.[2] This research was largely made

[1]Jerome S. Handler and Arnold A. Sio, "Barbados," in *Neither Slave Nor Free: The Freedman of African Descent in the Slave Societies of the New World*, ed. David W. Cohen and Jack P. Greene (Baltimore: The Johns Hopkins University Press, 1972), pp. 214–57.

[2]This research is described in Jerome S. Handler, "African Immigrants and Their Descendants in Barbados: The Social and Cultural Life of a West Indies Slave Population, 1640–1834," *American Philosophical Society, Yearbook 1969* (Philadelphia, 1970), pp. 384–86; and *idem*, "An Archaeological Investigation of the Domestic Life of Plantation Slaves in Barbados," *JBMHS*, 34 (1972): 64–72.

possible through grants from the National Science Foundation (GS-1154 and GS-30993), National Institute of Mental Health (MH 11434-01), American Philosophical Society (Johnson Fund, no. 750), Wenner-Gren Foundation for Anthropological Research (no. 2776), and a fellowship from the National Endowment for the Humanities (H69-1-138).

A good portion of the book was written while I was a Visiting Professor at Colgate University in 1971-72. I am especially grateful to my colleagues and students at Colgate for the congenial personal and intellectual atmosphere they provided, and to the Colgate University Research Council for a grant which permitted the typing of the final manuscript.

By inviting me to a conference on freedmen in New World slave societies, held at The Johns Hopkins University in April 1970, Jack P. Greene stimulated my interest in Barbadian freedmen, and the moral and practical encouragement given by both Greene and David W. Cohen was instrumental in leading to the expansion of the original essay into the present work. Sidney W. Mintz, H. A. Vaughan, and Michael Chandler read that essay and offered helpful suggestions for its improvement.

In the later phases of research, assistance was provided by Todd F. Brady, who gathered information from the wills and estate inventories located in the Barbados Department of Archives and who provided a preliminary statistical analysis of these materials which I found especially useful during the writing of Chapter 6; Darla Schecter took time out from other projects in Barbados to transcribe wills and to gather statistical information from manumission deeds; and Jane Malone helped in collecting manumission data from the *Parliamentary Papers*. I am also especially indebted to Arnold A. Sio for making available to me his notes on various manuscripts in the Barbados Department of Archives and the Public Record Office in London.

Sheila Duncker kindly gave me permission to duplicate her unpublished thesis on Jamaican freedmen, and I am thankful to Barry W. Higman for permission to cite his thesis on the slave population and economy of that island.

Jane Malone and Doris Vaughan bravely and cheerfully endured some badly scarred early drafts and managed to type a clean final manuscript. Finally, an immeasurable debt is owed Eugenia Handler, who, with great patience, understanding, and sensitivity, carefully read all drafts of the manuscript, offered countless suggestions for its improvement, and whose relentless criticism often made me wonder if the last word was ever to be written.

J.S.H.

NOTE ON SOURCES

No bibliography is appended to this book, but the primary sources upon which it is based are described in Jerome S. Handler, *A Guide to Source Materials for the Study of Barbados History, 1627-1834* (Carbondale: Southern Illinois University Press, 1971), which also discusses in detail the archival repositories and provides library locations for the printed works. In the present work, complete citations on all published materials and unpublished theses appear the first time they are mentioned in each chapter and by author's last name and short title thereafter. The following abbreviations are employed in the footnotes for items cited most frequently:

MANUSCRIPT COLLECTIONS AND ARCHIVAL REPOSITORIES

BDA	Barbados Department of Archives
BM	British Museum, London
BPL	Barbados Public Library
CMSA	Church Missionary Society Archives, London
CO	Colonial Office Group, Public Record Office, London
LPL	Lambeth Palace Library, London
MMSA	Methodist Missionary Society Archives, London
PRO	Public Record Office, London
RCS	Royal Commonwealth Society Library, London
SPGFP	Society for the Propagation of the Gospel in Foreign Parts, London
SRO	Scottish Record Office, Edinburgh
ULL	University of London Library
USPGA	United Society for the Propagation of the Gospel Archives, London
WIC	West India Committee Library, London

PUBLICATIONS

CSPCS   *Calendar of State Papers, Colonial Series: America and the*
          West Indies (London)
JBMHS   *Journal of the Barbados Museum and Historical Society*
          (Bridgetown)
PP   *Parliamentary Papers* (London)

The Unappropriated People

There is, however, a third description of people from whom I am more suspicious of evil than from either the whites or slaves: these are the Black and Coloured people who are not slaves, and yet whom I cannot bring myself to call free. I think *unappropriated people* would be a more proper denomination for them, for though not the property of other individuals they do not enjoy the shadow of any civil right.—Governor Seaforth to Lord Hobart, June 6, 1802

INTRODUCTION

From an early period of its history, the slave society in the southeastern Caribbean island of Barbados conformed to a wider West Indian model of essentially two broad social strata. Although each was internally segmented (albeit by different criteria), there was, on the one hand, a minority population of European birth or descent, which contained an even smaller group that controlled the island's means of production, state organization, and other national institutions; and, on the other hand, a slave population, which, with minor exceptions,[1] was composed of persons of African descent. Gradually, over the years, a third group emerged which was comprised of persons whose racial ancestry was mixed or solely Negroid, but whose legal status was that of free persons. Whether free-born or manumitted from slavery, persons in this third group were accorded a variety of privileges and rights which were not extended to slaves, but because of their racial ancestry they were denied other privileges and rights which white society reserved for itself. These freedmen are the subject of this book.

In the preface to her excellent and now classic study of the Leeward Islands, Elsa Goveia defined the "slave society" as "the whole community based on slavery, including masters and freedmen as well as slaves." Her objectives were

> to study the political, economic, and social organization of this society and the interrelationships of its component groups and to investigate how it was affected by its dependence on the institution of slavery. I have tried to identify the basic principles which held the white masters, coloured freedmen, and Negro slaves together as a community, and to trace the influence of these principles on the relations between the

---

[1]See Jerome S. Handler, "The Amerindian Slave Population of Barbados in the Seventeenth and Early Eighteenth Centuries," *Caribbean Studies*, 8 (1969): 38–64; see also *idem*, "Aspects of Amerindian Ethnography in 17th Century Barbados," *ibid.*, 9 (1970): 50–72.

Negro slave and his white master, which largely determined the form and content of the society.[2]

I have quoted Goveia's description of the aims of her study in order to clarify what the present work on Barbadian freedmen does and does not attempt to accomplish. The literature on the British Caribbean lacks a holistic description and analysis of Barbadian slave society which approaches the scope of Goveia's work on the Leewards or Brathwaite's recent study of Jamaica.[3] The present study, however, focuses on the freedmen as one segment of the slave society. It is concerned with describing and analyzing their legal and social status, demographic and sociocultural attributes, and especially the nature and degree of their participation in the island's national institutions. Although these interests must also involve considerations of the wider societal context, I have made no elaborate attempt to probe this context or to detail the nature of the island's institutions or other major population segments. I have considered the relationship of freedmen to whites and slaves, but largely from the perspective of how this relationship appeared to affect the freedmen. In a similar manner, external historical forces and insular social, political, and economic conditions and structural characteristics are briefly treated or alluded to only when they help clarify the status, activities, and aspirations of the freedman population per se. Thus, the present work does not pretend to be a study of the "slave society" as defined by Goveia, even though some crucial elements of this society inevitably emerge as one explores the position of freedmen within it.

Aspects of the freedman's life and involvement in Barbadian society have been treated to varying degrees in a few modern publications,[4] but, aside from a recent article by this author and Arnold A. Sio,[5] there have been no scholarly attempts to provide a comprehensive and systematic description of this population. Indeed, although recent major studies of British Caribbean slave societies, such as those by Goveia and Brathwaite, discuss freedmen, the discussions form part of wider concerns with the totality of the slave society and are largely confined to the late eighteenth and early nineteenth centuries. With the exception of a few modern

[2]Elsa V. Goveia, *Slave Society in the British Leeward Islands at the End of the Eighteenth Century* (New Haven: Yale University Press, 1965), p. vii.

[3]Edward Brathwaite, *The Development of Creole Society in Jamaica, 1770–1820* (London: Oxford University Press, 1971).

[4]See H. A. Vaughan, "Samuel Prescod: The Birth of a Hero," *New World Quarterly*, 3 (1966): 55–60; Claude Levy, "Barbados: The Last Years of Slavery, 1823–1833," *Journal of Negro History*, 44 (1959): 308–45; Neville Hall, "The Judicial System of a Plantation Society— Barbados on the Eve of Emancipation," in *Colloque d'Histoire Antillaise: Le Passage de la Société Esclavagiste a la Société post-Esclavagiste aux Antilles au XIXe Siècle* (Pointe-à-Pitre, Guadeloupe, 1969), pp. 38–70.

[5]Jerome S. Handler and Arnold A. Sio, "Barbados," in *Neither Slave Nor Free: The Freedman of African Descent in the Slave Societies of the New World*, ed. David W. Cohen and Jack P. Greene (Baltimore: The Johns Hopkins University Press, 1972), pp. 214–57.

works which focus exclusively on Jamaica, specialized studies of British West Indian freedman populations are generally lacking.[6] The present study, then, not only provides a detailed exposition of a segment of Barbadian slave society but also helps fill a gap in the literature on Caribbean—particularly British West Indian—slave societies; in so doing, it provides materials for the comparative study of these societies as well as of freedman populations in the New World.

This book focuses upon the period from the end of the eighteenth century to 1834. Although freedmen made their appearance early in Barbados's history, very little is known about their existence in the seventeenth century, and they were relatively few in number until the end of the eighteenth. The small number of freedmen in the earlier periods is reflected by the scarcity of references to them in the sources. Hence, although there is varying discussion of these earlier periods in the present study, the major period considered includes the pre-emancipation decades of the nineteenth century. Not only are the source materials richer for these years, but the period was also a crucial one for the freedman (indeed, for the society as a whole): his population grew significantly, his participation in commercial activities and the skilled trades greatly expanded, wealth and property holdings became more widespread, communal activities and associations increased, and major changes in his civil status culminated in the formal removal of all legal disabilities a few years before emancipation.

After the termination of slavery, Barbados, along with other British West Indian territories (with the exception of Antigua), passed through four years of what is commonly known as the Apprenticeship period. Despite its close resemblance to slavery, and the continued functioning of major pre-emancipation institutions, cultural patterns, and social practices, the Apprenticeship period brought in its wake a number of institutional modifications and a considerable increase in the freedman population. It is felt that these changes were of a sufficient order to merit separate discussion, and thus the Apprenticeship period is not generally treated in this book. However, materials that relate specifically to apprenticeship are sometimes considered when they permit a fuller description and understanding of institutions and the life of freedmen during the slave period.

[6]Sheila Duncker, "The Free Coloured and Their Fight for Civil Rights in Jamaica, 1800–1830" (M.A. thesis, University of London, [1960]); Douglas Hall, "Jamaica," in *Neither Slave Nor Free*, ed. Cohen and Greene, pp. 193–213; Samuel J. Hurwitz and Edith F. Hurwitz, "A Token of Freedom: Private Bill Legislation for Free Negroes in Eighteenth-Century Jamaica," *William and Mary Quarterly*, 3rd ser., 24 (1967): 423–31. See also Charles H. Wesley, "The Emancipation of the Free Coloured Population in the British Empire," *Journal of Negro History*, 19 (1934): 137–70; and Rawle Farley, "The Shadow and the Substance: A Study of Aspects of Economic and Social Structure and the Change in Economic and Social Relations between Whites and Coloured Free in Slave Society in British Guiana," *Caribbean Quarterly*, 4 (1955): 132–53.

Source materials relating to Barbados during the period of slavery are abundant,[7] but references to freedmen are relatively infrequent. Of the sources that mention freedmen, many make only brief and passing references to them, and few sources by themselves provide sufficient information on any one aspect of life to permit a reasonably comprehensive account. Since much of the literary or qualitative information that specifically treats freedmen is of a fragmentary nature, I found it necessary to rely upon a wide variety of source materials, and, when possible, I have employed statistical information to supplement qualitative evidence. Although the statistical information is not particularly rich, and is often imprecise and incomplete, it does give concrete expression to a number of social, demographic, and economic patterns. Furthermore, statistics sometimes yield information that is otherwise unavailable, or raise issues that literary sources do not suggest.

In general, the source materials are sufficient to permit a survey of the development of the freedman's civil and legal status and a description, in varying degrees of detail, of his participation in the island's major national institutions; however, the evidence is more restricted on the freedman's social and cultural life, many of his demographic characteristics, the internal organization of his community, and the nature and implications of its stratification. Furthermore, direct evidence is especially limited on topics such as the views freedmen held on Barbadian society, their values and how they regarded themselves, how they perceived the white and slave groups, and the subtleties and various dimensions of their interaction with, and relationship to, these groups.

The paucity of information on these topics is in large measure a reflection of the nature of the authorship of most of the source materials. There are no known books or pamphlets written by freedmen, no freedman newspapers existed during the slave period, and there are very few known letters by freedmen. Thus, the vast majority of sources were written by whites, most of whom were affected in one way or another by class and racial biases, and who were not particularly interested in describing at length, with dispassion, or with sympathy the island's freedman population. In general, then, the very nature of the source materials often makes it difficult not only to probe a variety of areas of the freedman's life but also to write with assurance about his perspectives and values. In many cases conjecture must of necessity take the place of concrete evidence; in other cases the evidence is so scant that only minimal treatment of important and relevant topics is possible.

Major exceptions to the general rule of source material authorship are the group petitions and addresses that freedmen submitted to legislative

---

[7]See Jerome S. Handler, *A Guide to Source Materials for the Study of Barbados History, 1627–1834* (Carbondale: Southern Illinois University Press, 1971).

bodies during their struggle for civil rights in the nineteenth century. Relatively few of these documents are available, and they sometimes represented the interests of small or elitest groups; furthermore, because the petitions and addresses usually requested or acknowledged legislation that was favorable to the freedman's civil and legal status, the language in the documents was often cautiously, if not conservatively, phrased. In general, although the petitions and addresses cannot be taken as full expressions of the sentiments of all freedmen, the rarity of documentary evidence produced by freedmen gives these documents an importance they might otherwise not have. Thus, despite various qualifications which must surround their use, the petitions and addresses constitute a unique body of source materials wherein freedmen directly conveyed their sentiments and aspirations and expressed their views on the society in which they lived. For such reasons, I have cited these documents frequently and have sometimes quoted them at length.

It is advisable to specify and define some of the major reference terms employed for the population categories discussed in the following pages. A definition and consistent use of major terminology is necessary because the sources are sometimes ambiguous and because various terms are employed, particularly for the free nonwhite population; in addition, there are differences in contemporary usage between, as well as among, West Indian and British scholars, on the one hand, and U.S. scholars, on the other.

The word *freedman*, which is of central concern, is occasionally employed in Caribbean literature to refer to free nonwhites in the slave society (although one variation or another of "free colored" is more common), but in the United States it generally refers to the former slave population after the abolition of slavery. In this book *freedman* is used to refer to any person in the slave (or apprenticeship) society, whether manumitted or freeborn, whose racial ancestry was mixed or solely Negroid; the term is applied to both sexual groups, but, where females are specifically discussed, the term *freedwoman* is employed. *Freedman* thus denotes a status group defined by legal attributes and physical criteria, but it does not necessarily imply specific phenotypic[8] or racial characteristics—that is, degrees of Negroid or Caucasoid ancestry. Such implications are sometimes conveyed by writers when they use, for example, "free Negro" or "free Colored," although they intend, in fact, to refer to the freedman group in general, and not to racial variations within it. Since these terms are also used for phenotypic categories, it can be unclear whether the categories or freedmen in general are under discussion. The term *freedman*

---

[8] *Phenotype* refers to the visible and observable physical characteristics of an individual; it is the outward manifestation of the genotype, or the totality of an individual's genetic endowment. Phenotypic characteristics include features such as skin and hair color, nose form, and so forth, but the value and social significance of these characteristics are, of course, culturally determined and vary from society to society.

is consistently used in this book because it is felt to be more useful as a general term and because it avoids possible misunderstandings about specific phenotypes.

At times, however, it is necessary to make phenotypic distinctions among freedmen. The sources on Barbados do not yield a "complex, multi-tiered color coding system,"[9] such as that historically employed in Jamaica. In Jamaica, phenotypic gradations between Negroid and Caucasoid were reflected in a terminology that included specific categories such as "quadroon," "mustee," "mustifino," "quintroon," and "octoroon"; all persons who were identified by such terms were considered to be of varying degrees of mixed racial ancestry, but those who were most Caucasoid could legally be defined as white.[10] In Barbados, however, no one of *known* Negroid ancestry, no matter how remote, could be considered *white* with respect to social or legal status, and the evidence does not indicate that Barbadians actively employed the phenotypic grading system found in Jamaica.

Two major phenotypic categories were socially recognized in Barbados, and neither of them had legal implications for freedmen. For purposes of this book, *free "colored"* is employed for persons of mixed racial ancestry, and *free black* refers to those of Negroid ancestry alone. Primary sources, such as the island's laws, often use *mulatto* and *Negro*, respectively, but, judging from the way Barbadian freedmen referred to themselves in their petitions and addresses, many apparently rejected these terms and preferred either *"colored"* or *black*. In this book *Negro* appears in direct quotations or in a context which makes it clear that the term is used to refer to nonwhites in general. Despite its widespread usage in the primary sources and contemporary scholarship, the term *mulatto* is avoided, and appears only in direct quotations. The meaning of "colored" in the sources is often ambiguous: sometimes it specifically refers to persons of mixed racial ancestry, sometimes to a segment of the freedman community defined in socioeconomic terms and by phenotype, and frequently, as in contemporary usage, it appears as a synonym for freedmen in general. In this book *"colored"* is employed for the sake of convenience to refer to persons of mixed racial ancestry, whether they were free or slave, but, since the term's connotations and social implications differ in contemporary West Indian–British and U.S. usage, it is retained within quotation marks.

Finally, *freeman* is used as a collective term to refer to the freedman and white groups—that is, to persons, regardless of sex or racial ancestry, who were not slaves; and, for want of a better term, *nonwhite* is used here as it is conventionally employed, to refer to the total population of freedmen and slaves.

---

[9]Cohen and Greene, Introduction to *Neither Slave Nor Free*, p. 7.
[10]Brathwaite, *Creole Society*, pp. 167–68; Duncker, "Free Coloured," pp. 20–22, 37–48.

I

BARBADOS AND THE FREEDMAN POPULATION

The first non-Amerindian settlement in Barbados was established in 1627, when a small group of Englishmen arrived directly from England, bringing with them a handful of Africans captured during the sea voyage. In its early years, the island's cash economy rested on the production of tobacco, cotton, and indigo, which were grown on relatively small farms that were largely, but not exclusively, cultivated by free and indentured Europeans. The island's white population grew rapidly, and the already established slave trade continued to bring Africans to Barbadian shores. Over time, there were marketing and other difficulties with the main cash crops, and, as a consequence, the commercial growth of sugar cane was encouraged. Although the cane plant had been brought to Barbados during the first year of the colony's life, it was not then grown as a cash crop; in the late 1630s, however, Dutchmen from Brazil reintroduced the plant and, more important, the technical knowledge to grind the cane and produce sugar. With the aid of Dutch capital and credit, Barbados became the first British possession in the Caribbean to cultivate sugar on a large scale, and during the 1640s its economy was transformed into one based upon plantation production and slave labor.

By the 1650s the plantation slave system was firmly entrenched and the island's flourishing sugar-based economy made it (until surpassed by Jamaica in the eighteenth century) the richest of Britain's Caribbean possessions. As the plantation system expanded, the number of small holdings was severely reduced and the number of landowners declined from between 8,300[1] and 11,200[2] in the mid-1640s to 2,639 in 1679.[3] Thousands of

[1]"Some Observations on the Island Barbadoes," [1667], CO 1/21, no. 170.

[2]John Scott, "The Description of Barbados," [1668], Sloane MSS 3662, fols. 54–62, BM. Richard S. Dunn finds Scott's figure "at a minimum five times too high," but Dunn's evidence for this statement is unclear (*Sugar and Slaves: The Rise of the Planter Class in the English West Indies, 1624–1713* [Chapel Hill: The University of North Carolina Press, 1972], p. 75).

[3]Richard S. Dunn, "The Barbados Census of 1680: Profile of the Richest Colony in English America," *William and Mary Quarterly*, 3rd ser., 26 (1969): 8–9.

Europeans left the island in search of land and other opportunities else-where. Many of these emigrants were "proprietors and tradesmen—wormed out of their small settlements by their more subtle and greedy neighbors,"[4] while considerable numbers were indentured servants whose contracts had expired. The heightened need for agricultural labor on the sugar plantations intensified the slave trade to Barbados. Despite enor-mous mortality rates, the island's African population grew from between 5,680[5] and 6,400[6] in the mid-1640s to "above 50,000" in 1666.[7] In the 1640s whites greatly outnumbered blacks, perhaps by a ratio as high as five or six to one, but during the 1650s the ratio declined considerably; by the 1660s and 1670s, blacks outnumbered whites two to one, and in the 1680s whites were outnumbered three to one.[8]

Barbados, "that fair jewell of your Majesty's Crown,"[9] reached the zenith of its prosperity around the 1660s and 1670s. By 1679 more than 54 percent of the island's land and slaves were owned by only 7 percent of its planters, but the combined efforts of both large and small planters appear "to have produced more sugar and employed more shipping than the other English islands combined."[10] Throughout the remainder of the seven-teenth century, the value of Barbados's exports to England was greater than that of any other British Caribbean territory, and "more valuable than the total from North America."[11] "Little Barbados, with its 166 square miles," wrote Eric Williams in his *Capitalism and Slavery*, "was worth more to British capitalism than New England, New York and Pennsylvania combined."[12]

From its earliest colonization Barbados was governed under proprietary patents. In the early 1650s, however, the "mother country" assumed direct control and formalized a tripartite political system whose major compo-

---

[4]"Some Observations on the Island Barbadoes."

[5]Scott, "Description of Barbados."

[6]"Some Observations on the Island Barbadoes."

[7]*Ibid.*

[8]These ratios are derived from population estimates given in the following sources: "Some Observations on the Island Barbadoes"; Scott, "Description of Barbados"; "An Estimate of the Barbadoes and of the Now Inhabitants There," n.d. [1650s], Edgerton MSS 2395, fols. 625–27, BM; Colleton to Council for Trade, May 28, 1673, *CSPCS, 1669–1674*, p. 495; Jonathan Atkins, "An Account of His Majesty's Island of Barbadoes and the Government Thereof," February 1676, CO 1/36; Richard Dutton, "An Account of Barbadoes and the Government Thereof," 1683/84, Sloane MSS 2441, BM; Willoughby to Lords of the Council, July 9, 1668, *CSPCS, 1661–1668*, p. 586; Blake to King, February 28, 1669, *ibid., 1699*, p. 590. See also the population figures given in V. T. Harlow, *A History of Barbados, 1625–1685* (London: Oxford University Press, 1926), pp. 45, 338; Carl Bridenbaugh and Roberta Briden-baugh, *No Peace beyond the Line: The English in the Caribbean, 1624–1690* (New York: Oxford University Press, 1972), p. 226; and Dunn, *Sugar and Slaves*, p. 312.

[9]Willoughby to Charles II, May 12, 1666, quoted in Alfred D. Chandler, "The Expansion of Barbados," *JBMHS*, 13 (1945–46): 106.

[10]Dunn, "Barbados Census of 1680," pp. 4, 17.

[11]*Ibid.*, pp. 4–5, n. 5.

[12]Eric Williams, *Capitalism and Slavery* (New York, 1961), p. 54.

nents had been established in previous years. This political system was to remain substantially unaltered throughout the eighteenth century and the pre-emancipation decades of the nineteenth. During this period it was structured along the following lines. A major element was the lower chamber, the House of Assembly, whose twenty-two members (two from each of the island's eleven parishes) were elected annually on a narrow franchise based on property, sexual, religious, and (by the early eighteenth century) explicitly defined racial criteria. Members of the Assembly were usually large plantation-owners and merchants who were intensely concerned with protecting the economic and political interests of the plantocracy. The second component of the political system was the twelve-man Council, whose members, also leading planters and merchants, were appointed by the Crown on the nomination of the governor (although, in actual fact, they often served at the pleasure of the governor). Although an advisory body to the governor, the Council was empowered to originate bills, with the exception of those relating to public finances, which were the Assembly's responsibility. The Council could, and often did, amend bills formulated by the lower chamber, but, regardless of where a bill originated, the approval of both chambers was needed before it could be forwarded to the governor. The governor was appointed by the Crown and was assigned to represent and protect its interests. Aside from a variety of judicial and administrative functions, he could recommend subjects for legislative consideration, and all bills passed by the Assembly and Council required his approval to become law.

These three bodies comprised the island's legislature, which in its major structural and organizational features was comparable to the system found in Britain's other Caribbean and American mainland colonies. Generally speaking, the British legal system operated in Barbados, but it was supplemented by colonial laws, including slave codes, which reflected local conditions; these were sanctioned by the Crown, or its representative, when they did not contradict British law or violate metropolitan political and economic interests. The nature of local interest groups, however, often brought them into conflict with "official policy," and Barbados's political history was marked by frequent clashes between the plantocracy and the governor, or the imperial government itself.

In addition to the legislative system and the judicial and political apparatus of national government, including various administrative personnel and committees, the island, in common with other British West Indian territories, had a system of local government which was framed around its parishes. The affairs of each parish were controlled by a vestry, whose members, all property-owners in the parish, were elected under the same franchise that applied to membership in the House of Assembly. The vestry maintained the parish church, looked after parish roads, collected taxes, distributed poor relief, and so forth. The churchwarden was chosen from among the vestrymen and functioned as the vestry's administrative officer.

The fundamental social, political, and economic institutions that were established during the seventeenth century persisted into the eighteenth and early nineteenth centuries. Although Barbados lost its earlier pre-eminence in the British Empire, sugar continued to be the mainstay of its economic life. Despite vicissitudes in its national economy, disruptions in its trading patterns, and threats to its external markets, sugar and its by-products, rum and molasses, accounted for over 90 percent of the value of the island's exports. The slave plantation continued to be an institution of major importance, one that helped shape the island's polity and society; it remained the major unit of sugar production, but proportionately less of its acreage was devoted to sugar than became the case in postemancipation times. The importation of foodstuffs (and many other goods) was considerable, although Barbadian plantations also grew food crops in various of their fields and often allotted slaves small gardens for their own use.

Absentee plantation owners were not uncommon, but Barbados had many locally based planters. There were also many small landowners who cultivated subsistence and minor cash crops, as well as sugar cane, which was milled at neighboring plantations. To varying degrees, all landowners were dependent on slave labor in agricultural production, but many slave-owners in Barbados owned no land, and by the nineteenth century, if not earlier, the total number of slaveowners exceeded the number of land-owners. In 1822 there were 5,206 slaveowners, 1,535 of whom (including 302 plantations with "sugar works") owned land, but 3,671 of whom were landless; by 1834, 3,055 of the island's 5,349 slaveowners possessed no land.[13] For their livelihood many of the landless slaveowners depended on the hiring out of slaves as agricultural workers or for various types of skilled and unskilled work, and slaves were universally employed in a multiplicity of domestic and household tasks by all categories of slave-holders.

Throughout most of its history, Barbados had a larger number and proportion of whites than did other British West Indian territories. By the late eighteenth century a good proportion of these whites were native-born, or creoles.[14] Although most were neither plantation-owners nor wealthy, and

---

[13]*A Report of a Committee of the Council of Barbadoes Appointed to Inquire into the Actual Condition of the Slaves in this Island* . . . (London, 1824), pp. 77–78, 127; MacGregor to Glenelg, December 6, 1836, *PP*, 1837–38, vol. 48, rept. 215; "A Memorial of the Council and Assembly of Barbadoes . . . ," November 4, 1834, *ibid.*, 1835, vol. 50, rept. 278, p. 83. See also pp. 149–51 of the present volume.

[14]The word *creole* can take on a variety of meanings. As used in this book, it refers to anyone, regardless of racial ancestry, who was born in Barbados. Creole culture is comprised of those beliefs and behavioral patterns which developed in the New World environment. Despite the often marked resemblance of these patterns to their Old World antecedents, creole culture has its own distinctive elements and patterning.

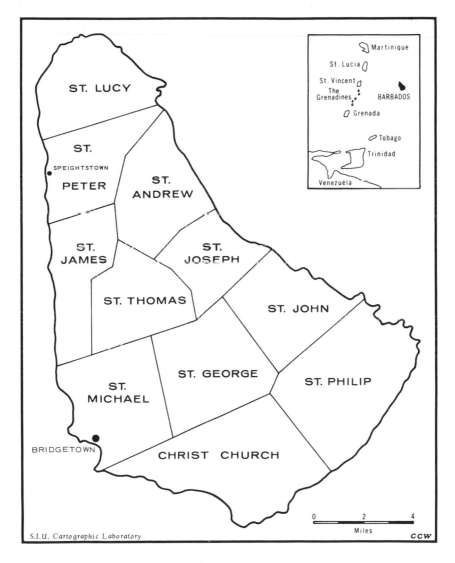

Figure 1. Barbados

considerable numbers were quite poor, as in other slave societies the white group as a whole encouraged a rigid stratification system based on racial origins and ardently defended the institution of slavery on which the Barbadian social order rested. Despite the efforts of the island's plantocracy and those whose sentiments it expressed, slavery legally ended in 1834, when slaves throughout the British colonies were formally emancipated. However, a number of crucial features of the slave system were to endure for many years after its termination. Not the least of these was an ideology of white racism, which, during the slave period, had been instrumental in precipitating and justifying the position of social and legal subordinacy to which the island's freedmen had been relegated.

DEMOGRAPHY

Contemporary accounts place the number of Africans who arrived at Barbados in 1627 between two or three and ten.[15] Whatever the actual number, these Africans appear to have been considered slaves, but it is difficult to determine whether their enslavement was defined as a lifetime condition. In any event, ambiguity surrounded the legal status of at least some of the Africans (and Amerindians) who arrived at the island in later years. This ambiguity was resolved in July 1636, when the governor and his council ordered "that Negroes and Indians, that came here to be sold, should serve for life, unless a contract was before made to the contrary."[16] This resolution, probably the earliest statement legalizing lifetime servitude for non-Europeans in England's New World colonies,[17] was passed before the expansion of the sugar plantation system, with its concomitant dependence on massive numbers of African slaves. The colony's early agricultural economy depended on the labor of thousands of whites, many of whom were indentured servants. White indentured servants performed their labor under contractual agreements which specified the length of their service, and it is likely that the 1636 resolution was modeled in accordance with the customary procedures by which indentured servants were acquired and served their labor obligations. It appears to have been implicit within the 1636 resolution that blacks need not have been, of

[15] Jerome S. Handler, "The Amerindian Slave Population of Barbados in the Seventeenth and Early Eighteenth Centuries," *Caribbean Studies*, 8 (1969): 40, n. 4.

[16] [William Duke], *Some Memoirs of the First Settlement of the Island of Barbados . . . to the Year 1741* (Barbados, 1741), p. 19. Written by the clerk of the House of Assembly, this book is based on documents which are no longer available and contains the only known reference to this early and important resolution.

[17] Bridenbaugh and Bridenbaugh, *No Peace beyond the Line*, p. 33. What was apparently the earliest Barbadian law specifically and solely concerned with regulating the behavior of slaves was passed in August 1644, but there is no known copy of its text or provisions; the law's title, "An Act Concerning Negroes," is listed in Richard Hall's comprehensive *Acts, Passed in the Island of Barbados. From 1643 to 1762, Inclusive* (London, 1764), p. 460.

necessity, slaves, and it may have been that *legally* the status of some was similar, if not identical, to that of white indentured servants.

It is uncertain when blacks were first granted free status, but suggestive evidence for the existence of free blacks occurs early in Barbados's legal code. In the early 1650s Governor Searle verified "the true substance" and legality of the island's laws, including one, attested to in October 1652, that aimed at curtailing the movements of indentured servants and slaves within the island. The law specified that anyone who "shall entertain any man or woman, White or Black, above one night, if he doth not know him to be a Free-man, shall . . . forfeit one hundred pounds of sugar, and if he know him to be a servant, or slave to another man . . . he shall forfeit five hundred pounds of sugar."[18] Although this law was attested to in 1652, it was probably passed at an earlier, albeit unknown, time. When, in 1651, the island's Royalists relinquished control to the representatives of Cromwell, both parties signed an agreement, known as the "Charter of Barbados," under which the island was to be governed. Article 22 of the Charter specified that "all laws made heretofore by General Assemblies, that are not repugnant to the law of England," were to be valid, and the laws verified by Governor Searle followed from this provision (although some new acts were passed during the early years of his administration).[19] Thus, the volume which contains the above-mentioned 1652 law includes the laws passed in Barbados since its first settlement which were in force as of 1654; the dates given for the laws are the dates at which their legitimacy was verified by the governor, not necessarily the dates at which they were originally passed.

Whenever it was first enacted, the law attested to in 1652 indicates that free status could have been theoretically associated with blacks at an early period, and it also suggests the existence of freedmen by the early 1650s. There is more concrete evidence of the existence of freedmen later in the 1650s, some of whom apparently won their freedom through manumission from slavery;[20] it is not definitely known, however, if there were some whose freedom had evolved from indentured, or similar, servitude. In any event, if, in the island's early history, there were blacks whose status was similar to that of white servants, their number must have been very small, and it is unlikely that island custom permitted this status by the time the sugar revolution was fully under way.

[18]John Jennings, *Acts and Statutes of the Island of Barbados*, 2nd ed. (London, 1656), pp. 20–21. In this volume all provisions concerning the behavior and status of slaves are incorporated in laws dealing with indentured servants; that is, there are no separate slave laws, and the provisions of the 1644 law referred to in the above note are probably included among the laws in Jenning's volume.

[19]For a copy of the "Charter of Barbados," see Robert H. Schomburgk, *The History of Barbados* (London, 1848), pp. 280–83.

[20]See Minutes of the Council of Barbados, March 20, 1655, October 5, 1658, and November 2, 1658, typescript volumes of Council Minutes for 1654–58, PRO.

The growth of a racially mixed population, albeit not necessarily a free one, also started in the seventeenth century, and by the early 1670s a wealthy planter's description of Barbados noted that its population included "mullato's and Negro's which are kept here, and accounted for slaves."[21] However, there are no figures on the "colored" population until 1684, when it was reported that there were 326 "mullatoes"; they comprised less than 0.5 percent of the island's total population.[22] A few of the 326 were probably free, but there are no statistics on the island's free "colored" population during the seventeenth century (or until the middle of the eighteenth). Indeed, no freedmen of any phenotypic category are mentioned either in detailed seventeenth-century population descriptions or statistics[23] or in intensive modern population studies of this period.[24] Although manumissions occurred during the seventeenth century, there were undoubtedly very few freedmen at any given time, and virtually nothing can be said about their demographic characteristics.

Population statistics for the eighteenth century and the pre-emancipation decades of the nineteenth are frequently imprecise and fragmentary and sometimes are contradictory for the same year; for freedmen, in particular, the statistics are discontinuous for significant runs of years. In most of these respects, Barbados's statistical picture does not significantly deviate from that of other British West Indian colonies during the slave period.

A systematic census of the island's white population was taken in 1715,[25] but nothing similar was conducted for freedmen or slaves during the eighteenth century. Although ample eighteenth-century figures for the total slave population derive from annual tax returns, owners frequently did not declare all of their slaves, and thus the figures are usually, if not entirely, underestimates. In 1787, for example, the number of slaves was given as 62,712,[26] but Joshua Steele, a knowledgeable planter, expressed an apparently widely held opinion that "there may be about four or five thousand slaves more" than the reported figure.[27] In 1817, as a result of pressures from the British government, the "slave registry bill" was passed.[28] This set forth elaborate procedures for ascertaining the size of

[21]Letter from Robert Rich, May 31, 1670, quoted in John Ogilby, *America: Being the Latest and Most Accurate Description of the New World* (London, 1671), p. 379.

[22]"An Account of Barbados and the Government Thereof," 1683/84, Sloane MSS 2441.

[23]See, for example, the primary sources listed in note 8 of this chapter; see also Richard Ligon, *A True and Exact History of the Island of Barbados* (London, 1657), and the very detailed "Census of Barbados, 1679, Supplied by Governor Jonathan Atkins to the Lords of Trade and Plantations in March–April 1680," CO 1/44, no. 47, fols. 141–379.

[24]Chandler, "Expansion of Barbados"; Dunn, "Barbados Census of 1680."

[25]"A Census of the Island of Barbados . . . Taken in the Months of October and November . . . 1715," CO 28/16.

[26]"An Account of the Number of Negro Slaves, of Free Negroes, and Mulattoes . . . ," 1764–88, *Report of a Committee of the General Assembly upon the Several Heads of Enquiry, etc., Relative to the Slave Trade* (London, 1790).

[27]Reply of Joshua Steele to Governor Parry, 1788, *PP*, 1789, vol. 26, p. 35.

[28]CO 30/20, no. 343; see also act of 1820, *ibid.*, no. 406.

the slave population and resulted in more reliable counts than had been made in previous years. The governor reported that the first census taken under this act yielded 5,000 more slaves "than were hitherto supposed to have been upon the island."[29] Thereafter, detailed returns on the slave population were reported triennially, and were presumably more accurate.

Fewer sets of figures are available on freedmen, especially in the eighteenth century. As the Council of Barbados reported in the late 1780s, "the exact number of Free Negroes in this island has never yet been ascertained,"[30] and eighteenth-century estimates of their numbers were usually little more than guesses by officials or legislative bodies. In most cases, if not in all, such figures were underestimates and could be disputed. In 1786, for example, the official island estimate placed the number of freedmen at 838, but Joshua Steele felt the number "cannot be less than about 5,000," although, he was quick to add, "there is no certain account of them by any legal authority."[31] Steele's estimate was based on the counting of nonwhites in funeral processions he observed in Bridgetown during the late 1780s. His method was of questionable reliability, and his figure of 5,000 was probably as inflated as the official one of 838 was deflated.

The problems faced by persons of Negroid ancestry in proving their free status led Governor Seaforth in 1802 to hope that a "register" for freedmen would be established by the island's legislature.[32] A registration system would have enormously facilitated the accumulation of more reliable population figures, but such a system was never adopted. Throughout the remainder of the slave period the number of freedmen (and whites) was usually determined by the rectors or churchwardens of each parish when the island's government required population figures for various purposes, usually as a result of requests from the Colonial Office. What appears to have been the earliest attempt to provide detailed statistical information on freedmen took place in 1802 and yielded parish-by-parish data on sex and relative age.[33] These data were collected by the churchwardens, but the methods employed in gathering them, as well as later figures, are unknown.

In general, then, the reliability of population statistics remains questionable, but, despite their incompleteness and imprecision, they do provide some idea about the freedman's demographic characteristics and trends in his population growth. The remainder of this chapter by and large summarizes the available statistical information, while subsequent

[29]Combermere to Bathurst, January 3, 1818, CO 28/87.

[30]Reply of Council of Barbados to query 28, "Report of the Lords of the Committee of Council . . . Submitting . . . the Evidence . . . concerning the Present State of the . . . Trade in Slaves; and . . . the Effects and Consequences of this Trade . . . in Africa and the West Indies . . . ," pt. 3, Barbados section, *PP*, 1789, vol. 26.

[31]Reply of Joshua Steele to Governor Parry, 1788, *PP*, 1789, vol. 26, p. 35.

[32]Seaforth to Alton, July 14, 1802, Seaforth Papers, 46/7/7, SRO.

[33]"Returns of Free Coloured People in the Island of Barbados, May 1802," CO 28/72.

chapters discuss in more detail the sociocultural patterns and practices which appear to have accounted for particular distributions.

Of primary importance is the fact that freedmen were a distinct minority in Barbados and always formed, even at their maximum number in the 1830s, a small percentage of the island's population. They averaged from 2.9 to 4.8 percent of the total population during most of the first third of the nineteenth century, and surpassed 6 percent only in the 1830s (Table 1). Similarly, they formed a small segment of the nonwhites (slaves and freedmen), ranging between a 3.6 percent average from 1809 to 1816 and a 5.8 percent average from 1825 to 1829; but they were still under 8.0 percent by the time of emancipation. Although their proportion was greater in relation to the total number of freemen (whites and freedmen), it was only in the late 1820s that they exceeded 25 percent of the free population, and during earlier years of the nineteenth century they averaged 14.1 percent (Table 1).

However, freedmen formed a proportionately larger segment of the population of the parish of Saint Michael than the island-wide numbers indicate. This parish contained, as it does today, Bridgetown, the island's capital and urban center. Most freedmen appear to have lived in Bridgetown (although there are no concrete figures on its population) and its immediate environs. Although a minority in Saint Michael, ranging between 6.3 percent in 1801 and 12.6 percent in 1829, this group appears to have been quite sizable if one eliminates the parish's slaves (many of whom lived in the rural or plantation areas) and considers only its free population: freedmen averaged 23.9 percent from 1809 to 1816, and 37.7 percent from 1825 through 1829 (Table 2).

By the latter years, at least, Bridgetown displayed a settlement pattern which is still evident today (albeit in a highly attenuated form); whites tended to cluster in certain areas. Although there was no legal residential segregation, some urban areas, as a visitor in 1825 observed, were "principally inhabited by the coloured people."[34] Poor whites lived in some of these areas, but there is little concrete information on residential patterns. However, given the nature of Barbadian slave society and the racism of its white population, it is likely that some kind of socially enforced residential segregation was characteristic of Bridgetown for much, if not all, of the slave period.

In any event, as a group, freedmen were concentrated in Saint Michael; although many were dispersed throughout the ten other parishes (which were fundamentally rural), it is in Saint Michael, as will be discussed in subsequent chapters, that one finds the most evidence of an organized community and proportionately greater participation in the island's national institutions. In 1801 about 45 percent of the freedman population

[34]Henry Nelson Coleridge, *Six Months in the West Indies in 1825* (London, 1826), p. 51.

lived in Saint Michael, but by 1809, and for the next twenty years, this parish contained an average of about 61 percent; that is, the freedman population of Saint Michael (principally Bridgetown) increased in absolute and proportional terms during the late eighteenth and early nineteenth centuries (Table 2), with the most significant growth period apparently starting in the 1790s.[35]

Some of the growth of the freedman population in Saint Michael must be attributed to natural increase and some to manumission. The latter factor, for example, was given special weight by J. W. Orderson, a white creole, in accounting for the increase in the parish's freedmen between 1802 and 1812; and close to 60 percent of the manumissions for which there is information on place of manumission (from 1832 to 1834) took place in Saint Michael.[36] Aside from manumissions and natural increase in Saint Michael itself, there was also a tendency for slaves manumitted in the rural areas to gravitate to Bridgetown. Rural freedmen also sought the towns, including Speightstown in Saint Peter (the island's second-largest town, but considerably smaller than Bridgetown), for the greater economic opportunities they provided.

Statistical information on the major phenotypic categories of "colored" and black freedmen is restricted to the years 1773 and 1825–29, but not for all of the island's parishes (Table 3). In 1773, 63.6 percent of Saint Michael's freedmen were "colored," which suggests that, in the eighteenth century, freedmen tended to be of mixed racial ancestry. An impression gained from the sources is that this tendency continued over the following decades; freedmen even referred to the signatories of their early petitions and addresses only as "free colored." In later years, however, freedman petitioners referred to themselves as "free colored" *and* "free black," which reflected the increasing number of free blacks in the freedman population as a whole. The data indicate that as the years progressed the proportion of black freedmen became larger than it had been in earlier years. During the five-year period 1825–29, when the reliability of colonial statistics was greater than eighteenth-century statistics (and the sample was numerically more significant and accounted for about 85 percent of the total freedman population reported), an average of 46.6 percent of freedmen were black, while 53.3 percent were "colored." That free "coloreds" were in a majority is not surprising, but it would be an obvious distortion to generalize and discuss the freedman group as simply one of mixed racial ancestry (a tendency which is found in some modern writings) when blacks formed such a significant minority within it.

[35]Garnett to Beckwith, December 5, 1811, *PP*, 1814–15, vol. 7, rept. 478.

[36]J. W. [I. W.] Orderson, *Cursory Remarks and Plain Facts Connected with the Question Produced by the Proposed Slave Registry Bill* (London, 1816), pp. 15–17; see also pp. 51–54 of the present volume.

Table 1. Population of Barbados

Year	Number				Percentage			Freedmen as Percentage of	
	Slaves	Freedmen	Whites	Total	Slaves	Freedmen	Whites	Total Free	Total Nonwhite
1748	47,025	107	15,192	62,324	75.4	0.2	24.4	0.6	0.2
1768	66,379	448	16,139	82,966	80.0	0.5	19.5	2.7	0.6
1773	68,548	534	18,532	87,614	78.2	0.6	21.2	2.8	0.7
1786	62,115	838	16,167	79,120	78.5	1.1	20.4	4.9	1.3
1801	64,196	2,209	15,887	82,292	78.0	2.7	19.3	12.2	3.3
1809	69,369	2,663	15,566	87,598	79.2	3.0	17.8	14.6	3.6
1810	69,119	2,526	15,517	87,162	79.3	2.9	17.8	13.9	3.5
1811	69,132	2,613	15,794	87,539	79.0	3.0	18.0	14.1	3.6
1812	68,569	2,529	15,120	86,218	79.5	2.9	17.5	14.3	3.5
1813	65,995	2,412	15,561	83,968	78.6	2.9	18.5	13.4	3.5
1814	66,663	2,317	15,920	84,900	78.5	2.7	18.8	12.7	3.3
1815	69,280	3,139	16,145	88,564	78.2	3.5	18.2	16.2	4.3
1816	71,286	3,007	16,072	90,365	78.9	3.3	17.8	15.7	4.0
1825	78,096	4,524	14,630	97,250	80.3	4.7	15.0	23.6	6.0

1826	80,551	4,777	14,584	99,932	80.6	4.8	14.6	24.8	5.6
1827	79,383	4,896	14,687	98,966	80.2	4.9	14.8	25.0	5.8
1828	80,050	5,020	14,824	99,894	80.1	5.0	14.8	25.2	5.9
1829	81,902	5,146	14,959	102,007	80.3	5.0	14.7	25.5	5.9
1833–34	82,807	6,584	14,592	103,983	79.6	6.3	14.0	33.1	7.4

Sources: 1748 ("A List of the Number of Planters and Inhabitants . . .," June 20, 1748, CO 28/89); 1768 ("Report of the Lords of the Committee of Council . . .; Submitting . . . the Evidence . . . Concerning the Present State of the . . . Trade in Slaves; and . . . the Effects and Consequences of this Trade, . . . in Africa and . . . the West Indies . . .," pt. 4, 3rd suppl. to no. 15, *PP*, 1789, vol. 26); 1773 (CO 318/2, cited in David H. Makinson, *Barbados: A Study of North-American–West-Indian Relations, 1739–1789* [The Hague, 1964], p. 15); 1786 ("Report of the Lords," pt. 4, no. 15); 1801 and 1809–11 (*PP*, 1814–15, vol. 7, rept. 478); 1812–16 (compiled from statistics in "General Return of the Clergy of Barbados," 1817, CO 28/86; *PP*, 1823, vol. 18, rept. 80; *ibid.*, 1826, vol. 26, rept. 350. J. W. [I. W.] Orderson reported that in 1812 the island-wide freedman population was 4,071 persons, but he provided no information on how this figure was acquired [*Cursory Remarks and Plain Facts Connected with the Question Produced by the Proposed Slave Registry Bill* (London, 1816), p. 15]); 1825–29 (*PP*, 1830, vol. 21, rept. 674. The 1825 slave population is given as an estimate for all parishes; the other years were presumably based on systematic counts. The 1826 and 1829 slave populations are taken from "Slave Population of Barbadoes," *PP*, 1833, vol. 26, rept. 539. In "West India Miscellaneous, Volume 4, Slavery Abolition, Part 2" [CO 318/117], the population for 1829 is given as 4,326 freedmen, 15,029 whites, and 81,200 slaves); 1833–34 (whites and freedmen, R. Montgomery Martin, *History of the Colonies of the British Empire* [London, 1843], p. 64. No statistics are given for the white population in Saint Peter and Saint Thomas, and for the purposes of this table these have been estimated on the basis of returns in the late 1820s; statistics on slaves are from *PP*, 1835, vol. 51, rept. 420. In 1833 the governor reported a population of 12,000 freedmen, 15,000 whites, and 83,000 slaves [Smith to Stanley, October 29, 1833, CO 28/111]; the last two figures are credible, but it is hard to explain the first).

Table 2. Population of Barbados by Parish

| | Number | | | | | | | Percentage of Population of Barbados Residing in Saint Michael | | | Percentage of Population of Saint Michael | | |
| | Saint Michael | | | | All Parishes | | | | | | | | |
Year	Slaves	Freedmen	Whites	Total	Slaves	Freedmen	Whites	Slaves	Freedmen	Whites	Slaves	Freedmen	Whites
1748	9,906	64	4,407	14,377	47,025	107	15,192	21.0	59.8	29.0	68.9	0.4	30.7
1773	13,760	214	4,613	18,587	68,548	534	18,532	20.0	40.0	24.8	74.0	1.2	24.8
1801	10,519	1,000	4,336	15,855	64,196	2,209	15,887	16.3	45.2	27.2	66.3	6.3	27.3
1809	12,262	1,668	5,313	19,243	69,369	2,663	15,566	17.6	62.6	34.1	63.7	8.7	27.6
1810	12,001	1,466	5,161	18,628	69,119	2,526	15,517	17.3	58.0	33.2	64.4	7.9	27.7
1811	12,293	1,551	5,406	19,250	69,132	2,613	15,794	17.7	59.4	34.2	63.8	8.1	28.1
1812	12,070	1,540	4,519	18,129	68,569	2,529	15,120	17.6	60.8	29.8	66.6	8.5	24.9
1813	11,509	1,370	4,977	17,856	65,995	2,412	15,561	17.4	56.7	31.9	64.5	7.7	27.8
1814	11,277	1,264	5,130	17,671	66,663	2,317	15,920	16.9	54.5	32.2	63.8	7.2	29.0
1815	11,558	2,071	5,374	19,003	69,280	3,139	16,145	16.6	65.9	33.2	60.8	10.9	28.3
1816	13,695	1,933	5,038	20,666	71,286	3,007	16,072	19.2	64.2	31.3	66.3	9.4	24.3
1825	17,000	2,825	4,942	24,767	78,096	4,524	14,630	21.7	62.4	33.7	68.6	11.4	20.0
1826	16,439	3,045	4,965	24,449	80,551	4,777	14,584	20.4	63.7	34.0	67.2	12.5	20.3
1827	16,722	3,065	5,001	24,788	79,383	4,896	14,687	21.0	62.6	34.0	67.5	12.4	20.1
1828	16,719	3,095	5,020	24,834	80,050	5,020	14,824	20.8	61.6	33.8	67.3	12.5	20.2
1829	16,807	3,140	5,050	24,997	81,902	5,146	14,959	20.5	61.0	33.7	67.2	12.6	20.2

Sources: Saint Michael, 1773 (Report of a Committee of the General Assembly upon the Several Heads of Enquiry, etc., Relative to the Slave Trade [London, 1790]); other sources are the same as those for Table 1.

Table 3. Freedman Population by Phenotype

Year	Number			Percentage	
	"Colored"	Black	Total	"Colored"	Black
1773	136	78	214	63.6	36.4
1825	2,066	1,760	3,829	54.0	46.0
1826	2,169	1,905	4,074	53.2	46.8
1827	2,201	1,947	4,148	53.1	46.9
1828	2,259	1,989	4,248	53.2	46.8
1829	2,313	2,027	4,340	53.3	46.7

Sources: 1773 ("An Account of the Number of Negro Slaves, of Free Negroes and Mulattoes . . . ," 1764–88, in *Report of a Committee of the General Assembly*; these figures are only for Saint Michael, which in 1773 contained 40 percent of the island's freedmen); 1825–29 (compiled from "Return of the White, Free Coloured, Free Black and Slave Population of Barbados, from 1825 to 1829 Inclusive," *PP*, 1830, vol. 21, rept. 674; figures are available for only eight of the parishes – Saint Andrew, Saint Thomas, and Saint Peter are excluded – but these eight contained 85 percent of the total freedman population).

As throughout New World slave societies, in Barbados, sexual relationships ranging from relatively stable ones to those that were highly transitory were not uncommon between female slaves and white men. Such liaisons increased the number of racially mixed slaves, and when a white father manumitted his children by a slave mother the number of "colored" freedmen increased. Freedwomen also participated in sexual relationships with whites, and these liaisons produced children who were not only "colored" but also, because of their mothers' status, free at birth.

The age distribution of freedmen is of interest because the qualitative and limited statistical information that is available indicates that a considerable number of them were children. There is no information on absolute age groupings, but in 1802, the only year for which there are statistical data on relative age, 393 men and 762 women were reported—that is, the adult population totaled 1,155; in addition, there were 499 boys and 514 girls, or 1,013 children.[37] Thus, adults comprised about 53 percent of the freedman population and children comprised 47 percent. It is difficult to determine how much of this age division persisted during the remainder of the slave period. However, birth rates (Table 5) and the efforts made by freed parents to manumit their still-enslaved children suggest that the number of children continued to be large and that they formed a significant proportion of the freedman population. Thus, it must be kept in mind

[37]"Returns of Free Coloured People in the Island of Barbados, May 1802," CO 28/72. Age breakdowns are given for ten of the parishes (exclusive of Saint Lucy); these contained 97 percent of the freedman population reported.

that, although much of the discussion in subsequent chapters implicitly focuses on the status, institutional participation, and behavior of adults, one is, in effect, dealing with a group that was considerably smaller than the gross population figures given in Table 1 indicate.

In considering the adult group, sexual composition is important for a variety of reasons pertaining to the organization of the freedman community and the participation of its members in various national institutions; in addition, the number of freedwomen of child-bearing age was a variable in the rate of natural increase of the freedman population. However, as noted above, figures for 1802 are the only ones which permit an estimate of the number of women of child-bearing age. In this year 60 percent of the women were adults.[38] Although it is known that older female slaves were manumitted, the lack of statistical or qualitative evidence makes it impossible to hazard a guess as to what percentage of women in 1802, or in later years, were beyond the child-bearing age.

A late-eighteenth-century informant estimated that the sexual ratio of freedmen in Barbados was "two males to three females."[39] Yet, as Joshua Steele reported around the same time, "we have no accurate account of the numbers and proportions of the sexes among the free Negroes,"[40] and until 1801 there was no statistical information on the sexual composition of the freedman group. The nineteenth-century information is distributed over a nineteen-year period; for only six of these years, however, does the information relate to the entire freedman population, and the remaining years treat varying fractions of the total (Table 4). Because there is a great deal of proportional consistency between the fractional and total population figures given in Table 4, the two sets of figures can be summarized together. During 1801 and 1802, the two earliest years, females averaged 58 percent of the freedman population, while during the remaining seventeen years, starting in 1809, they averaged 49.6 percent. It thus appears that, during the second and third decades of the nineteenth century, the freedman population was roughly equally divided between males and females. Although these figures portray some annual fluctuations, they do convey a picture of a population that was not, on the whole, disproportionately represented by one sex alone.

Yet, according to manumission figures for 1809–29, a consistently high percentage (averaging 62 percent during the period) of slaves manumitted were females (see Table 6). These figures are consistent with other statistical and qualitative evidence which indicates that female slaves had a greater chance of being freed than male slaves did. One might thus expect that the nineteenth-century population figures would indicate a greater number of females rather than a tendency toward equalization of the

[38] *Ibid.*
[39] Anonymous respondant in *Report of a Committee of the General Assembly*, p. 5.
[40] Reply of Joshua Steele to Governor Parry, 1788, *PP*, 1789, vol. 26, p. 35.

sexes. The sources make it difficult to explain this discrepancy. It may be a result of deficiencies in the figures themselves or it may be that manumission figures were often not included in population statistics. In either event, females certainly formed a significant proportion of the freedman population and may even have been in a majority for most of the period focused on in this study.

Gross population figures undoubtedly underestimate the size of the freedman population, but with respect to population growth the figures do show definite trends. As can be gathered from Table 1, the number of freedmen had risen significantly by the end of the eighteenth century, and it continued to grow steadily during the nineteenth. Increasing from a reported 2,209 persons in 1801 to 5,146 in 1829, the number approached 7,000 on the eve of emancipation; thus, the reported figures indicate that in a little more than three decades the freedman population had tripled in size. Freedmen showed a proportionately greater rate of growth than did the island's slaves, and, while both of these groups increased in size, the number and proportion of whites declined.

For all intents and purposes, slave importations ceased in 1807 with Britain's abolition of the slave trade; thus, whatever growth occurred in the slave population was a result of natural increase. However, an emigration phase that started in the late eighteenth century appears to have been largely responsible for the reduction in the number of whites. Many left the island in search of economic opportunities elsewhere. In 1811, for example, the rector of Saint Thomas reported that the parish's white population "for more than ten years past has been considerably diminished by emigrations to the Southern Colonies, where mechanics and planters meet with more tempting offers of emolument than are to be obtained here"; the rector of Saint George gave similar reasons for the "regular and gradual decrease" in the number of whites in his parish.[41] Aside from emigration, no other variable seems to have been significant in accounting for the gradual decrease in the white population. The average annual crude rate of natural increase among whites from 1826 to 1829 (as calculated from Table 5) was nil. It should be noted, however, that 329 whites died as a result of a massive hurricane in 1831 (compared to a loss of 1,189 slaves, and 73 freedmen).[42] In all, as the number of whites declined and that of freedmen increased, the latter came to form an increasingly significant minority among the island's freemen, a population trend that had implications for plantocratic reactions and legislation relative to the freedman's civil status.

[41]Als to Beckwith, 1811, and Thomas to Beckwith, November 30, 1811, *ibid.*, 1814–15, vol. 7, rept. 478, pp. 10, 11. See also Hinds to Husbands, November 21, 1825, *ibid.*, 1826, vol. 26, rept. 350; John Poyer, *History of Barbados from 1801 to 1803, Inclusive* (Bridgetown, 1808), *passim*; and [John Poyer], *A Letter Addressed to His Excellency . . . Francis Lord Seaforth, by a Barbadian* (Bridgetown, 1801), pp. 21–22.

[42]Schomburgk, *History of Barbados*, p. 440.

Table 4. Population of Barbados by Sex

Year	Slaves				Freedmen				Whites			
	Males		Females		Males		Females		Males		Females	
	No.	%	No.	%	No.	%	No.	%	No.	%	No.	%
1712	–	–	–	–	–	–	–	–	3,537	50.1	3,529	49.9
1715	–	–	–	–	–	–	–	–	8,419	49.9	8,469	50.1
1748	–	–	–	–	–	–	–	–	3,840	42.4	5,209	57.6
1757	–	–	–	–	–	–	–	–	4,608	45.4	5,549	54.6
1783	–	–	–	–	–	–	–	–	4,466	43.1	5,903	56.9
1801	29,872	46.5	34,324	53.5	942	42.6	1,267	57.4	7,147	45.0	8,740	55.0
1802	–	–	–	–	892	41.1	1,276	58.9	–	–	–	–
1809	–	–	–	–	136	48.6	144	51.4	1,102	41.8	1,534	58.2
1810	–	–	–	–	139	48.6	147	51.4	1,141	42.2	1,562	57.8
1811	–	–	–	–	181	50.3	179	49.7	1,507	43.0	1,996	57.0
1812	–	–	–	–	180	50.0	180	50.0	1,802	47.5	1,992	52.5
1813	–	–	–	–	196	50.8	190	49.2	1,737	46.7	1,985	53.3
1814	–	–	–	–	201	52.1	185	47.9	1,792	47.0	2,021	53.0
1815	–	–	–	–	203	54.0	173	46.0	1,757	46.6	2,011	53.4
1816	–	–	–	–	207	52.9	184	47.1	1,899	47.8	2,076	52.2
1817	35,354	45.6	42,139	54.4	224	48.9	234	51.1	1,804	45.7	2,147	54.3

Year											
1818	–	–	–	241	49.0	251	51.0	1,784	45.6	2,130	54.4
1819	–	–	–	251	48.9	262	51.1	1,790	46.8	2,034	53.2
1820	46.9	41,612	53.1	338	50.2	335	49.8	2,237	47.1	2,516	52.9
1823	45.9	42,657	54.1	–	–	–	–	–	–	–	–
1825	–	–	–	2,258	49.9	2,266	50.1	6,827	46.7	7,803	53.3
1826	45.9	43,556	54.1	2,386	49.9	2,391	50.1	6,859	47.0	7,725	53.0
1827	–	–	–	2,454	50.1	2,442	49.9	6,924	47.1	7,763	52.9
1828	–	–	–	2,562	51.0	2,458	49.0	6,986	47.1	7,838	52.9
1829	46.0	44,211	54.0	2,609	50.7	2,537	49.3	7,049	47.1	7,910	52.9
1832	46.3	43,738	53.7	–	–	–	–	–	–	–	–

Sources: 1712 ("A List of Inhabitants, Men, Women, and Children . . .", August 16, 1712, CO 28/14. No figures are given for the parish of Christ Church. Sample does not include an additional 5,462 children for whom no sex is given); 1715 (derived from the 1715 census of the white population, cited in E. M. Shilstone, "The Population of Barbados," *JBMHS*, 13 [1945]: 14; no figures are given for Saint James); 1748 ("A List of the Number of Planters and Inhabitants . . .", June 20, 1748, CO 28/29; sample includes adults from all parishes, but excludes 6,143 children for whom no sex is given); 1757 and 1783 ("Report of the Lords," pt. 4, 3rd suppl. to no. 15, *PP*, 1789, vol. 26; sample includes all parishes, but excludes 6,615 children in 1757 and 5,798 in 1783 for whom no sex is given); 1801 (*PP*, 1814–15, vol. 7, rept. 478; all parishes included); 1802 ("Returns of Free Coloured People in the Island of Barbados, May 1802," CO 28/72; excluded are 61 freedmen in Saint Lucy for whom no sex is given); 1809–10 (*PP*, 1814–15, vol. 7, rept. 478; sample includes only Saint Lucy, Saint Peter, and Saint James); 1811 (*ibid.*; includes Saint Lucy, Saint Peter, Saint James, and Saint Thomas); 1812–16 (*ibid.*, 1823, vol. 18, rept. 80; includes Saint George, Saint James, Saint Thomas, and Saint Philip); 1817 (freedmen and whites, *ibid.*; includes same parishes as in 1812–16. Slaves, *ibid.*, 1833, vol. 26, rept. 539; all parishes are included); 1818–19 (*ibid.*, 1823, vol. 18, rept. 80; includes same parishes as in 1812–16); 1820 (freedmen and whites, *ibid.*; includes same parishes as in 1812–16 and Saint John. Slaves, *ibid.*, 1833, vol. 26, rept. 539; all parishes included); 1823 (*ibid.*; all parishes included); 1825 (*ibid.*, 1830, vol. 21, rept. 674; all parishes included); 1826 (freedmen and whites, *ibid.*; all parishes included. Slaves, *ibid.*, 1833, vol. 26, rept. 539; all parishes included). Slaves; 1827–28 (*ibid.*, 1830, vol. 21, rept. 674; all parishes included); 1829 (freedmen and whites, *ibid.*; all parishes included. Slaves, *ibid.*, 1833, vol. 26, rept. 539; all parishes included); 1832 (*ibid.*, 1833, vol. 26, rept. 700; all parishes included).

There is some evidence that, in the late eighteenth and early nineteenth centuries, Barbados's freedmen included immigrants from neighboring islands; in addition, after the abolition of the slave trade, some Africans captured from slavers by British ships, as well as slaves who had escaped from neighboring islands, appear to have been ultimately freed in Barbados.[43] However, there is no indication that voluntary immigrants, captured Africans, or foreign runaway slaves, as a group, ever formed more than a very small fraction of the total freedman population. For all intents and purposes, therefore, one must attribute the growth of the freedman population to manumissions and natural increase (births minus deaths). It is, however, difficult to ascertain with precision which of these factors was most influential, and to determine how their influence varied at different periods of time.

What appear to be reasonably useful figures on the births and deaths of freedmen are limited to the four-year period 1826–29 (Table 5). During these years (it is not known how they compare to earlier ones), the annual natural increase was 127, 114, 148, and 120, respectively. Projecting these figures onto the population totals available for 1827, 1828, and 1829, the projections roughly coincide with the actual figures reported. One might thus conclude that natural increase was largely responsible for the growth of the freedman population during these years. However, other sets of figures indicate that the population during this period was also growing as a result of slave manumissions. During the three-year period 1827–29, the natural increase in the number of freedmen was 382, but during the same triennium a *minimum* of 670 manumissions were reported (Table 6), although the actual number of manumissions exceeded this number.[44] Combining manumission figures with those of natural increase yields a larger population than is reported in the sources. This discrepancy cannot be attributed only to the inadequacy of the statistical data themselves, but it may also be due to the fact, as suggested above, that manumission figures were often not included when population figures were reported. In any event, despite the considerable difficulties involved in determining the extent to which natural increase contributed to the growth of the freedman population, it does appear that, at least during the later years of the slave period, manumission played an important role.

In summary, during the pre-emancipation decades of the nineteenth century, the freedman population of Barbados was a minority population; it was vastly outnumbered by the island's slaves and was considerably smaller than the white group.[45] The freedmen were also in a minority in

[43]See pp. 38–39.

[44]See pp. 48–49.

[45]In the latter respect, by the last fifteen years or so of the slave period Barbados appears to have become unique in the British West Indian islands; the general pattern was that the freedman population was larger than the white one (Charles H. Wesley, "The Emancipation

Table 5. Population of Barbados: Births and Deaths

Year	Slaves				Freedmen				Whites			
	Total Population	Number of Births	Number of Deaths	Natural Increase	Total Population	Number of Births	Number of Deaths	Natural Increase	Total Population	Number of Births	Number of Deaths	Natural Increase and Decrease
1826	78,543	3,200	2,237	963	4,797	343	216	127	14,584	469	549	−80
1827	79,383	3,083	2,271	812	4,896	265	151	114	14,687	422	353	+69
1828	80,050	3,083	2,271	812	5,020	349	201	148	14,824	529	437	+92
1829	80,086	3,083	2,271	812	5,146	373	253	120	14,959	506	594	−88

Sources: Freedmen and whites (PP, 1830, vol. 21, rept. 674); slaves (total population, ibid.; births and deaths, ibid., 1833, vol. 26, rept. 359. Birth and death figures for slaves are available only as totals for triennium; for purposes of this table the annual averages have been calculated from each triennium).

the major urban parish of Saint Michael, although proportionately more
freedmen lived in towns than did whites or slaves, and freedmen were
particularly prominent in Bridgetown, the island's capital. A considerable
number of freedmen were children, and, although a majority of the population was "colored," or of mixed racial ancestry, a consequential minority
was black, and for a number of years a majority was female. The freedman
population grew steadily and increased in size significantly from the beginning of the nineteenth century to emancipation. Natural increase
accounted for some of this growth, but manumission from slavery was
also an important variable.

Manumission was of more importance in the society than is indicated
by the number of slaves who actually won their freedom. It was something
to which slaves aspired, and it motivated many in their behavior toward
slaveowners. It was also of vital concern to freedmen whose kin or spouses
were enslaved, and freedmen slaveowners themselves were involved in the
manumission process. In addition, the legislature periodically turned its
attention to manumission when, for example, it became anxious over the
growing number of freedmen or uncomfortable with various of the activities in which they engaged. For such reasons, and because it reflected
some significant characteristics of Barbados's slave society, manumission
is discussed in detail in Chapter 2.

---

of the Free Colored Population in the British Empire," *Journal of Negro History*, 19 (1934):
139–40, 150). Although this seems to have been true for Jamaica as well, the Jamaican statistics appear to contain the greatest ambiguity on white/freedman ratios, but that island
clearly contained more freedmen than any of the others (Edward Brathwaite, *The Development of Creole Society in Jamaica, 1770–1820* [London: Oxford University Press, 1971], pp.
151–52, 168–69; Sheila Duncker, "The Free Coloured and Their Fight for Civil Rights in
Jamaica, 1800–1830" [M.A. thesis, University of London, (1960)], pp. 1–10; Barry W.
Higman, "Slave Population and Economy in Jamaica at the Time of Emancipation" [Ph.D.
diss., University of the West Indies, 1970], pp. 135, 142–43).

II

MANUMISSION
AND THE VALIDATION
OF FREE STATUS

Let me tell you, it will doubtless be very acceptable to the Lord, if so be that masters of families here [in Barbados] would deal so with their servants, the Negroes and Blacks, whom they have bought with their money, to let them go free after a considerable term of years, if they have served them faithfully; and when they go, and are made free, let them not go away empty-handed.

The above words, "taken from the mouth of George Fox at a Mens meeting . . . in Barbadoes in the year 1671," were uttered while the Quaker leader was giving his views on "the government of families according to the law of Jesus."[1] Relative to the state of Barbadian society at the time, Fox's exhortation that masters had a moral obligation to free certain slaves and materially reward them was a radical one. Although his teachings on how masters should treat their slaves had some influence on the ways in which Quaker slaveholders related to their human property, there is no evidence that his advice on manumission was followed to any extent; it is even less likely that non-Quaker slaveholders accepted this advice, given the scorn and hostility with which they viewed the island's Quaker community.[2]

[1]George Fox, *Gospel Family-Order: Being a Short Discourse concerning the Ordering of Families, Both of Whites, Blacks, and Indians* ([London], 1676), p. 16. John Hull, a Quaker who accompanied Fox to Barbados, attended the meeting at which the discourse published in *Gospel Family-Order* was delivered. In a letter written not long after this meeting, Hull reported that Fox's directive on manumission was "to make them free after thirty years servitude" (Hull to Mann, November 1, 1671, quoted in *The Journals of George Fox*, ed. John L. Nickalls [London, 1952], pp. 598–99).

[2]Modern writers often imply or assume that the seventeenth-century persecutions of Quakers in Barbados were largely a result of their involvement in the Christianization of slaves. There is no strong evidence, however, that Quakers became involved in such efforts prior to Fox's visit during late 1671 and early 1672. Before this time Quakers were already being persecuted for a variety of reasons, such as their refusal to participate in the island's militia and to pay for the upkeep of the Anglican ministry, as well as their outspoken criticism of the morality and behavior of the island's whites. Attempts to Christianize slaves after Fox's visit added another reason for the persecutions and exacerbated them, but the old reasons were still present.

29

Direct evidence for slave manumissions dates from the early 1650s, when a handful of Amerindians were granted their freedom through the will of a deceased owner,[3] but manumissions were rare at this early period.[4] By the time George Fox visited Barbados, manumissions of African slaves had taken place, but, although a few slaves continued to win their freedom during the remainder of the seventeenth century (primarily, it appears, through the wills of owners), manumission was not a variable of relative significance in the growth of the freedman population until the end of the eighteenth century.

A few devices for gaining freedom involved direct intervention by the British Crown (for example, as a result of escheatment, or the freeing of Africans captured after the abolition of the slave trade), but throughout the slave period the main forms of manumission under colonial law were the wills and deeds of slaveowners; in addition, the legislature could manumit slaves as a reward for their role in helping to prevent revolts or in defense of the island against foreign invasion. In general, however, and this should not be lost sight of during the following discussion, manumission was extremely difficult to achieve, and for the vast majority of Barbadian slaves there was little or no hope of gaining freedom while the slave society persisted.

MANUMISSION BY ACTS OF THE LEGISLATURE

The concern with slave revolts in Barbados, especially in the seventeenth century, led the plantocracy to discover the useful role that slave informers could play in checking rebellions. A revolt planned in 1675 was discovered through information provided by a female slave; as a consequence of "her eminent service to the good of this country," the House of Assembly recommended her manumission.[5] This procedure was formalized in 1692, when, after a particularly threatening slave plot, an act was passed which provided for the manumission of slaves who informed on their peers who were planning "to commit or abet any insurrection or rebellion."[6] This act was of little significance, however, for, despite another plot in 1702, there were no slave revolts on the island until 1816; even then, a special bill, passed early in 1817 "for manumitting certain slaves for their good conduct during and since the rebellion," resulted in the

[3]Jerome S. Handler, "The Amerindian Slave Population of Barbados in the Seventeenth and Early Eighteenth Centuries," *Caribbean Studies*, 8 (1969): 53–54.

[4]See, for example, Berkenhead to Thurloe, February 17, 1655, *A Collection of State Papers of John Thurloe*, ed. Thomas Birch, 7 vols. (London, 1742), 3: 159.

[5]Minutes of the Assembly of Barbados, November 25, 1675, CO 31/2.

[6]Richard Hall, *Acts, Passed in the Island of Barbados. From 1643 to 1762, Inclusive* (London, 1764), pp. 129–30.

freeing of only four persons.[7] For similar reasons of security and in recognition that "there are many Negroes and other slaves . . . who are worthy of trust and confidence to be reposed in them and therefore may be of great service" in defense of the island, the legislature in 1707 passed an act whereby any slave who killed an invading enemy would be manumitted.[8] This act also was of little significance, for the island was never invaded, despite, as in the Napoleonic Wars, occasional threats. Although unimportant as sources of manumission, the laws of 1692 and 1707 were the only ones which contained specific conditions by which freedom could be granted. Both laws remained in force until the 1820s, when the substance of their clauses was incorporated, with elaborations, into two clauses of the "slave consolidation act," the most comprehensive slave law in the island's history. This law provided for the manumission of any slave whose information led to the conviction of any person, slave or free, who plotted, or engaged in, rebellion or insurrection; the liberated slave could be, at the expense of the public treasury, "sent wherever his or her wishes may point out" and receive an annuity of £10, but, if the slave preferred "remaining in his or her owner's possession to being freed," then he would receive a £25 lifetime annuity. In addition, if, during an invasion by a foreign force or an internal insurrection, a slave "shall engage and courageously behave in battle," or kill one or more of the enemy or rebels, he was to be "rewarded . . . as the legislature may think fit to direct"; if the legislature decided the slave "should be rewarded with freedom," it was empowered to do so, but no provision was made for an annuity in this case.[9] There is no indication that the above provisions resulted in the manumission of any slave, but it is relevant to note that the greatest reward the plantocracy could give for defending its interests and the island's security was the slave's freedom.

These two clauses and the earlier acts which contained similar provisions were, as noted, the only ones which specified the reasons and conditions by which slaves could gain their freedom. In all other cases it was an owner's decision when a slave should be manumitted, and the reason behind this decision varied with the inclination and desires of the owner

[7]See Journals of the House of Assembly, October 8 and December 17, 1816, and January 7, 1817, CO 31/47. A copy of the act is on file in CO 28/97. Another case of this kind was an 1824 "Act to Manumit a Slave Named Anthony for His Fidelity to the White Inhabitants of This Island"; Anthony, the property of the Rev. William Maynard Payne, had given "information of certain rebellious designs of a slave named Joseph" (CO 30/20, no. 442).

[8]Hall, Acts, pp. 175–76. The phrase "and other slaves" referred to Amerindians; see Handler, "Amerindian Slave Population," pp. 59–60.

[9]See clauses 48 and 50, "An Act to Repeal Several Acts and Clauses of Acts Respecting Slaves, and for Consolidating and Bringing into one Act, the Several Laws Relating Thereto . . . ," October 23, 1826, PP, 1826–27, vol. 25, unnumbered rept., pp. 205–30 of Barbados section.

concerned. A slave could be manumitted during the owner's lifetime under a variety of deed conveyances, or provision could be made for the slave's manumission in the owner's will.

MANUMISSION BY WILL AND DEED

Manumissions by will resulted from a special relationship between master and slave; for example, they were granted as a reward for "fidelity" in domestic service and/or a sexual relationship, or to a master's children by a slave woman. The particular conditions of the will, however, varied more widely: the 1658 will of Philip Bell specified that after his wife's death his "mulatto woman" Arabella was to be set free together with Mango, a "Negro man . . . which used to run along with me";[10] in 1679 the master of Asha stipulated that she continue to "serve for the space of 12 months after my decease (in such services as my executors shall appoint) and not longer, and then she be manumitted";[11] and Thomas Wardall's 1683 will "directed that certain of his slaves were to be set free, and that all the children of his slaves born after 9 April 1673 . . . were to be free on attaining thirty-four years of age, provided they were willing to be baptized in the Christian faith."[12] In 1764, Ann Hothersal provided that her "Negro woman slave," Moll Lumsley, was to be "supported at the expense of my estate in such manner as may hereafter make her life most agreeable to her and as if she was a white servant. And if it should be made appear by her to any of my children that she has any just cause of complaint, then I manumit . . . the said Negro woman."[13]

Manumitted slaves could also be given a bequest that might include money, housing, or even other slaves (slaves could not inherit slaves, and their inheritance would have to be held in trust until their manumission was legally recognized): in a will dated 1798, Sir John Gay Alleyne, a prominent member of the plantocracy, maumitted "my old and faithful slave Henry Buckingham and give him an annuity of £16";[14] in 1772, an owner freed his "Negro woman, Murria, and two children Thomas and Becky, the said Murria to have the use of the house where she lives and £12 half-year for life, also the use and services of a Negro slave-girl . . . and

[10]Transcript of the will of Philip Bell, 1658, Davis Collection, Box 15, item J, RCS.
[11]Transcript of the will of Peter Hanckock, December 4, 1769, *ibid.*, Box 8, no. 11.
[12]E. M. Shilstone, "Historic Sites Re-Visited: 1. Andrews Plantation, St. Joseph," *JBMHS*, 1 (1934): 95.
[13]Will of Ann Hothersal, March 12, 1764, Wills Books, vol. 1, pp. 411–12, BDA.
[14]Quoted in Louise R. Allen, "Alleyne of Barbados," *JBMHS*, 3 (1936): 231. Alleyne died in December 1801 and the will was proved in May 1802. However, sometime after making the original will, Alleyne changed his mind and entered a codicil which revoked Buckingham's freedom—to the surprise of one of the executors, who speculated that although Buckingham was due "a certain reward . . . for his services through a long period of Sir John's life . . . [perhaps] by his ill conduct . . . he had forfeited all claim to the promised favour" (J. F. Alleyne to Cobham, March 20, 1802, Alleyne Letters, pp. 191–92, WIC).

daily allowance from my plantations as long as she shall live, said Thomas to be put to school and decently clothed and bound to apprentice a trade."[15] Robert Harrison, in a 1766 will, specified: "I set free my Negro woman Betty and give her £150 and two mulatto girl slaves, Phillis and Rachel. I set free my Negro woman Grace and give her £100 and a mulatto girl slave Mary. A house to be provided for Grace and Betty."[16]

On the basis of available information, it is difficult to determine precisely the frequency of manumissions by will; yet an impression, gained from reading numerous transcripts of seventeenth- and early-eighteenth-century wills, as well as a sampling of late-eighteenth- and early-nineteenth-century ones in the Barbados Department of Archives, is that manumission by this means was relatively infrequent. This impression is reinforced by the limited figures that are available. From the beginning of 1821 to the end of 1825, the island's deputy secretary reported the manumission of 411 slaves by 146 different owners.[17] Only 25, or 6 percent, of these slaves (owned by 10 different persons) were manumitted as a result of a bequest made in their owners' wills.

During a slaveowner's lifetime, manumissions by deed were made for a variety of reasons and motives and could be effected in a number of customary ways. One reason commonly reported was manumission as a favor to a slave mistress, and deed manumissions resulting from such a relationship were regarded as an important source of the freedman population. As Waller observed in 1807–8, "The natives [white creoles] cohabit with people of colour at a very early age; and I have observed many instances of their being perfectly captivated by their mulatto mistresses, who thus obtain their freedom, and that of their children, from the master who cohabits with them."[18] Waller placed the emphasis upon the sexual licentiousness of white creoles. Joseph Husbands, a white creole who emigrated from Barbados in 1812 and was very critical of Waller's assessment of white behavior, placed the onus on nonwhites; in so doing, however, Husbands also reported that "by far the greater number of free colored persons in Barbadoes have either obtained their freedom by their own prostitution, or claim it under some of their female ancestors who in like manner obtained it and have transmitted it to their descendants."[19] In a slave society such as Barbados, sexual alliances with white men were one of the few devices that slave women could employ to achieve their freedom, and in 1811 the rector of Saint Michael, reporting on the "very rapid" increase in the number of freedmen

[15]Will of Francis Ford, April 29, 1772, quoted in *The Barbadian Diary of Gen. Robert Haynes, 1787–1836*, ed. E. M. W. Cracknell (Medstead, Hampshire, 1934), pp. 59–60.

[16]Quoted in E. M. Shilstone, "Harrison of Barbados," *JBMHS*, 8 (1941): 30–31.

[17]W. Husbands, "A Return of the Number of Manumissions Effected by Purchase, from 1st January 1821 to [31 December 1825]," *PP*, 1826, vol. 28, rept. 353.

[18]John A. Waller, *A Voyage in the West Indies* (London, 1820), p. 20.

[19]Joseph D. Husbands, *An Answer to the Charge of Immorality against the Inhabitants of Barbadoes* (Cooperstown, [N.Y.], 1831), p. 19.

in the parish since 1802, observed that "great numbers of them obtain their freedom every year . . . [and] out of every four at least three are females, who obtain that privilege by becoming the favourites of white men."[20] (Estimates such as the above, which emphasize the preponderance of female slave manumissions, are supported by statistical materials [see Table 6] and by the higher fees that were placed, in 1801, on the manumission of females.)

Another reason for manumission during an owner's lifetime derived from slaves' becoming nonproductive or incapable of performing their duties effectively. Because such slaves generally were not marketable, owners either manumitted them, and thus rid themselves of the necessity of their upkeep and of paying taxes on them,[21] or simply permitted them to wander and fend for themselves. The latter practice was much more common than immediate manumission, and it became so widespread that in 1785 a law was passed to curtail it. "Some persons," the law's preamble noted, "possessing Negroes who, from old age and infirmities, are incapable of further service to their inhuman owners, . . . drive them from their plantations to beg, steal or starve; which said unhappy objects are daily infesting the public streets of the several towns in this island"; if an owner did not recall such a slave, he was subject to a fine of £5 in island currency.[22] As with other laws designed to prevent or curtail a particular behavioral pattern, this one had limited effect, and the practice of turning out nonproductive slaves continued.[23] These slaves, however, although of little economic use to their owners, could sometimes engage in activities through which they were able to accumulate some cash. This money could then be paid to the master, who, if he agreed to the sum paid, would execute a deed of manumission. This process was commonly known as self-purchase.

Self-purchase was a practice related to deed manumission which was accepted in custom rather than specified in law. The process is best described by a contemporary writer who was familiar with conditions in Bridgetown:

> A man, possessing more slaves than the necessary duties of his house require, suffers one or more of them to . . . *go at large*, that is, permits them to follow, without control, whatever line of life they please—so long as they punctually pay the fixed weekly stipend. . . . Prone to in-

[20]Garnett to Beckwith, December 1811, *PP*, 1814–15, vol. 7, rept. 478, p. 3.

[21]An annual head tax on slaves, usually around 1s. (which could be raised if special needs arose), was used to pay the governor's salary and to take care of other governmental expenses.

[22]Samuel Moore, *The Public Acts in Force, Passed by the Legislature of Barbados, from May 11th, 1762, to April 8th, 1800, Inclusive* (London, 1801), pp. 258–60.

[23]William Dickson, *Mitigation of Slavery in Two Parts* (London, 1814), pp. 154, 448; George Pinckard, *Notes on the West Indies*, 3 vols. (London, 1806), 2: 109.

dustry, desirous of becoming free, and careful of their profits, they presently amass money with which they purchase themselves, that being the principal object in view. *Purchasing themselves* means the depositing in the hands of the master the sum which he values them at . . . before he can give his consent to manumission; this then may also be termed *buying consent.*[24]

Once the purchase price was fully paid the master would then execute a deed of manumission. Of course, the slave had no legal protection in the event that a master refused to draw up a deed, and the only evidence that masters largely honored their self-purchase agreements derives from pro-slavery sources. Although slaves were sometimes able to save money from activities engaged in while "going at large" or from the sale of garden crops, small livestock, or poultry, few field slaves could accumulate the money to purchase their freedom;[25] a similar situation prevailed in the Leeward Islands, where, as well, slave tradesmen and domestic servants had the greatest opportunities to "go at large" or to be hired out, and, as a consequence, had the best chances to acquire funds to purchase their freedom.[26] In Barbados, one knowledgeable writer was of the opinion that self-purchase applied mainly to male slaves, while females were more prone to being liberated through purchase from their masters by white men.[27]

It appears, however, that self-purchase was relatively difficult to achieve. Forster Clarke, a prominent planter, offered the general "opinion that very few [slaves] ever possess the means of purchasing their freedom"; he cited only five cases within the period 1822–28 on the Codrington plantations, owned by the Church of England's Society for the Propagation of the Gospel in Foreign Parts.[28] Even when the necessary funds could be acquired, owners were reluctant to permit the practice. In 1832 the archdeacon of Barbados, who strongly felt that "the possessor of slaves is bound on Christian principles . . . to grant unhesitatingly freedom to his dependents, whenever they, or their friends, are able to purchase it," delineated three common rationalizations given by whites for preventing or criticizing self-purchase: "[1] the master's interest will be impaired by

---

[24]*Letter from a Gentleman in Barbadoes to His Friend in London, on the Subject of Manumission from Slavery, Granted in the City of London and in the West India Colonies* (London, 1803), pp. 20–21; italics in the original. See also J. W. [I. W.] Orderson, *Cursory Remarks and Plain Facts Connected with the Question Produced by the Proposed Slave Registry Bill* (London, 1816), pp. 15–16.

[25]See, for example, Clarke to Secretary of the SPGFP, May 7, 1828, quoted in SPGFP, *Annual Report* (London, 1828), pp. 217–18; Haynes to Lane, April 7, 1806, Newton Estate Papers, 523/601, ULL; and testimony of Captain Cook, *PP*, 1791, vol. 34, p. 204.

[26]Elsa V. Goveia, *Slave Society in the British Leeward Islands at the End of the Eighteenth Century* (New Haven: Yale University Press, 1965), pp. 141, 147, 239.

[27]Orderson, *Cursory Remarks*, p. 16.

[28]Clarke to Secretary of the SPGFP, May 7, 1828, quoted in SPGFP, *Annual Report*, (1828), pp. 217–18.

the withdrawal of a slave whose services he will often be unable to replace at the price at which he is sold. . . . [2] the master, from a personal regard for the slave, or from a more accurate knowledge of his worth, will estimate him far above the market price. . . . [3] the slave will lessen his value by wilful misconduct, with a view to obtain his freedom at a low price."[29]

As a rule, however, self-purchase—indeed, manumission in general—was denied when it fundamentally contravened what the owner defined as his own self-interest, economic or otherwise. Thus, during his visit to Barbados in 1829–30, William Bell reported that the bishop of Barbados had told him "the planters objected to grant manumissions to their best & oldest servants for fear of losing their services altogether";[30] yet, as noted previously, when such persons, as well as other slaves, became nonproductive or incapable of performing their duties effectively, they sometimes gained direct manumission as a "reward" for their past services, or were permitted to purchase their freedom. For example, in 1802 a plantation owner notified his manager: "There is a mulatto woman belonging to Mount Standfast . . . [who] is now and has long been I believe useless to the estate . . . [and] I am . . . ready to accept the offer she had made of

---

[29]Edward Eliot, *Christianity and Slavery: In a Course of Lectures Preached at the Cathedral and Parish Church of St. Michael, Barbados* (London, 1833), pp. 139, 222–24.

[30]Joseph Boromé, ed., "William Bell and His Second Visit to Barbados, 1829–1830," *JBMHS*, 30 (1962): 22.

Britain's slave emancipation act, which went into effect on August 1, 1834, declared that all emancipated slaves above the age of six years were to serve as apprentices to their masters until 1838 or 1840, depending on whether they had been domestic or field slaves. The act, however, permitted ex-slaves to buy themselves out of apprenticeship if they could pay their masters the value of the remaining years of their service. Thus, self-purchase was made somewhat easier than it had been under slavery, and, as a result, the number of self-purchases increased. There were two ways by which self-purchase could be effected during the Apprenticeship period: one involved the apprentice paying the value of his remaining years of service as this value was determined by the master and approved by judges charged with appraisal; the other way avoided formal appraisal and simply involved a personal financial agreement made directly between the master and apprentice. The "amicable arrangement" and "appraisal" appear to have accounted for the majority of manuissions during the Apprenticeship period. For example, during the nine months August 1836–April 1837, a minimum of 775 manumissions was reported by the island's eight stipendiary magistrates. Although this figure does not represent all the manumissions that occurred during this period (occasionally a magistrate would omit figures in his monthly report), it probably includes the great majority and it indicates the relative importance of self-purchase. Of the 775 manumissions, 660 yield information on the method by which the manumission was effected. Of these 660, 151 (22.8 percent) were won by "gratuitous discharge," while 505 (76.5 percent) were achieved through self-purchase (mostly by private arrangements between apprentices and their masters); the remaining 4 were discharged by the stipendiary magistrates because of "the cruelty of their owners." However, the widespread desire of apprentices to purchase their freedom is not accurately reflected in the manumission figures. Many apprentices were unable to pay their appraised value, and others were so discouraged by the high prices that they never attempted self-purchase. See the monthly reports of the stipendiary magistrates in "Papers . . . in Explanation of the Measures Adopted . . . for Giving Effect to the Act for the Abolition of Slavery . . . ," pt. 4, *PP*, 1837, vol. 53, rept. 521-1, pp. 384–421; J. A. Thome and J. H. Kimball, *Emancipation in the West Indies* (New York, 1838), p. 67; and Sylvester Hovey, *Letters from the West Indies* (New York, 1838), p. 109.

£40 as the price of herself."[31] The reason why the attorney for the Newton plantation recommended the self-purchase of two female domestic slaves of advanced years was that both of them "certainly are useless people in the estate, and perhaps be better gotten rid of."[32]

For similar reasons of incapacity or nonproductivity, owners would sometimes permit freedmen to purchase their own kinsmen whom they ultimately hoped to manumit. This process is well illustrated in the case of Jenny (or Jane) Lane, one of the elder women at the Newton plantation referred to above. About five or six years after her manumission, she attempted to purchase her sons, who were still slaves on Newton. Although perhaps an unusual device, her letter (one of the few on record that were written by emancipated slaves) to the plantation-owner clearly states why she felt the plantation would find it acceptable to sell her sons:

> I have taken the liberty to write to you, hopes you will excuse me requesting the favour of your goodness to oblige me with my two mullato sons at Newtons. The name of one is Robert, a joiner by trade, but one of his arms is affected and no use to the estate. The other is name William Henry, a taylor by trade and a poor constitution that I think is but little use to the estate. If I thought or knew they was any great use, you may depend I would not taken the liberty   but my having a little to depend on and they poorly [I] would wish to have them to own.[33]

The owner requested the plantation attorney's advice, and he recommended the sale of the two men: "I am convinced of the propriety of so doing as their value to the estate is but trifling and the sooner we are rid of them, the better."[34] Jenny Lane had offered £150 island currency for each of her sons, and by a deed executed in 1818 (more than five years after she first made the request) her sons were sold to her and became her slaves.[35]

Another practice which had the same effect as manumission by deed involved white men, often British army officers, purchasing their slave mistresses from "their owners, in many instances their own parent, and subsequently giving a certificate on the back of the deed of sale, annulling their right of property in the person of their favourite"; this gave the slave mistresses "a freedom not recognized by the laws, but tacitly assented to by the community,"[36] although it is not known how common the practice was.

---

[31]Alleyne to Smittens, March 24, 1802, Alleyne Letters, pp. 203–4.

[32]Haynes to Lane, April 7, 1806, Newton Estate Papers, 523/601.

[33]Jane Lane to John and Thomas Lane, March 4, 1813, *ibid.*, 523/690; except for punctuation, the letter is transcribed as it appears in the original document.

[34]Haynes to Lane, October 18, 1818, *ibid.*, 523/811.

[35]Indentures between John and Thomas Lane and "Jenny, a free black woman," May 8, 1818, *ibid.*, 523/976.

[36]Orderson, *Cursory Remarks*, p. 16.

MANUMISSION BY IMPERIAL AUTHORITY

Aside from special legislative enactments relating to the island's security, wills, and deeds, there were four other ways by which slaves could be manumitted, but all of these together apparently contributed only a small percentage to the island's freedman population. One way involved slaves who, subsequent to Britain's abolition of the slave trade in 1807, were either shipwrecked on Barbadian shores or captured from slavers by British naval vessels. Under directives from the Colonial Office, such slaves were apprenticed for seven years to persons who were willing to accept them or they were inducted into the British army; in both cases, "upon their term being expired, they were . . . to be free from all restraint."[37] In 1828, Barbados's collector of customs notified the president of the island's Council that, "a great many years ago, there were eighty-four in all, male and female," apprenticed Africans.[38]

A second minor way by which slaves were manumitted occurred as a consequence of their escheatment to the Crown. These slaves were owned by persons who died intestate and without legal heirs; because of their indeterminate status, the slaves were claimed as Crown property. During the period from August 1822 to September 1832, at least seventy slaves (belonging to seventeen different owners) were escheated to the Crown, and fifty were manumitted, usually after successfully petitioning "his Majesty to cede his right to them."[39] Some of the manumitted slaves are identifiable as having been owned by freedmen, and the case of John T. Atherley is illustrative, though perhaps not typical, in its details. Atherley was born a slave, but had managed to pay his master £100 (sterling) for his freedom, and had deposited the manumission fee required by island law. After obtaining his freedom, he was able to purchase his wife and four children, who were still enslaved; although he intended to manumit his family, he was unsuccessful in raising the fee "to render their manumission complete in law." Atherley died suddenly without having made a will, and, since he had no "relations who were free in law," there were no legal heirs. Thus, all of Atherley's material property, as well as his wife and children, who were legally his slaves, escheated to the Crown. The wife and children petitioned the Crown for their freedom and, because their case was found to be "of extreme severity and most deserving of the interference of his Majesty's government," the lords commissioners of the British Treasury ordered their manumission.[40]

---

[37] Aberdein to Skeete, February 14, 1828, CO 28/102; see also Bathurst to Combermere, May 11, 1819, CO 28/88.

[38] Aberdein to Skeete, February 14, 1828, CO 28/102.

[39] See *PP*, 1826, vol. 28, rept. 353; *ibid.*, 1833, vol. 26, rept. 453; and *ibid.*, 1831–32, vol. 47, rept. 660, p. 23.

[40] Macaulay to Bathurst, November 11, 1821, CO 28/94; *PP*, 1826, vol. 28, rept. 353.

Runaway or fugitive slaves from neighboring territories in the West Indies were another source of the island's freedman population, although no statistics are available on the number of persons in this category. In 1826 the colonial secretary ordered the Barbados legislature not to remove foreign runaway slaves from the island and to treat them as alien freedmen.[41] He based his order on the interpretations that Crown lawyers gave of Britain's act to abolish the slave trade. "All the rules and regulations," the Barbados Assembly complained, "distinguishing the slave from the freeman, are at the sole will of the Colonial Secretary, to vanish. . . . in defiance of our existing laws."[42] Despite the Assembly's objections, however, foreign runaway slaves did win their freedom on the island.

A final method by which slaves were manumitted occurred during the twilight of the slave period, when Barbados's collector of customs gave "certificates of freedom to certain slaves, who had formerly been in England [presumably as servants accompanying their masters] . . . . On such persons coming to him, he merely gave them a bit of paper, stating that by the 3rd clause of the Act of Parliament for the Emancipation of Slaves [passed in 1833] 'all slaves who have been in England or Ireland previous to the passing of the Act, shall be free.' "[43]

Apprenticed Africans and slaves who escaped from neighboring territories, as well as those freed after escheatment to the Crown or through Britain's 1833 emancipation act, contributed relatively few freedmen to the island's population. They won their freedom through directives from the British government and not through colonial legislation. Will and deed manumissions, on the other hand, were not considered legal under colonial law from 1739 to 1831 until a manumission fee or tax had been paid to the vestry of the parish in which the slave was manumitted. Since these fees were a significant variable in the manumission process, it is necessary to discuss the legislation which established them.

MANUMISSION FEES

Although manumission occurred early in the history of slavery in Barbados, the island's legislature did not control the process until 1739, when it passed a law requiring manumission fees. The reasons for this act stemmed from the long-standing practice, as noted earlier, of owners manumitting slaves, often old and infirm, "without making proper provision for their maintenance and support [and] they continuing their baseness, have in-

[41]Bathurst to Barbados Council, September 14, 1826, Minutes of the Barbados Council, October 31, 1826, CO 31/50.

[42]"An Address to the Governor from the Assembly," Minutes of the Barbados House of Assembly, January 2, 1827, CO 31/51.

[43]From Minutes of the Barbados House of Assembly, October 16, 1833, reported in Studholme Hodgson, *Truths from the West Indies* (London, 1838), p. 192.

stead of supporting themselves by honest labour and industry, through idleness and other vices been greatly injurious to the inhabitants, in enticing and corrupting other slaves to steal and rob their owners."[44] In order to provide for the support of manumitted slaves "to prevent their becoming burdensome to the parish," the manumitter was obliged to pay £50 in island currency to the parish government, which in turn would provide the freed slave with an annuity of £4; failure to pay the fee could result in court action by the parish against the manumitter.[45] In the Leeward Islands, where owners also manumitted old and diseased slaves, comparable legislation was enacted; when they passed such legislation, the plantocracies in these islands, as Elsa Goveia points out, were interested in "considerations of public order, rather than of humanity."[46] Similarly, the Barbadian plantocracy was less concerned with the material well-being of the emancipated slave than with discouraging him from engaging in illicit trading activities. The Barbadian economy at this time provided very few opportunities for emancipated slaves, and the most important area in which they could involve themselves was, as will be discussed in Chapter 6, the island's internal marketing system. The manumission-fee act was also implicitly designed to limit the number of freedmen, but it was not entirely successful; however, a 1744 bill that was introduced into the House of Assembly for these reasons involved raising the manumission fee on female slaves to £100, but was defeated by a vote of eleven to five.

The arguments presented by the main speaker against the bill, John Gay Alleyne, were probably instrumental in preventing the bill's passage. He strongly felt that it would impose a restraint "upon the justice and gratitude of an owner," and was injurious to the "most deserving part of our slaves, the females who . . . have generally recommended themselves to our kindest notice." An increased manumission fee, Alleyne remarked, would deprive an owner "of the satisfaction of bestowing upon" a female slave "the only adequate reward of such an endearing service," and he could not see how the manumission of old women would stop the increase in the number of freedmen; in addition, old women would not live very long and therefore would not require much support from the parish. Not only would the bill prevent an owner's act of gratitude toward an old female, but it would also prevent an act of affection toward a young female slave, who might well be the owner's child. An increase in fees, Alleyne felt, would not restrain the "passions" of white masters, and therefore would not prevent them from producing nonwhite children. Some manumitted females, Alleyne acknowledged, became prostitutes in order to support themselves, while others became involved in illegal huckstering ac-

[44]Hall, *Acts*, pp. 323–25.
[45]*Ibid.*
[46]Goveia, *Slave Society*, pp. 172–73; see also *ibid.*, pp. 168, 191–92.

tivities with slaves, but not all engaged in such activities, and the act would have the effect of penalizing the innocent for the crimes of the guilty. Finally, Alleyne was extremely doubtful that the Crown would approve such a bill, and he felt it would certainly be returned to the legislature with "severe reproaches."[47]

Although the 1739 manumission fee continued in force, owners who wanted to manumit slaves were able to evade paying fees. They did this by transferring ownership of the slave to some "insolvent" person who would then execute a deed of manumission. Since the new owner would not have the £50, nothing could be paid into the parish; the slave was thus manumitted without the fee payment, and the law was circumvented.[48] In order to remedy this situation, the 1739 act was amended in 1783 to require that the manumitter "shall actually deposit or pay into the hands of the [parish] churchwarden" the £50, and that a receipt be issued; without the latter the manumission would be "void and of no effect," and the slave for whom the manumission was intended would remain a slave.[49] This law was apparently more effective in producing the desired results, but it inadvertently contributed to another form of circumvention, which, as will be discussed below, involved manumitting the slave in England, where manumission fees were not required.

By the end of the century the number of manumitted slaves was rising, and in 1801 Lord Seaforth, the new governor, proposed to the Assembly a bill which "might insure to those people the means of existence when age, sickness or misfortunes render them incapable of procuring it by their own exertions."[50] The act, which raised manumission fees and the annuity for support, was passed during that year,[51] and, not long after he had signed the bill, Seaforth applauded this action: "for the better provision of freed Negroes was loudly called for both by humanity and good policy as the smallness of the sum attending the manumission of the slave was accumulating the number of freed people of colour to a most alarming extent and the smallness of the sum allowed for their support . . . joined to their naturally idle and dissipated habits, made by far the major part of them public nuisances."[52] Once again, the plantocracy was less concerned with humanitarian considerations than with the increasing number of freedmen and the growing wealth and economic diversification of their community. The new law was thus "calculated to prevent the artificial encrease of the

[47]Minutes of the Barbados House of Assembly, March 15, 1744, BDA.

[48]*Letter from a Gentleman*, p. 33.

[49]Moore, *Public Acts*, pp. 223–25.

[50]John Poyer, *History of Barbados from 1801 to 1803, Inclusive* (Bridgetown, 1808), p. 11. Poyer could not agree with this reasoning: "If liberty is such a blessing as the advocates for the abolition of slavery contend for, is it not enough that the owner should restore his slave to freedom without being compelled to provide for his future support?" (*ibid.*, p. 12).

[51]CO 30/17, no. 225.

[52]Seaforth to Duke of Portland, July 27, 1810, Seaforth Papers, 46/7/4, SRO.

free coloured people,"[53] and was aimed at "the preservation of that preponderance of the white population . . . considered essential to the security and stability of [white] property."[54]

Manumission fees were now raised to £300 island currency for females
and £200 for males, while the annual subsidy was raised to £18 and £12,
respectively, "in consequence of the increased price of all the necessary
articles of life"; all other provisions of the 1783 manumission fee law were
retained.[55] The differential in manumission fees reflected the preponderance of female manumissions and the fact that only females could contrib-
ute to the natural increase of the freedman population since slave children
inherited the status of their mothers. "The Governor on this occasion,"
wrote John Poyer, a contemporary historian, "seems to have been forsaken
by his usual sagacity; while blinded by an erroneous humanity, he was de-
ceived into a concurrence in a measure which holding out the specious
prospect of affording a better support to the object of his benevolence, was
prudently calculated to prevent the evil it ostensibly professed to
remedy."[56] John Foster Alleyne, a wealthy planter and member of the
Council, expressed the majority plantocratic view when he observed that
by the new manumission bill "an increase in the number of that description of people has been wisely checked."[57] The existence of fees had traditionally inhibited manumissions under island law. However, with its increased fees, the new bill once again further encouraged manumissions in
England and thus the circumvention of colonial law.

In 1816 the 1801 act was repealed. Manumission fees were reduced to
£50 and included an annuity of £4 (regardless of sex), as specified in the
1783 law.[58] The rationale behind the new law's passage was, as a committee of the Barbados Council reported,

> the fidelity and good conduct of the [freedman] . . . in the [slave] insur-
> rection of 1816 [which] removed all apprehensions on that score from
> the minds of our legislature . . . . and as it now appeared that there was

[53][John Poyer], *A Letter Addressed to His Excellency . . . Francis Lord Seaforth, by a Barbadian* (Bridgetown, 1801), p. 25.

[54]*A Report of a Committee of the Council of Barbadoes Appointed to Inquire into the Actual Condition of the Slaves in This Island . . .* (London, 1824), p. 81.

[55]CO 30/17, no. 225.

[56]Poyer, *History of Barbados from 1801 to 1803*, p. 14.

[57]Alleyne to Wiltshire, February 1, 1802, Alleyne Letters, p. 133. "The number of manumitted slaves and mulattoes had increased of late years so considerably," Alleyne wrote
another friend, "that I began to think the period was at no great distance when the same
scenes which had been acted in some of the neighboring colonies would be more successfully, and perhaps to the utter destruction of the white inhabitants, performed in our own
island. This law I hope will operate to our preservation" (Alleyne to Hinds, September 10,
1802, *ibid.*, pp. 108–9).

[58]"An Act to Repeal an Act Entitled An Act to Increase the Sums Made Payable by
Former Laws on the Manumission of Slaves and for Their Better Support and Maintenance,"
August 19, 1816, Acts, Original, BDA.

no good reason for opposing the increase of their numbers, the deposit on a manumission was reduced to a sum which was thought barely sufficient to prevent unkind and ungrateful owners from ridding themselves of the burthen of maintaining their old and infirm slaves, and also for providing in some measure for the support of the enfranchised slave.[59]

Freedmen had largely remained loyal to white interests during the 1816 slave revolt, and this loyalty was a great factor in producing the first legislation that ameliorated their status. However, increasing pressures from Britain also contributed to changes on the island, and in 1823 the British government formally declared itself in favor of eventual emancipation and began pressuring colonial legislatures to pass ameliorative slave laws. The major thrust in this direction was embodied in a July 1823 dispatch sent to island legislatures by Lord Bathurst, the colonial secretary, in which he recommended a number of reform measures for the colonial slave codes. Among these were provisions that related to manumission, including the removal of fees, the registration of all manumissions, and a recommendation that slaves desiring manumission "not become chargeable if under 6 or above 50 years old, or labouring under sickness, disease, or infirmity." Close to three years later another set of recommendations included one that slaves were "under certain restrictions to be enabled . . . to purchase their freedom and that of their families and relations."[60] Some of these recommendations virtually amounted to compulsory manumission.

The Barbadian plantocracy, like plantocracies in the other islands, strenuously objected to what it defined as the unwarranted intrusion of the British government into an area which was felt to be the sole concern of the colonial legislature. In fact, in the "slave consolidation act," as the Colonial Office noted, "on the subject of manumission, the legislature have declined entirely to adopt the recommendations of His Majesty's government, and no enactments are substituted which could be compared with those suggested in Lord Bathurst's despatch."[61] In defending the legislature's action, the Speaker of the House of Assembly unequivocally stated that "compulsory manumission is such a direct invasion of the right of property . . . that the Assembly felt they could not, without violating the sacred trust reposed in them by their constituents, contemplate a measure absolutely destructive of that right by investing slaves with the power, at their own will, and against the will of their owners, of purchasing their freedom."[62] Only continual prodding from the Colonial Office itself finally produced a manumission law that the British government was willing to

[59] *Report of a Committee of the Council of Barbadoes*, pp. 81–83.

[60] *PP*, 1831–32, vol. 47, rept. 739, pp. 2–3.

[61] Huskisson to Skeete, October 18, 1827, *ibid.*, 1828, vol. 27, unnumbered rept., pp. 37–41 of Barbados section.

[62] Haynes to Warde, [1826], CO 28/102.

accept; this bill, however, still did not include any provisions that amounted to compulsory manumission.

In 1831, finding that "it is expedient to remove pecuniary deposits upon the manumission of slaves," the legislature repealed earlier laws that had established fees and declared "that no duty, tax, impost or deposit of any nature or kind whatsoever shall be paid . . . in respect of the manumission of any slave or slaves."[63] By repealing manumission fees, the Barbados legislature not only partially complied with the wishes of the British government but also, in effect, expanded the right of owners to freely dispose of their property. Even if owners had not necessarily interpreted fees as a direct infringement on property rights (although they may have, it can be assumed that this interpretation was offset by accepting that, in the long run, the status quo could be better served by the existence of fees), fees were intended to inhibit the number of manumissions and thereby curtail the growth of the freedman population. It is not known how often slaves were refused manumission because of the existence of fees, but to avoid paying them, owners, as indicated above, "frequently manumitted [slaves] by the authority of the Lord Mayor of London,"[64] under a device which was ultimately accepted by island custom, even though it was not specified in colonial law.

MANUMISSION IN ENGLAND AND OTHER ISLANDS

Manumissions in England were made possible by the interpretation of a law passed by the British Parliament in 1732, "An Act for the More Easy Recovery of Debts in His Majesty's Plantations and Colonies in America"; this law provided that colonial property, including slaves, could be attached as assets for the payment of debts, taxes, and the like, that were owed to the Crown or any British subject "in like manner as real estates are by the law of England."[65]

The slaveowner who desired to manumit a slave would go, for example, to the lord mayor's office in London (although this was the most common place, one could go to other cities as well) with a deed of manumission. This deed not only attested to the rights the manumitter held over the

[63]CO 31/21, no. 542. In October 1826 the legislature passed a law which removed manumission fees, but for technical reasons the governor did not give his assent. The same bill also extended the right of testimony to certain categories of freedmen, but, lacking the governor's assent, neither legislative action went into effect until years later, when new and separate laws were passed to cover manumission fees and testimony. See *PP*, 1826–27, vol. 25, unnumbered rept., p. 279 of Barbados section; and Huskisson to Skeete, October 18, 1827, *ibid.*, 1828, vol. 27, unnumbered rept., pp. 37–41 of Barbados section.

[64]Beckwith to Liverpool, January 13, 1812, CO 28/81. In 1816 Orderson estimated that, of the freedmen "who have obtained their freedom within the last ten years, . . . not one in twenty" complied with the provisions of the manumission fee law (*Cursory Remarks*, p. 15).

[65]Quoted in *Letter from a Gentleman*, pp. 12–13, which includes the full text of the law and discusses how its interpretation permitted slave manumissions in Great Britain.

slave, including the original bill of sale, or conveyance of title, but also included a standard phraseology which declared that, "in consideration of the faithful services . . . and for divers other good causes and valuable considerations," the owner has "manumized, enfranchized, and for ever set free," the slave or slaves named in the document. An affidavit was then sworn to attest the truth of the details contained in the manumission deed, and the lord mayor, in accordance with the 1732 British law, executed the manumission by putting his seal of office on the deed.[66]

English manumissions were not regularly employed in Barbados until the late eighteenth century. A major reason for this was probably the 1783 law which required that the £50 manumission fee actually be deposited with the parish before a manumission could be legalized. Prior to this date, as described previously, owners often avoided fee payment by simply conveying the title to their slaves to impoverished persons, who then executed the deed of manumission. Thus, just as owners had circumvented the payment of fees after 1739 by transferring ownership to poor persons, they turned to England after 1783 to achieve the same end.

Early manumissions effected in England resulted in an ambiguous status for the emancipated slave, and opinions were divided as to whether such manumissions were actually valid. For example, in one late-eighteenth-century case, a slave manumitted by the lord mayor of London "subjected himself to the resentment of a white person who, hearing of the doubtful tenure of his freedom, had recourse to the [Barbadian] law which prescribes corporal punishment for the insolence of slaves"; the manumitted slave, not wanting to be treated as a slave again, ultimately received a legal opinion which suggested that he pay the manumission fee required by island law "in order that his freedom should not in future be deemed disputable."[67] By 1823 a committee of the Barbados Council could explain that, although deeds of manumission executed in England "were not originally legalized by any statute of the island, . . . their validity has for a series of years been recognized by all our courts, and they are now considered as good and effectual for their purpose as any other form of manumission."[68]

In the late eighteenth century, English manumissions were apparently largely executed while the slave was actually in the "mother country." A writer, whose discussion of English manumissions is the most extensive available, reported that when West Indian owners came to England they were frequently accompanied by domestic slaves, "favourites of the

[66] Ibid., pp. 12–16.

[67] Ibid., pp. 17–18.

[68] Report of a Committee of the Council of Barbadoes, pp. 82–83. See also Letter from a Gentleman, p. 19; and F. Dwarris, Substance of Three Reports of the Commission of Inquiry into the Administration of Civil and Criminal Justice in the West Indies (London, 1827), p. 71.

family," and these owners would sometimes "consent to manumit them"; the writer found this to be "the general mode" by which slaves were manumitted in England.[69] Another method he described involved slaves who were able to raise the price of their self-purchase, but who wanted to avoid paying the manumission fee; the slave would obtain a job as a steward or cook on a ship bound for England or would enlist himself as a servant to one of the ship's passengers. The slave's ownership would then be transferred to either the ship's captain or the passenger. Upon arrival in England, the new "owner" would then manumit the slave "for a *master* must appear at the Lord Mayor's office . . . and *in due form of law* deliver the deed of manumission."[70] As the years progressed, these manumissions did not involve the actual presence of the slave; the necessary papers were simply sent to someone in England who executed them and returned the deed of manumission to Barbados, where in some cases it was registered at the island secretary's office.[71]

English manumissions came to play an increasingly important role in the manumission process in general. In late 1802 one writer estimated "that they are not only numerous, but that they have multiplied exceedingly within the last five or six years"; his prediction that, as a result of the 1801 increase in manumission fees, "they will proportionately increase annually," proved correct.[72] By 1823 a committee of the Barbados Council, finding that manumission fees were "constantly evaded by the connivance or rather by the consent of public opinion," estimated that "at least nine-tenths of the slaves who have been emancipated during the last six years, have obtained their freedom by virtue of English manumissions."[73]

[69] *Letter from a Gentleman*, pp. 19–20.

[70] *Ibid.*, pp. 25–26, italics in the original. It would seem that both of these methods applied to slaves who, for whatever reasons, wanted to return to Barbados as freedmen. Lord Mansfield's 1772 decision in the Somersett case set a precedent whereby slaves could become free once on English soil and could not be compelled to return to the West Indies as slaves (Goveia, *Slave Society*, pp. 154, 256; Lowell J. Ragatz, *The Fall of the Planter Class in the British Caribbean, 1763–1833* [New York, 1963], p. 246; see also M. Dorothy George, *London Life in the Eighteenth Century* [New York: Harper Torchbooks, 1965], pp. 134–36). Therefore, after 1772 there would have been no need to effect manumission papers if a slave was in England, unless that slave wanted to return to Barbados, and masters who took their domestic slaves abroad were, as Joshua Steele wrote in the late 1780s, "in danger of losing them, on their arrival in England, for want of being able to produce some legal title to the perpetual service of such slaves, conformable to the laws of England" (quoted in Dickson, *Mitigation of Slavery*, p. 102).

It is also necessary to emphasize that self-purchase and English manumission were not mutually exclusive processes; that is, self-purchase was a means for activating a manumission deed and did not result in manumission in and of itself.

[71] Husbands to Warde, [1821], *PP*, 1823, vol. 18, rept. 80; see also Orderson, *Cursory Remarks*, pp. 16–17. For particular cases, see Haynes to Lane, March 9, 1807, and November 24, 1808, Newton Estate Papers, 523/630 and 523/666.

[72] *Letter from a Gentleman*, p. 19.

[73] *Report of a Committee of the Council of Barbadoes*, pp. 82–83; see also Orderson, *Cursory Remarks*, p. 17.

A more concrete statement of the proportion of manumissions in England can be derived from information in a report by the island's deputy secretary for the period 1808–21; during these years 1,713 manumissions went on record in the secretary's office. But from 1808 to August 18, 1816, (when the £200 and £300 fees enacted in 1801 were in force) only 15 manumissions were processed in accordance with Barbadian law; from August 19, 1816, to September 30, 1821 (while the manumission fee was £50), 250 manumissions were carried out under colonial law, the remainder being "with few exceptions enfranchise[ments] by persons in England."[74] Thus, for the fourteen-year period 1808–21, about 85 percent of the reported manumissions were effected in England, although for the earlier period, 1808–August 18, 1816, English manumissions came close to 98 percent.

The extent to which colonial law was evaded in manumissions can also be seen in another set of statistics for the fourteen-year period 1817–1830. During these years, the deputy secretary reported 1,688 manumissions, 315 (18 percent) of which took place in Barbados through payment of the manumission fee. The remaining manumissions were largely accomplished in England, but there were also an unspecified number of persons "who have been set free by their owners in this island for a nominal consideration and without requisite deposit to the churchwarden, but who nevertheless enjoy all the privileges of free subjects."[75]

By the early nineteenth century some Barbadian slaves were obtaining their freedom through manumissions in other British West Indian islands, particularly Grenada. "The obvious and persuasive reason why many quit Barbadoes to sue for freedom in Grenada," wrote a critic of this process, was that manumission fees were only £10 in Grenada while they were £300 in Barbados.[76] The same writer, questioning whether the laws passed in one island were enforceable in another, felt that Grenadian manumissions should not be valid in Barbados; for this reason, as well as his generally proslavery attitudes, he may have been exaggerating when he reported that "many" Barbadian slaves obtained Grenadian manumissions. However, there is no record of the number of manumissions that took place in other West Indian islands at the turn of the century, and it is believed that the numbers either were small or subsided considerably as the years progressed. During the five-year period 1821–25, for example, an official return listed 411 slave manumissions, only 1 of which occurred in Grenada and 2 in Antigua; 86 (21 percent) slaves were manumitted under Barbadian law, and 322 (78 percent) were manumitted in England.[77]

[74] *PP*, 1823, vol. 18, rept. 80.
[75] Husbands to Goderich, September 22, 1832, CO 28/109.
[76] *Letter from a Gentleman*, pp. 29–30.
[77] *PP*, 1826, vol. 28, rept. 353.

NUMBER AND CHARACTERISTICS OF MANUMITTED SLAVES

The reports quoted above, from which manumission figures for 1808–21 and 1817–30 were derived, permit some definitive statements about the percentage of manumissions that occurred in England, but contain statistics only on those recorded in the secretary's office; thus, the total number of Barbadian slave manumissions was greater than the figures cited. In a later report, the deputy secretary explained the difficulty in determining the total number of manumissions; slaves "manumitted by persons in England," he noted, "are . . . first . . . conveyed by their owners to such persons, . . . but as these conveyances are seldom or never recorded [in the secretary's office], it is impossible to give a correct answer."[78] Even when such conveyances of title were reported, "the former owners return those slaves to the Registrar as sold, and the persons to whom the conveyances are made, being generally non-residents, no return is made by them of having purchased and manumitted those slaves."[79]

Because of such difficulties the sources contain not only incomplete, but often contradictory, statistical information. For example, one official source cites 412 slaves as being manumitted during the three-year period 1818–20, while another sets the figure at 308;[80] the latter source also reports 451 manumissions during 1821–25, while another reports 411 for the same period.[81] For the years 1827–29, one source reports 497 manumissions, while another places the figure at 670.[82] And none of the above sources claim that their figures represent all manumissions of Barbadian slaves. Because it is difficult to be precise on the total number of manumissions in any given year, the figures presented in Table 6 must be viewed in light of these qualifications and only as indications of the minimum number of slave manumissions that occurred during the years cited.

However, it is evident that the number of manumissions increased by the late 1820s and jumped considerably with the elimination of manumission fees in 1831 (this jump, however, may partially reflect more accurate counting rather than an actual increase in the number of manumissions). For example, in the trienniums 1824–26 and 1827–29, 322 and 670 persons, respectively, were reported freed, and in 1830–32 (which includes part of the period in which manumission fees were eliminated), a figure of 1,089 was reported (Table 6); from January 1832 to July 1834 (a period in which no manumission fees were required), at least 698 slaves were manumitted by deed.[83] None of these figures precisely indicates the total number of slave manumissions, but by 1831, as a white creole wrote, the num-

---

[78]*Ibid.*
[79]*Ibid.*, 1833, vol. 26, rept. 700.
[80]*Ibid.*, 1823, vol. 18, rept. 80; Husbands to Goderich, September 22, 1832, CO 28/109.
[81]Husbands to Goderich, September 22, 1832, CO 28/109; *PP*, 1826, vol. 28, rept. 353.
[82]Husbands to Goderich, September 22, 1832, CO 28/109; *PP*, 1833, vol. 26, rept. 539.
[83]Manumission deeds, Miscellaneous and Powers Record Books, RB 7/26–27, BDA.

Table 6. Slave Manumissions in Barbados by Sex

	Number			Percentage	
Triennium	Males	Females	Total	Males	Females
1809–11	168	263	431	39.0	61.0
1812–14	88	148	236	37.3	62.7
1815–17	191	279	470	40.6	59.4
1818–20	167	245	412	41.0	59.0
1821–23	131	166	297	44.1	55.9
1824–26	126	196	322	39.1	60.9
1827–29	212	458	670	31.6	68.4
1830–32	–	–	1,089	–	–

Sources: 1809–20 (*PP*, 1823, vol. 18, rept. 80, p. 36); 1821–29 (*ibid.*, 1833, vol. 26, rept. 539); 1830–32 (*ibid.*, rept. 700). All of these figures are the highest ones available for the years reported, but, as explained above, they still represent only the minimum number of manumissions.

ber of emancipated slaves was "daily augmenting."[84] One can surmise that by the early 1830s a significant number of freedmen were relatively recently manumitted slaves.

As the period of slavery drew to a close, manumissions were a substantial source of the island's freedman population; thus, the manumission process itself was important if one focuses upon this population and the factors responsible for its growth. However, it cannot be emphasized too strongly that manumission was of limited significance when viewed within the context of the society at large. One must not lose sight of the fact that Barbados was a slave society, and that the efforts of its slaveowners were largely directed toward the acquisition of more slaves or the retention of those already owned. It can safely be assumed that those owners who never manumitted any of their slaves were in the vast majority, and that those owners who did usually freed no more than one or two.[85]

How difficult, in fact, was it for a slave to become manumitted? This seemingly simple, but important, question is very difficult to answer with precision. There is little doubt that most slaves desired freedom, and that many attempted to achieve their manumission. There are no data, how-

[84]I. W. Orderson, *Spare Minutes at the Pier: Or a Short Discussion on the Equality of Rights That May Be Granted to the Free Coloured Inhabitants of This Island* (Barbados, 1831), p. 9.

[85]For example, during the five-year period 1821–25 the names of 146 manumitters were reported; 86 of these persons freed one slave each, 21 manumitted two slaves each, and 9 freed three slaves each. The number of manumitters who freed four or more slaves progressively decreased; the maximum number of slaves manumitted by one owner was twenty-nine, but there was only a single recorded case of this kind (*PP*, 1826, vol. 28, rept. 353).

ever, on the number of slaves who were refused the manumission they requested, and thus it is not possible to judge the number of requests or attempts in relation to the number of manumissions. Lacking such data, another way of dealing with the question is to establish the annual number of manumissions in relation to the total slave population.

Although manumission statistics are available for various years in the nineteenth century (Table 6), these statistics, as discussed above, represent the minimum number of manumissions. Nonetheless, the statistical data can be employed to give a rough idea of the approximate percentage of slaves manumitted annually from 1817 on (when, because of the slave registry, population figures were more accurate than those of earlier years). These data are compiled in Table 7, which indicates that the number of annual manumissions was always far below 1 percent of the total slave population. Even in 1832, when the number of manumissions exceeded that of previous years (and when it may be assumed that the reported figures were more accurate), the percentage was still less than 0.5 percent; although the percentage in actual fact was higher, because the manumission figure is the minimum one, an arbitrary doubling of the 1832 figure still results in less than 1 percent. Clearly, for the vast majority of Barbadian slaves it was extraordinarily difficult or impossible to achieve manumission.

To place this conclusion within a wider framework, the Barbadian data can be compared to those from other territories in the British West Indies. Available statistics from Jamaica (Table 7) and Saint Christopher, Grenada, Dominica, and Antigua (Table 8) show that Barbados fell within a general pattern in the British West Indies wherein manumissions were very infrequent, and, with the exception of Antigua in 1831–32, were less than 1 percent in relation to the total slave population.[86] As with the Barbadian statistics, the manumissions from the other islands cannot be taken as precise indicators of the total number of manumissions, but they do yield suggestive evidence of what the actual situation probably was. More refined conclusions and comparisons must depend upon further research, including a more intensive and careful scrutiny of the statistical data than the present study was able to accomplish.

As an indicator of the characteristics of the manumitted population, Barbados displays similarities with other islands in the British West Indies. In Barbados, for the period 1809–29, 2,838 manumission docu-

---

[86]Trinidad also appears to have conformed to this general pattern. For manumission figures in the late 1820s, see Eric Williams, *Capitalism and Slavery* (New York, 1961), p. 259. For figures on the slave population, see *idem, History of the People of Trinidad and Tobago* (London, 1962), pp. 67–68, 78, 83; Donald Wood, *Trinidad in Transition* (London: Oxford University Press, 1968), p. 191; Alan Burns, *History of the British West Indies* (London, 1954), p. 633; and F. R. Augier et al., *The Making of the West Indies* (London, 1969), p. 183.

ments contain sex identification. Of this total, 62 percent were females and 38 percent were males; although the figures indicate triennial percentage fluctuations throughout the period, females always significantly out-numbered males (Table 6). Similarly, of 698 slaves who were reported as manumitted by deed from January 1832 to July 1834, 60 percent were females.[87] Phenotypic information is restricted to 427 cases, during the years 1832–34, of which 63 percent were "colored" and 37 percent were black.[88] Of the 707 cases for which the parish of manumission was stated (also during the 1832–34 period), 58 percent were freed in Saint Michael, while Christ Church, with the second-largest number of manumissions, accounted for only 8 percent.[89] In sum, the evidence indicates that, during the period for which there is information, most of the Barbadian slaves manumitted were females, of mixed racial ancestry, and living in Saint Michael (that is, the urban area)—and this distribution is remarkably similar to that reported by Higman in his elaborate statistical study of Jamaica in the final years of the slave period.[90]

Female slaves had a greater chance for manumission largely because of the sexual alliances they were able to form with white men, a pattern that

Table 7. Slaves Manumitted as Percentage of Total
Slave Population: Barbados and Jamaica

	Barbados			Jamaica		
Year	No. of Slaves	No. of Manumis-sions	% of Slaves Manu-mitted	No. of Slaves	No. of Manumis-sions	% of Slaves Manu-mitted
1817	77,493	157	0.2	345,252	818	0.2
1820	78,345	137	0.2	342,382	632	0.2
1823	78,816	99	0.1	336,253	443	0.1
1826	80,551	107	0.1	331,119	448	0.1
1829	81,902	223	0.3	322,421	516	0.2
1832	81,500	363	0.4	312,876	454	0.1

Sources: Number of Slaves: 1817–29 (Barbados, PP, 1833, vol. 26, rept. 539; Jamaica, Orlando Patterson, The Sociology of Slavery [London, 1967], p. 96); 1832 (Barbados, PP, 1833, vol. 26, rept. 700; Jamaica, Barry W. Higman, "Slave Population and Economy in Jamaica at the Time of Emancipation" [Ph.D. diss., University of the West Indies, 1970], p. 39). Number of Manumissions: Barbados (calculated averages from triennium figures given in Table 6); Jamaica (Higman, "Slave Population," pp. 189, 194).

[87] Manumission deeds, Miscellaneous and Powers Record Books, RB 7/26–27, BDA.
[88] Ibid.
[89] Ibid.
[90] Barry W. Higman, "Slave Population and Economy in Jamaica at the Time of Eman-cipation" (Ph.D. diss., University of the West Indies, 1970), pp. 190, 191–93, 195.

Table 8. Slaves Manumitted as Percentage of Total Slave Population: Saint Christopher, Grenada, Dominica, and Antigua

Year	Saint Christopher			Grenada			Dominica			Antigua		
	No. of Slaves	No. of Manumissions	% of Slaves Manumitted	No. of Slaves	No. of Manumissions	% of Slaves Manumitted	No. of Slaves	No. of Manumissions	% of Slaves Manumitted	No. of Slaves	No. of Manumissions	% of Slaves Manumitted
1817	20,137	92	0.5	–	–	–	17,959	85	0.5	28,847	211	0.7
1820	16,139	71	0.4	26,910	41	0.2	16,554	113	0.7	29,172	106	0.4
1823–24	19,817	72	0.4	25,310	104	0.4	15,714	103	0.7	30,314	186	0.6
1826–27	19,516	88	0.5	29,307	91	0.3	–	–	–	29,839	228	0.8
1829	19,310	81	0.4	24,145	95	0.4	–	–	–	–	–	–
1831–32	19,085	81	0.4	23,411	115	0.5	–	–	–	29,537	314	1.1

Sources: Number of Slaves: 1817 (Saint Christopher, *PP*, 1833, vol. 26, rept. 539; Dominica and Antigua, *ibid.*, 1823, vol. 18, rept. 80); 1820 (Saint Christopher, Grenada, and Antigua, *ibid.*; Dominica, *ibid.*, 1833, vol. 26, rept. 542); 1823–24 (all islands, *ibid.*, rept. 539); 1826–27 (Saint Christopher and Antigua, *ibid.*, Grenada, *ibid.*, 1830, vol. 21, rept. 674); 1829 (Saint Christopher and Grenada, *ibid.*, 1833, vol. 26, rept. 539); 1831–32 (Saint Christopher, *ibid.*; Antigua, *ibid.*, rept. 700; Grenada, *ibid.*, 1835, vol. 51, rept. 420). Number of Manumissions: 1817 (all islands, *ibid.*, 1823, vol. 18, rept. 80); 1820 (Saint Christopher and Antigua, *ibid.*; Grenada, *ibid.*, 1833, vol. 26, rept. 539; Dominica, *ibid.*, rept. 542); 1823–24 (Saint Christopher, Grenada, and Dominica, *ibid.*, rept. 539; Antigua, *ibid.*, 1826–27, vol. 22, rept. 128); 1826–27 (all islands, *ibid.*, 1833, vol. 26, rept. 539); 1829 (all islands, *ibid.*); 1831–32 (Saint Christopher and Grenada, *ibid.*; Antigua, *ibid.*, rept. 700). The annual manumission figures for Saint Christopher for 1823–32 are calculated averages from triennium figures given in the sources; all other manumission figures for Saint Christopher and the other islands are the figures that were reported annually.

also existed in the Leeward Islands,[91] and presumably in Jamaica as well. In Barbados these whites were either creole masters or British military personnel or civilians who owned or hired the slaves as domestic servants (subsequently purchasing and then liberating them). Children born of such alliances also were sometimes freed.[92] No statistics exist on the ages of slaves at the time of their manumission, but it can be noted that slave mothers (as well as their children) were not necessarily young when manumitted, and that the elderly also received their manumissions (whether or not a sexual relationship had been involved) as a reward for domestic service.

Because the domestic or house slave was in close personal contact with the master, the relationship itself created a higher likelihood of reward for personal or sexual services, even though masters were often reluctant to manumit their best and oldest servants; in addition, the domestic slave had opportunities to be hired out or to "go at large," thus expanding the possibilities of forming sexual alliances or acquiring money for self-purchase.

Little concrete evidence exists on the occupational status of manumitted slaves in Barbados; however, the situation on the island was probably not very different from that elsewhere in the West Indies, for slave domestics and tradesmen generally had greater chances for manumission than did field slaves. This was so not only because domestics and artisans had more personal contact with their masters but also because they had relatively greater opportunities to acquire cash resources to effect self-purchase.[93] (In addition, a slave's personal relationship with his or her master could also have been a causative factor which permitted the slave to attempt self-purchase in the first place.)

In the Leewards and Jamaica, "colored" slaves were apt to be chosen as domestics and tradesmen because whites were generally reluctant to employ them as field laborers.[94] The materials on Barbados yield little discussion or information that consistently links phenotype and occupational category; that is, both black and "colored" slaves were tradesmen and domestics (the latter were both males and females), and only slight evidence suggests that "coloreds" were disproportionately represented in

[91]Goveia, *Slave Society*, pp. 217, 231–32.

[92]See Higman, "Slave Population," p. 132.

[93]William Dickson, *Letters on Slavery, to Which Are Added Addresses to the Whites and to the Free Negroes of Barbados* (London, 1789), p. 6. See also Goveia, *Slave Society*, pp. 231, 232; and Orlando Patterson, *The Sociology of Slavery* (London, 1967), p. 62. In Trinidad from 1825 to October 29, 1830, 743 manumissions were reported, of which 556 (74.8 percent) were of domestic slaves and the remainder of field slaves (Williams, *Capitalism and Slavery*, p. 259).

[94]Goveia, *Slave Society*, pp. 231–32; and Patterson, *Sociology of Slavery*, pp. 59, 61–62, 64. Higman writes that in Jamaica this reluctance was born of the whites' feeling that "colored" slaves were less capable of arduous labor than black ones ("Slave Population," pp. 368–72). See also Goveia, *Slave Society*, p. 317.

these categories.[95] However, the situation in Barbados may not have differed a great deal from that in the Leewards and Jamaica. Thus, the racial characteristics of "colored" slaves would have placed them in a better position to follow those occupations which were sexually and economically advantageous for potential manumission. This social pattern (which, in its widest sense, included the children of white fathers) helps explain why, in the statistics cited above, 63 percent of the manumitted slaves were "colored."

As in Jamaica, manumission in Barbados was to a considerable degree an urban phenomenon,[96] and it appears to have favored nonplantation slaves. The large percentage of slaves freed in Saint Michael can be accounted for by the fact that Bridgetown provided the greatest employment opportunities for tradesmen and domestics, which, as assumed above, were the occupational categories that offered the greatest chances for manumission.

THE FREEDMAN AS MANUMITTER

Although the discussion thus far has largely focused on manumissions by white slaveowners, freedman owners also participated in the manumission process. They were, however, in a definite minority. For example, in a list of 146 manumitters during the years 1821-25, 9 were identified as freedmen,[97] and of the 338 manumitters named on deeds from January 1832 to July 1834 only 34 were freedmen.[98] These are the only periods for which statistics provide racial distinctions among manumitters. Although it is not certain that all freedmen were explicitly identified in the sources, most probably were; at any rate, it is clear that white manumitters were numerically preponderant throughout the slave period.

---

[95]Among the plantation inventories that were available for this study, two give the phenotypes of slaves and suggest that there was a tendency for "colored" slaves to be disproportionately represented among the tradesmen and domestics. Of the total 237 slaves on the Staple Grove plantation in 1820, one-third were "colored" and two-thirds were black; a similar ratio existed among the field laborers, but one-half of the tradesmen and domestics were "colored" (Deed Books, vol. 287, pp. 322-28, BDA). During the same year the Guinea plantation had 180 slaves, three-fourths of whom were black; slightly more than one-half of the tradesmen and domestics were black and more than three-fourths of the field laborers were black (Privately held inventory, courtesy of Mr. Lionel Ward, Staple Grove Plantation, Barbados). Twelve of the fifteen house servants who were listed for both plantations were "colored." An intensive survey of estate inventories for the later periods of slavery would undoubtedly help to clarify this issue considerably.

Speaking generally of the French and English islands, but clearly having Barbados in mind among the latter, Waller wrote: "Of the field slaves there are none but Negroes; a master cannot send a mulatto into the field" (Waller, *Voyage in the West Indies*, p. 89). There is little doubt, however, that he overstated the case with respect to Barbados.

[96]Higman, "Slave Population," pp. 135, 191-93, 195.

[97]*PP*, 1826, vol. 28, rept. 353.

[98]Manumission deeds, Miscellaneous and Powers Record Books, RB 7/26-27, BDA.

However, one question immediately arises: Did white slaveowners also manumit at a proportionately higher rate than freedman slaveowners? That is, were there any significant differences in the propensity of white and freedman owners to manumit their slaves? There is no qualitative evidence on this, and the statistical data yield only rough indications. During the five-year period 1821–25, 411 slave manumissions were reported by 146 manumitters. Nine freedmen manumitted a total of 15 slaves. Thus, freedmen comprised 6.1 percent of the manumitters, but they manumitted only 3.6 percent of the slaves, or a rate of 1.6 slaves per owner; the rate for whites was 2.8 slaves per owner.[99] From January 1832 to July 1834 (when racial identifications of the manumitters appear to be more complete), 698 slaves were freed by 338 manumitters; of these, 34 freedmen manumitted 64 slaves. Thus, in this sample, freedmen comprised 10 percent of the manumitters and manumitted 9.1 percent of the slaves, a rate of 1.8 slaves per owner; the rate for whites was 2.1 slaves per owner.[100] These figures also must be used with caution because, as noted above, it is not certain that all freedmen manumitters were identified as such in the sources. But the figures indicate that freedmen manumitted at a rate that was roughly comparable to, or even somewhat below, that of whites, and give the impression that freedmen were not disproportionately inclined to manumit their slaves. In general, inability to acquire the manumission fee (as well as a lack of social contacts in Great Britain) may have limited freedman slaveholders more than whites in effecting manumissions; however, the relative conservatism of freedmen in the manumission process is indicated not only in the statistics cited above but more so in what is ascertainable about their slaveholding (the evidence for which is reviewed in Chapter 6) and in an analysis of a small number of their wills.

In a random search of wills for the period 1789 to 1833, the wills of twenty-five freedmen who owned slaves were located.[101] Within these twenty-five wills, 266 slaves are mentioned, but only 12 were designated for immediate manumission upon the death of their owners. These 12 were manumitted by seven owners who owned a total of 86 slaves. Eleven out of 13 slaves owned by four other owners were to be manumitted only if they could purchase themselves, and fourteen owners (who together owned 167 slaves) made no provision for either immediate or eventual manumission through self-purchase. In actual fact, then, only 4.5 percent of the slaves mentioned in the will sample were assured of liberation upon the death of their freedman owners. Again, these figures must be used cautiously because most manumissions were by deed, and at least some of the freedmen

[99] *PP*, 1826, vol. 28, rept. 353.

[100] Manumission deeds, Miscellaneous and Powers Record Books, RB 7/26–27, BDA.

[101] All of the wills are located in the BDA. It is not known what percentage of all freedman wills during the period 1789–1833 these twenty-five represent. In addition, many freedmen undoubtedly died intestate.

in the will sample may have manumitted some of their slaves by deed before their deaths. A great deal of research time and resources would probably yield data from wills and deeds that would permit a more comprehensive analysis of freedman manumission tendencies, as well as a more systematic comparison of white and freedman manumission rates. But, as noted above, the available data suggest that freedmen were neither reluctant to own slaves nor unusually disposed to manumit those they did own.

In discussing freedman manumissions, however, it is important to emphasize that the slaves they owned were of two very different social categories. Freedmen themselves recognized these categories and made them operative in the way in which they participated in the manumission process. One category comprised slaves to whom freedmen bore no relationship as mate, spouse, parent, or child; such slaves apparently had no greater chance for manumission than those owned by whites, and they were used in similar ways. For example, in the freedman wills referred to above, most of the 239 slaves who were not designated for immediate manumission were simply bequeathed to various heirs (on occasion these heirs were slaves themselves); others were to be sold to pay the debts of the deceased, to cover funeral expenses, or to raise cash to be divided among the heirs.

The other category of slaves (there is no way of determining an actual number or percentage) included the mates, spouses, parents, or children of freedman owners. These slaves had a greater chance for manumission. There is little doubt that freedmen frequently tried to liberate persons with whom they shared relationships of close sentimentality; in fact, it can be reasonably argued that it was *expected* that an emancipated slave would ultimately attempt to manumit his close kin, mate, or spouse. Some of the slaves in this category had been purchased by freedmen as a first step toward manumission, while others had been inherited.[102] In some instances manumissions were effected soon after the slaves were acquired, or, at any rate, sometime during the owner's lifetime; in other cases manumission did not occur, either because the fee could not be raised or because some other arrangement, such as manumission in England, could not be made.

For example, London Bourne, who by 1837 was a "wealthy merchant" in Bridgetown, had been born a slave but had been manumitted by his

---

[102]For example, in 1807–8 Waller related the case of a freedwoman who "informed me that she had always lived very respectably as the *chere amie* of an officer of rank . . . ; he had purchased her, and died . . . leaving her a female child; . . . before his death, he had made her free, but that her daughter was not included in the manumission, and was her slave, left to her by will"; Waller reported that, in general, as a result of the high manumission fees required during his stay on the island and because children born to a freedwoman before she was manumitted "must be freed separately, . . . it frequently happens that the children of a free woman are her slaves" (Waller, *Voyage in the West Indies*, p. 93).

father, a freedman, who first purchased him, as well as his mother and four brothers, for a total sum of $3,000.[103] Phoebe Forde also had been a slave, but was able to purchase her freedom; after her manumission she "kept a retail shop and by her assiduity and industry she procured a sufficient sum of money to purchase . . . her illegitimate offspring who were then slaves, and . . . after having purchased [them] she also manumitted them."[104] However, John T. Atherley, a freedman whose case was discussed earlier, purchased his wife and children with the intention of manumitting them, but died before he could raise the manumission fee; his family was freed only subsequent to their being escheated to the Crown. As in the case of many other freedmen, Atherley died intestate, but still others left wills that provided for the manumission of kinsmen. In her 1789 will Bettey Burk freed her own daughter, who she owned as a slave, and declared that her two other slaves be sold to raise the money for the daughter's manumission fee.[105] Providence Padmore specified that after all his debts were fully paid the residue of his estate be used for "manumitting and setting free according to law my daughter Avis."[106] George Gill, on the other hand, wanting to avoid the manumission fee, directed his executors to "execute a good and sufficient deed of sale or conveyance to some person in whom [they] can place confidence, resident in England . . . [of] my son a Negro man slave named Prince for the purpose of having the said slave manumitted in England by such a person so resident there."[107]

Other freedmen, unable to acquire rights over their kinsmen or mates during their lifetimes, attempted to provide for their purchase and subsequent manumission in their wills. Thomas Massiah, for example, ordered that his executor "shall as soon as possible purchase my girl child, Anna Maria by name, at present the property of Doctor Dummett, out of what property my late father . . . bequeathed to me . . . and the said child . . . to be manumitted as soon as possible."[108] Samuel Hall declared that part of his estate be set aside for purchasing his daughter and her two children owned by "Mr. Read of Newfoundland," and "as soon as they are purchased they are to be immediately manumitted according to the laws and custom of Great Britain."[109] Elizabeth Christian Sergeant directed her executors to purchase from a Samuel Game "my reputed mother named Mary Pollard . . . [and to] emancipate and set [her] free . . . according to the laws of this island, and that the money requisite to give effect to the

[103]Thome and Kimball, *Emancipation in the West Indies*, p. 75.
[104]"Petition of Samuel Gabriel, Catherine Abel Duke, and William Collins Ford, Coloured Persons Inhabitants of This Island of Barbados," March 8, 1823, CO 28/92, no. 16x.
[105]Will of Bettey Burk, November 6, 1789, RB 6/19, BDA.
[106]Will of Providence Padmore, February 21, 1825, RB 4/63, *ibid.*
[107]Will of George Gill, August 20, 1811, RB 4/59, *ibid.*
[108]Will of Thomas Massiah, January 28, 1828, RB 4/65, *ibid.*
[109]Will of Samuel Hall, April 7, 1812, RB 4/59, *ibid.*

purchase and emancipation . . . I will and direct be paid out of my general estate."[110] Elizabeth Sergeant also bequeathed the residue of her estate to her mother, specifying that it was to be held in trust by the executors until the mother was fully manumitted and thus legally entitled to inherit.

In leaving property to a kinsman, Sergeant was following an inheritance pattern that freedmen shared with whites—a pattern that obviously was not unique to Barbados—wherein property, as well as other guarantees for material support, was generally bequeathed to kinsmen, spouses, and mates. Thomas Massiah, in his above-quoted will, mentions having inherited property from his father; Willy Blacket directed that the rental income from her house and land was to be used for the maintenance and education of her two nieces;[111] and Coobah Gibbs's property, including a house, household goods, and two slaves, was to be sold and the proceeds divided among her four children and one grandchild.[112]

Also, as among whites, freedmen sometimes bequeathed property to slaves they manumitted, but it appears that such slaves were more apt to inherit something if they were kinsmen or mates of their freedman manumitters. In the sample of twenty-five freedman wills from the period 1789–1833 (discussed above), twelve slaves were to be manumitted immediately and eleven others were to be manumitted if they could purchase themselves. No slaves in the latter category, and only three in the former, were bequeathed property; of the three who received property, only one was specified as a kinsman of the manumitter, and this one was also the only person identified as a kinsman among the total of twenty-three slaves. Phrased another way, of the twenty-three slaves who were designated for immediate or ultimate manumission, only one was specifically identified as a kinsman, and this one received property, while of the twenty-two nonkinsmen only two received property. In another sampling of freedman wills, which was specifically oriented to gathering information on the manumission of kinsmen, seven wills were located which identified the manumitted slaves as kinsmen.[113] Where financial circumstances permitted it, these slaves also inherited property. Hamlet Sealy, for example, bequeathed to "my beloved wife Hester my house . . . and all the household furniture," but required that the property be left "in trust to my beloved brother Charles Sealy Beckles, free mulatto, to hold the possession until my said wife obtain her legal manumission."[114] In other wills referred to previously, Elizabeth Sergeant followed a similar pattern; Samuel Hall set aside a sum of money for the purchase of his enslaved daughter

[110]Will of Elizabeth Christian Sargeant, February 21, 1825, RB 4/63, *ibid.*

[111]Will of Willy Rachel Blacket, June 20, 1825, RB 4/63, *ibid.*

[112]Will of Coobah Gibbs, April 18, 1830, RB 4/66, *ibid.*

[113]A spot check was conducted of will volumes for the years 1811, 1812, 1813, 1823, 1825, and 1828, *ibid.*

[114]Will of Hamlet Sealy, July 29, 1813, RB 4/59, *ibid.*

and two grandchildren and specified that upon their manumission they were to receive his "house, the land upon which it stands, and all appurtenances contained therein"; and Thomas Massiah not only provided for the purchase and manumission of his daughter, but it was also his "earnest request" that she be "maintained as far as my . . . funds will admit."

Although the number of cases referred to above is small, there is every reason to believe that they accurately reflect a general pattern. This pattern involved the bequeathal of property to close kinsmen and mates who were already free; if these kinsmen were not free, efforts were made to manumit them, and, financial circumstances permitting, to provide them with property or some other form of material support. If they did not own their own kinsmen or mates, freedmen attempted to purchase them, either by provisions in a will or, preferably, during their lifetime. In order to purchase their kinsmen and mates, freedmen were faced not only with acquiring the necessary money (a considerable chore for many who were emancipated slaves themselves) but also with obtaining the consent of the owner. It appears that this consent, or agreement to sell property, was largely given under principles that governed the sale of slaves in general. That is, slaves were primarily sold only when the owner perceived that it was in his self-interest to do so. And one can only speculate on the frustration and chagrin of parents, for example, whose desire to purchase (and then manumit) their own children was thwarted or obstructed by owners who refused to relinquish their human property. Similarly, one can only guess at the reactions of freedmen to another problem they often faced in the slave society—that of validating or proving their free status.

VALIDATION OF FREE STATUS

"It was admitted to be a rule," observed a parliamentary commission which investigated Barbados's legal and judicial system in 1823, "that every Negro is presumed to be a slave, unless he can legally prove the contrary."[115] This principle, one of a number the island shared with societies that defined slave status by racial criteria, was employed in a multiplicity of ways by the dominant white group to control, degrade, and humiliate the freedman. And the application of this principle did not stop with death: For holding an inquest "on the body of a white person, or free coloured person known to be such," a coroner in 1823 was paid £5, but he received only £3 15s. "on a slave or on a coloured person unknown."[116]

No statistics are available on the number and types of situations in which freedmen were compelled to prove or validate their status, but it appears that such cases were frequent, and could arise under a variety of

[115]Dwarris, *Substance of Three Reports*, p. 123.
[116]CO 28/92, no. 22.

conditions. A freedman could be arrested for violating a slave law and confined as a slave until his free status was established; or wages might be withheld from a skilled workman by claiming that he was a slave, thus forcing him to prove his free status.[117] (Even so, the legal prohibition of freedman testimony against whites for almost a century after 1721 made it extremely difficult to recover wages in cases of this kind.) Children could be seized from their mothers, or kept in slavery, under the claim that they had been born prior to their mothers' manumissions. In fact, in 1658, one of the earliest legal cases involving a freedwoman and a white slaveowner concerned her claims to the freedom of her children; the governor and the Council resolved the legal query as to "whether Negroes be real or personal estate" by giving the opinion that "if the said Mary was a slave at the time when the three children was born . . . then her master . . . ought to have them."[118] Especially in cases of this kind, one is largely forced to conjecture on the personal tragedies and frustrations involved in validating claims to free status. For example, Elizabeth Ann Miler, a freedwoman, had four children, all of whom she claimed were freeborn. They lived on the lands of the Newton plantation and "were seized as slaves" by the plantation's manager and "at different times [were] very severely treated." Elizabeth Miler's concern led her to England to make a direct appeal to the plantation-owner for her children's freedom, but upon arrival she discovered that the owner had recently died. She returned to Barbados and after six years was able to locate the new owner in England; she then petitioned him "to grant her, under his hand, . . . an order upon his agent for the release of her children."[119] In another case, the executors of a will delayed a woman's manumission and held her children in slavery, although they had been born after the date upon which her manumission should have been executed. She was forced not only to validate her own claim to freedom but to establish that her children had been born subsequent to her owner's death. Although Governor Seaforth found this to be "a most base and cruel case," in which the executors were guilty of "dishonest deeds," he was not surprised, "having had . . . experience how these people [white creoles] can dress up their own cases" and make their actions with respect to nonwhites appear both legally and ethically beyond reproach.[120]

In addition to the examples cited above, freedmen could be seized as runaway slaves by town constables or other whites, and, if unclaimed by an owner, could be sold as slaves if their free status was not successfully

[117]See, for example, Ford to Butcher, April 2, 1806, Seaforth Papers, 46/7/13; "An Act for Granting a Sum of Money to Thomas Henry Marshall . . . ," September 2, 1825, CO 30/21, no. 465.

[118]Minutes of the Council of Barbados, October 5 and November 2, 1658, typescript volumes of Council Minutes for 1654–58, PRO.

[119]Miler to Lane, May 25, 1801, Newton Estate Papers, 523/441.

[120]Seaforth to Beckles, June 23, 1806, Seaforth Papers, 46/7/13.

proven.[121] This problem was greatly exacerbated for the freedman by numbers of slaves who carried out their daily lives under the pretext of being free. That is, slaves who hoped for temporary or permanent escape from their masters left their plantations and went to another rural area, or, more commonly, sought the relative anonymity the towns afforded. This tendency increased over the years, and in the early nineteenth century the governor spoke of the "innundation of pretended free people," especially in the Bridgetown area.[122] The practice (which, it should be noted, was not confined to Barbados)[123] did not abate, however; in fact, it continued for the remainder of the slave period, and one finds slaveowners, such as Henry Grimes, advertising in island newspapers for the return of runaway slaves: "Notice is hereby given to all persons, that a Negro man slave by name Andrew, absented himself from my service. . . . I have understood he has been seeking some employment—he has represented himself to persons as a free man when making for employ. A handsome reward will be given to any person who will apprehend said slave."[124] As late as 1833 the governor wrote to the Colonial Office that "some anxiety exists here at the great number of runaways from the estates. . . . They now amount to between 4 [00] and 500, but many of these have been absent two and three years, which shows the wretched state of the police, as runaways almost always conceal themselves in towns."[125]

One cannot determine the frequency of cases wherein persons who actually knew themselves to be slaves claimed that they were free. But there were undoubtedly many who sincerely believed that they had been manumitted, or born free, only to discover that an irregularity in the manumission process could be used to threaten or nullify their freedom. In 1823 the commissioners investigating the island's legal system found a number of cases of this kind. "A black man complained 'that his manumission had been withheld, in a case where the [£] 50 had been paid.' On inquiry the commissioners learnt that the fact of payment was disputed. No such item appeared in the churchwarden's account (that officer being dead); and the parish . . . insisted upon some proof of the money having reached his hands." Sometimes a slave left his master after being told he was free, but the manumission was later voided because the owner neglected, either willfully or unwittingly, to pay the manumission fee. In other cases a master would promise to manumit a slave in his will, and upon the owner's death the slave, assuming that he was now free, would quite innocently

[121]For particular cases, see *CSPCS, 1701,* p. 49; *1702,* p. 692; and *1702–1703,* pp. 491, 771.
[122]Seaforth to Alton, July 14, 1802, Seaforth Papers, 46/7/7.
[123]A 1783 law in the Virgin Islands, for example, took note of how "many vagrant Negroes, Mulattoes and Mustees daily wander throughout these islands, under fictitious pretensions of freedom," and this pattern also existed in other of the Leeward Islands (Goveia, *Slave Society,* pp. 171–72).
[124]*Barbadian,* March 15, 1831.
[125]Smith to Stanley, November 26, 1833, CO 28/111.

take up a new life; only at some later date would the slave learn that in fact the will had made no provisions for his manumission and/or the fee payment, or that any number of legal technicalities could be used to deny the freedom he was confident he possessed. Sometimes slaves pursued their lives as freedmen while, unknown to them, executors delayed their manumission because an estate's debts had not been paid off; or manumission was "often . . . delayed and excused" by the executors "for want of assets." In still other cases "the enfranchisement of particular slaves was recommended to the heir," who might not choose to comply with the legator's request.[126] In all of these cases the slave could easily assume that he was free and thus inadvertently join the ranks of the "pretended free people."

In one especially complex case a legal technicality seriously threatened the freedom of five adults (and their children) twenty-four years after they thought they had been manumitted. This case merits a summary because it aptly illustrates the excessive price that people could pay for their racial origins, as well as the complicated path that could be followed in the course of trying to achieve freedom. In the late 1770s, John Kirton, a young Scottish bachelor, came to Barbados and "formed a connection" with Luckey, a "colored" slave whose master lived in Bridgetown. Luckey had five children by Kirton and he, "being much attached" to her and the children, was able, after about a dozen years of coresidence, to purchase them in order to effect their manumissions. In 1791 Kirton succeeded in freeing Luckey under island law, but could not raise the money for the children's manumission; instead he deeded them to Luckey, at the same time giving her six other slaves who he hoped, through their being hired out, would enable her to "bestow upon her children the blessings of freedom." Not long after, while Kirton and Luckey were still cohabiting, she became seriously ill and, with her death imminent, made a will bequeathing the six slaves and her children back to Kirton, "knowing that this would assure [the children's] being manumitted at some future date." However, by an omission of some legal wording in the will, Kirton acquired only a "life estate" in all the slaves, and this did not give him the power to manumit or bequeath them. Kirton was not aware of "these strict and technical rules of law," and not long after Luckey's death he returned to Scotland, where he executed a deed of manumission for his five children. Thereafter Kirton married, moved to England, and in his will bequeathed the six other slaves to his wife. After his death in 1816 or 1817, Kirton's wife went to Barbados to claim her bequest. In the process of trying to prove her claim, it was discovered that, under Luckey's will, "whatever might have been her wishes," Kirton did not have the author-

---

[126]Dwarris, *Substance of Three Reports*, pp. 110–11.

ity to manumit his children, and that, technically, all her property should have escheated to the Crown. In a petition to the governor, in which they requested the Crown to annul its rights over them and validate their freedom, Luckey's children expressed the mental anguish and "utmost dismay and alarm" they experienced as a result of "sudden[ly being] reduced to a state of unqualified slavery, and all this under a flaw or a supposed flaw in the will of Luckey"; as a result of Kirton's manumission, they "and their descendants were always considered and passed as free persons, . . . and not even a doubt or suspicion has been entertained for . . . twenty-four years of the validity of their freedom."[127] The request to the Crown was ultimately granted, but, as escheated property, Luckey's family had a clear direction to take in claiming and validating their free status. Most others in their position were forced to go through more conventional channels to establish their freedom against the claims of private owners.

"I wish very much to see the coloured people equitably protected in their real rights," wrote Governor Seaforth; "but," he added, "before they can claim the rights of freemen they must produce proofs that they are free."[128] "Proofs" that were variously found acceptable included documents such as receipts issued by churchwardens upon payment of manumission fees, deeds of manumission executed in England, wills, or, as the senior justice of the peace reported to the Commission of Inquiry in 1823, "the evidence of free persons."[129]

Proving one's freedom, however, was no easy matter, not only because persons of Negroid ancestry were denied protection in the legal and judicial system, but also because there was no effective system for registering freedmen and manumissions. Early in his administration, Seaforth, bothered by the problems involved in validating freedmen's status, hoped to "induce the legislature to . . . establish a Register for the Free Coloured People. This would evidently be of great utility to the whites, and I think not less so to the really free coloured people, as it would render their situation more respectable and less equivocal."[130] Twelve years later, Orderson, a white creole, made a similar argument:

A general registry of the free people of colour would be a measure towards them of as sound policy in securing their liberties, as that of a registry of slaves could be for ascertaining the actual villanage they are liable to. By this double registry, a principle would at once be estab-

[127]Petition of Anderson and Kirton to Lord Combermere, [1818], CO 28/87. See also Combermere to Bathurst, May 19, 1818; Brookshank to Bathurst, August 24, 1818; Bathurst to Combermere, September 8, 1818; and Combermere to Bathurst, November 4, 1818; all in *ibid.*

[128]Seaforth to Alton, July 14, 1802, Seaforth Papers, 46/7/7.

[129]Reply to query 30, "First Report of the Commissioner of Inquiry into the Administration of Civil and Criminal Justice in the West Indies," *PP*, 1825, vol. 15, rept. 517.

[130]Seaforth to Alton, July 14, 1802, Seaforth Papers, 46/7/7.

lished, by which these respective classes of the population would be clearly defined, and an insuperable barrier interposed to all future injustice towards both the white slave owner and the free man of colour.[131]

As noted earlier, registration of manumissions was one of the recommendations made by the colonial secretary in his 1823 circular dispatch concerning amelioration of colonial slave laws; although a number of manumissions came to be registered in the Barbados secretary's office, many, especially those that were effected in England, went unrecorded.

The validation of freedmen's status was also made difficult by the lack of systematic judicial procedures for the adjudication of contested manumission cases. Thus, the 1823 Commission of Inquiry reported:

> In Barbados, applications are constantly made to the governor in cases of this nature. It is impossible to discover *how* the governor derives any authority upon the subject. He has no jurisdiction, that is apparent; and it is clear that his decisions upon a question of property cannot be binding. Claims founded on manumission are sometimes incidentally considered before justices of the peace; but there nowhere exists *a regular court for the trial of such questions.*[132]

Since justices of the peace were white and were slaveholders themselves, it is highly unlikely that many proceedings, especially where the issues were ambiguous, worked to the benefit of nonwhites.

The 1826 "slave consolidation act" did provide a formal procedure and legal authority for establishing the status of persons who claimed their freedom, but only with respect to those who were arrested and confined in jail as slaves. If a jailed nonwhite claimed that he was a freedman, but was unable "satisfactorily to prove the same," the provost marshall was authorized to advertise in the newspapers describing the prisoner and requiring anyone "knowing the reputed slave" to appear and testify "whether such person or persons is free or not." The advertisement was to continue for three months; if, by the end of this period, no "satisfactory information of the freedom of such persons" was received, the provost marshall was to notify the governor and the Council. The law authorized the governor and the Council to "hear and determine upon the case . . . and unless it shall be proved to the[ir] satisfaction . . . that the person so claiming to be free is *bona fide* a slave," they were to "set him or her at liberty."[133] It is not known how many cases were brought up under this law, nor can it be established whether any such cases resulted in a decision that favored the nonwhite claimant to freedom.

[131]Orderson, *Cursory Remarks*, pp. 26–27.
[132]Dwarris, *Substance of Three Reports*, p. 110, italics in the original.
[133]Clause 14, "An Act to Repeal Several Acts and Clauses of Acts respecting Slaves . . . ," October 13, 1826, *PP*, 1826–27, vol. 25, unnumbered rept., pp. 205–30 of Barbados section.

In general, then, during most of the slave period, the courses of action that a freedman could take when his freedom was contested were extremely limited. If he did not have unequivocal documentary evidence, he could either plead with an owner to confirm his manumission or appeal to the governor, and through him hope for the Crown's intervention. Up to 1721, freedmen were allowed to testify in legal cases against whites, and some of the earliest litigations involving nonwhites were cases of contested manumissions or validation of free status.[134] Between 1721 and 1817, however, freedmen were denied the right to testify, because of their racial ancestry; it was thus more difficult to validate one's claim to freedom when this claim necessitated, in the absence of documentary evidence, a freedman's contradicting the legal evidence of a white who claimed him as a slave. The ramifications of debarment from legal testimony went far beyond contested manumission cases and were one dimension of the restricted civil status ascribed to freedmen by white society. The nature of this status and the freedman's participation in the island's judicial and political systems will be discussed in subsequent chapters.

---

[134]Minutes of the Council of Barbados, March 20, 1655, and October 5 and November 2, 1658, typescript volumes of Council Minutes for 1654–58, PRO. For a case involving Amerindians in the early 1650s, see Handler, "Amerindian Slave Population," pp. 53–54.

III

THE POLITICO-JUDICIAL SYSTEM: LEGAL STATUS AND THE REDUCTION OF CIVIL RIGHTS

At the turn of the nineteenth century, John Poyer aptly expressed the ideology that rationalized the constraints placed on Barbados's freedmen:

In every well constituted society, a state of subordination necessarily arises from the nature of civil government. Without this no political union could long subsist. To maintain this fundamental principle, it becomes absolutely necessary to preserve the distinctions which naturally exist or are accidentally introduced into the community. With us, two grand distinctions result from the state of society: First, between the white inhabitants and free people of colour, and secondly, between masters and slaves. Nature has strongly defined the difference [not] only in complexion, but in the mental, intellectual and corporeal faculties of the different species. Our colonial code has acknowledged and adopted the distinction. . . . I am not an advocate for cruelty or oppression. . . . Neither am I inclined to recommend the practice of unnecessary severity towards those who have obtained their freedom. They ought to enjoy every privilege which can be granted them consistent with a just and liberal policy. All that I contend for is that they should not be suffered to exceed the bounds of that subordinate state in which divine providence has placed them and to which the welfare of the colony requires they should be restricted.[1]

To see how the Barbadian plantocracy (as represented by its legislative bodies) controlled freedmen and legally defined "that subordinate state in which divine providence has placed them," this and the following chapter chronicle the major events and legislative decisions that affected their civil status and participation in the politico-judicial system. This chapter concentrates on the way in which the status of the freedman, as a *freeman*, was early defined and curtailed; Chapter 4 discusses the events and processes by which this status was expanded.

---

[1][John Poyer], *A Letter Addressed to His Excellency . . . Francis Lord Seaforth, by a Barbadian* (Bridgetown, 1801), pp. 22–24.

During the seventeenth century and the first two decades of the eighteenth, all Barbadian laws that mentioned "Negroes" or "mulattoes" focused on regulating the behavior and defining the status of the slave population.[2] No laws specifically concerned freedmen, and, although they undoubtedly suffered considerable social discrimination, their legal status was, for all intents and purposes, the same as that of white freemen.

In the first century of the slave period, there were few freedmen. The first population estimate, 107, was made in 1748 and was probably on the low side, but there is every indication that in earlier decades freedmen comprised no more than a slight percentage of the total free population. Very little can be said about freedmen during this early period, but assuredly only a handful could have possessed property sufficient to enfranchise them under Barbadian law. However, it was apparently the presence of such persons, and the likelihood that more would appear, which first caused the legislature to circumscribe the freedman's civil status.

This circumscription was contained within a major law, passed in 1721, which modified procedures and qualifications concerning the eligibility to vote, hold elective office, and serve on juries. Those entitled to enfranchisement were required to be "freeholders," twenty-one-year-old males who were "natural born" or naturalized British subjects, Christians, and who owned at least ten acres of land or a house having an annual taxable value of £10 island currency.[3] Earlier electoral laws, which generally followed those of England, had contained similar qualifications and thus, of course, they had disenfranchised the poorest whites, women, and the island's Jewish community.[4] Unlike previous laws, however, this one added the requirement that a "freeholder" had to be *white*, and one of its clauses stipulated that "no person whatsoever . . . whose original extraction shall be proved to have

[2]See William Rawlin, *The Laws of Barbados* (London, 1699), *passim*; and Richard Hall, *Acts, Passed in the Island of Barbados. From 1643 to 1762, Inclusive* (London, 1764), *passim*.
[3]Hall, *Acts*, pp. 252–69.
[4]For these earlier laws, see *ibid.*, nos. 4, 26, 95. William Dickson found that

the qualifications of the electors are so pitifully low as to admit in that quality . . . a rabble of poor, ignorant, incorrigible white men, nursed up in all the deplorable, not to call them savage and brutal, prejudices of the slave-system. The favourite candidates of those voters, are men who support what they, with incredible absurdity, call their "constitutional rights"; that is, their *rights* of doing all manner of *wrongs* to the unprotected Negro race. . . . the members [of the Assembly], who in general are fully as desirous of retaining their seats as those of the British House of Commons, are kept dependent on the popular opinion (such as it is). . . . The unlucky member who should dare to propose or to support any measure understood to favour the Negroes, or to trench on the *unbounded and absolute supremacy* of all white men over all black and tawny men, would be sure to lose his seat in a few weeks or months. And thus the very class of men from whose injustice, rapacity, and brutality the laws *ought* to protect, the unhappy Negroes and people of colour, may themselves be said to make the laws, or to control or powerfully influence, those who do! White men are held both by the laws, and by the general opinion, to be the only *legitimate* defenders of their country.

Mitigation of Slavery in Two Parts (London, 1814), pp. 355–56, italics in the original.

been from a Negro" could testify in court cases or other legal proceedings involving whites; nonwhites, including slaves, could give "evidence . . . only on the trial of Negroes and other slaves";[5] and, as the law was later interpreted, freedmen were also prevented from giving "evidence . . . either in civil or criminal cases, even among themselves."[6]

The 1721 law had the obvious effect of stripping freedmen of a fundamental aspect of their citizenship by denying them the right to participate in the politico-judicial system. They were also sheared of a major device that protected against assault, theft, and similar offenses against property and person. In addition, although there is little information on legal cases involving freedmen prior to 1721, some of the known cases stemmed from complaints that they were seized and illegally held as slaves;[7] debarment from legal testimony assuredly made it more difficult to win cases of this kind and to validate their claims to free status.

By denying the right of testimony to all persons "whose original extraction shall be proved to have been from a Negro," the 1721 law also implicitly provided the racial basis for a broader principle whereby the status of free nonwhites would be defined. That is, in neither the 1721 law nor any subsequent legislative action were phenotypic differences among nonwhites recognized. Although the laws often made terminological distinctions between free "Negroes," or "blacks," and free "mulattoes," or "coloreds," these terms never carried legal implications. Furthermore, the island's legal code contained no definition (and apparently no attempt was ever made to establish one) of the point at which Caucasoid characteristics would permit a freedman to be defined as white. Caucasoid features facilitated some relationships, such as the sexual liaisons freedwomen formed with whites, manumissions, and apparently entrée into certain occupational categories or economic pursuits. No one, however, who was known to be of Negroid ancestry could become legally or socially white, "even though," as Pinckard observed in the late eighteenth century, that person "should be of fairer skin than the fairest European."[8] In striking contrast to the legal code of Jamaica,

[5]Hall, Acts, p. 256.

[6]Seaforth to Hobart, June 6, 1802, Seaforth Papers, 46/7/7, SRO; see also Beckwith to Liverpool, November 2, 1811, CO 28/80.

[7]See Minutes of the Barbados Council, January 23, 1701, CSPCS, 1701, p. 49; October 27, 1702, ibid., 1702, p. 692; and June 9 and October 26, 1703, ibid., 1702–1703, pp. 491, 771. For earlier cases, see Minutes of the Barbados Council, March 20, 1655, and October 5 and November 2, 1658, typescript volumes of Council Minutes for 1654–58, PRO.

[8]George Pinckard, Notes on the West Indies, 3 vols. (London, 1806), 1: 244. Waller related that a freedwoman offered to sell him her very light-skinned slave daughter to serve as his mistress—under the condition that he would manumit her when he left the island. The mother "observed also as a greater inducement, that there would be no need to purchase the freedom of her [daughter's] children [of whom Waller was to be the father] as she was herself of the last degree of colour that could be enslaved, and that her children would necessarily be free, and entitled to all the privileges of white people" (John A. Waller, A Voyage in the West Indies [London, 1820], p. 94). There is, however, no corroboration for the statute or social custom that Waller's narrative implied, and in the 1820s a parliamentary commis-

where miscegenation was apparently much greater, the Barbadian code did not contain provisions which permitted freedmen, after a certain generation or with primarily Caucasian features, to be defined as white.[9] In general, then, in Barbados, for legal (and, to a considerable degree, social) purposes anyone with a hint of Negroid ancestry was considered a Negro, and the island's plantocracy devised a relatively simple method, as implied in the 1721 law, for distinguishing between free whites and free nonwhites.

In 1739, a second law specifically related to freedmen established manumission fees (thus indirectly attempting to control the growth of their numbers) and permitted "the evidence or testimony of any slave, where the same is supported with very good and sufficient corroborating circumstances, against any free Negro, Indian, or Mulatto."[10] Permitting slaves to testify was not a gesture designed to ameliorate their legal condition, but rather a device which made it less cumbersome for whites to recover stolen property or press charges against freedmen who engaged in illicit trade with slaves. At this early period, marketing activities with slaves were important to freedmen. The goods exchanged often involved items stolen by the slaves from their masters' properties, and quite often slaves were the only witnesses to the transactions. By establishing manumission fees and thus making legal provisions for the support of manumitted slaves, it was hoped that freedmen would be discouraged from engaging in illicit activities.

Thus, by 1740 a handful of provisions in the island's legal code particularly referred to freedmen, but throughout the remainder of the eighteenth century no other major statutes were in force and none apparently were passed (except for a 1783 law which sought to close a loophole in manumission procedures) that specifically curtailed their legal or civil status.[11] The social discrimination that restricted the freedman's behavior and opportunities was sufficient to perpetuate white dominance, and the plantocracy apparently felt no need to impose, for example, legal restrictions on the occupational roles freedmen could fill or the nature and value of property they could hold or inherit. By contrast, by the latter half of the eighteenth century, freedmen in Jamaica were prevented from inheriting property from whites beyond a certain value, had limits placed on the amount of land they

---

sion investigating the island's legal and judicial system inquired, "Do descendants of a slave ever and when become free by a commixture with whites?" The answer was an unequivocal "Never" (reply to query 39, "First Report of the Commissioner of Inquiry into the Administration of Civil and Criminal Justice in the West Indies," *PP*, 1825, vol. 15, rept. 517). The system remained unchanged in this respect for the rest of the slave period.

[9]Sheila Duncker, "The Free Coloured and Their Fight for Civil Rights in Jamaica, 1800–1830" (M.A. thesis, University of London, [1960]), pp. 20–22, 37–48; Barry W. Higman, "Slave Population and Economy in Jamaica at the Time of Emancipation" (Ph.D. diss., University of the West Indies, 1970), pp. 128, 130; Edward Brathwaite, *The Development of Creole Society in Jamaica, 1770–1820* (London: Oxford University Press, 1971), pp. 167–68.

[10]Hall, *Acts*, pp. 323–25.

[11]See *ibid., passim*; and Samuel Moore, *The Public Acts in Force, Passed by the Legislature of Barbados, from May 11th, 1762, to April 8th, 1800, Inclusive* (London, 1801), *passim*.

could purchase, and, if employed on plantations, were legally confined to
subordinate positions.[12] This is not to suggest that the Barbadian plantocracy was more "liberal" than the Jamaican one, but merely to indicate
that repressive laws were enacted in Jamaica in response to a socioeconomic
situation which was inconsequential in Barbados.

Generally speaking, in Barbados there were no legal restrictions on the
economic activities of freedmen, although a short-lived exception to this
occurred between 1774 and 1779. In the former year a major law was passed
which regulated the internal marketing system; one of its clauses prohibited
a few common trading practices followed by slaves and freedmen, including
the buying of goods directly from newly arrived vessels before they had
unloaded their cargoes.[13] Five years later the legislature acknowledged the
ineffectiveness of this clause and conceded to the continuance of the practice, but it required freedman hucksters to buy an annual license; at the
same time, however, a license, with the same fee, was also made mandatory
for "all white hucksters."[14]

In general, when the laws specified sanctions for violations, distinctions
were made between slave and free, but not among freemen themselves.
Slaves usually received up to thirty-nine lashes for a first offense in a minor
"crime," while freedmen and whites received the same fines or terms of
imprisonment. For example, the above-mentioned marketing law imposed
a £50 fine on all unlicensed freeman hucksters, and a 1784 law invoked a
three-month jail sentence for "every white person, Free Mulatto, or Free
Negro" who violated it;[15] in 1762 all freemen who threw garbage into the
streets of the towns were given a 10s. fine; and in 1764 a fine of £10 was imposed on those who concealed deserters from the British army.[16] In fact,
when in 1805 the House of Assembly debated a bill that would have made
the wanton murder of a slave a capital offense, the Speaker supported its
passage by stressing that "the [present] exemption from death . . . is not
confined to white men, but extends equally to all free persons. . . . and is
there a man who will say, that the black or mulatto murderer ought not to
suffer death?"[17] It cannot be assumed that the island's legal code was interpreted or applied with equal fairness to freemen of both races, but the
equality implied in most laws is important to the legal definition of the status
that freedmen, as freemen, possessed.

As in the legal sanctions they imposed, the vast majority of the laws
passed in the eighteenth century—which did not specifically or indirectly
relate to the rights of freeholders—did not limit the activities or the legal

[12]Duncker, "Free Coloured," pp. 22, 30, 88; Brathwaite, Creole Society, p. 170.
[13]Moore, Public Acts, pp. 166–67.
[14]Ibid., pp. 215–16.
[15]Ibid., pp. 251–57; see also ibid., pp. 218–19, 238–47, 381–408.
[16]Hall, Acts, pp. 218–19, 441.
[17]"Meeting of the House of Assembly, July 9, 1805," Barbados Mercury and Bridgetown
Gazette, April 16, 1805.

protection of freedmen.[18] With major exceptions stemming from the law of 1721, freedmen *theoretically* shared many of the rights and privileges held by white British subjects. They were considered freemen. Although their free status was qualified by their racial ancestry, which led Governor Seaforth to designate them "*the unappropriated people,*"[19] there was no legally defined intermediate status for freedmen—that is, a status which by law placed them between whites and slaves. Undoubtedly, the lack of such an intermediate status and the fact that they were freemen and British subjects made it extraordinarily difficult, as the years progressed, for freedmen to accept the subordinate position into which white colonial society placed them.

Freedmen, after all, were not slaves. They were no one's property, and they were not the subjects of the many laws that defined the property status of slaves and restricted their behavior and movements. "In Barbadoes," Governor Parry reported in the late 1780s, "the power of masters over their slaves is at present unlimited by law, excepting by a small fine on the person who wantonly kills his slave."[20] Although the wanton murder of a freedman might go unpunished, under the law the murder of a freedman was as much a capital offense as the murder of a white.

Because of the supreme power the master held over his slave, he could choose, for example, to prevent the slave from marrying, attending the Anglican church, or becoming literate; he could sexually degrade the slave, beat him at whim, and compel his labor at all times. Slaves had no real legal protection, lacked civil rights, and were surrounded by a diversity of repressive laws and social conventions that stemmed from the power a master wielded over his human property. Although repressive legislative enactments were often evaded, their mere presence underscored the profound differences between the legal status of slaves and that of freedmen.

As freemen, freedmen shared with whites many of the privileges and obligations of citizenship that were totally denied slaves, either by law or through social convention. Freedmen were entitled to form their own associations, petition legislative bodies, and hold public meetings; as with

[18]There were some exceptions, such as a 1774 law which attempted to curtail the growth of parochial relief rolls by penalizing the mothers or reputed fathers of illegitimate children who became wards of the parish because they were not adequately supported by their parents; the increasing numbers of such children were straining the resources of the vestries, especially in Saint Michael. The law, however, applied only to whites (Moore, *Public Acts*, pp. 171–75). A similar law was enacted in Antigua in 1786 (Elsa V. Goveia, *Slave Society in the British Leeward Islands at the End of the Eighteenth Century* [New Haven: Yale University Press, 1965], pp. 219–20), and in that island, as well as in Barbados, the law was associated with a social convention that denied freedmen various forms of relief provided by the vestries out of parochial tax revenues—despite the fact that freedmen had to pay such taxes.

[19]Seaforth to Hobart, June 6, 1802, Seaforth Papers, 46/7/7.

[20]Reply of Governor Parry to query 1, "Report of the Lords of the Committee of Council . . . ; Submitting . . . the Evidence concerning the Present State of the . . . Trade in Slaves; and . . . the Effects and Consequences of this Trade, . . . in Africa and the West Indies . . . ," pt. 3, Barbados section, *PP*, 1789, vol. 26.

whites, the law required them to pay taxes (there was no differential rate) and to serve in the militia, and they were allowed to possess and carry firearms; they were not legally restricted from traveling on the island or abroad, and were not prevented from owning or bequeathing property.

The laws which guaranteed the property rights of whites and protected them from fraud, theft, assault, and so forth, were, albeit sometimes implicitly, equally applicable to freedmen. For example, freedmen were included under the protective umbrellas of 1688 and 1749 laws that made it a crime for slaves to "offer any violence to any Christian, by striking or the like," and to use "any insolent language or gesture to any white or free person."[21] As with whites, freedmen were "considered subject to the criminal code of England, where it is in force with free persons," while slaves were governed by a separately constructed colonial code. All freemen accused of criminal offenses were tried in the island's criminal courts, particularly the Court of Grand Sessions, while slaves were tried in a "slave court," which consisted of five judicial officials when the offense was capital, and only one when it was minor—there were no juries in the "slave courts."[22]

Freedmen could not testify in the courts nor sit in judgment, for they were debarred from magistracies, judgeships, and jury duty; nor could freedmen participate in the legislative process as voters or officeholders. As noted above, these major rights were denied them by virtue of their racial ancestry, and acquisition of these rights was to become a major political issue in the nineteenth century. Another, related issue involved exemption from arrest. A clause in a 1672 law specified that debtors who intended to leave Barbados were immune from arrest while suits against them were pending if they owned ten or more acres of land.[23] This privilege was granted to encourage whites at this early period to settle on the island and become landed proprietors. As the years passed, the law was frequently circumvented, and in 1770 another law was designed to remedy the situation.[24] Neither of these laws explicitly denied freedmen immunity from arrest, but the judiciary disqualified landless whites, as well as other persons who could not qualify as freeholders under the island's electoral laws. By the mid-1820s freedmen were seeking, in the words of one of their leaders, "to be exempt from arrests when possessed of property sufficient to exempt other persons."[25] (Although the number of freedman property-holders had increased by this period, very few owned more than ten acres of land; thus,

[21]Hall, *Acts*, pp. 114, 355.

[22]F. Dwarris, *Substance of Three Reports of the Commission of Inquiry into the Administration of Civil and Criminal Justice in the West Indies* (London, 1827), pp. 85–90.

[23]Hall, *Acts*, pp. 87–93.

[24]Moore, *Public Acts*, pp. 80–82.

[25]Testimony of Samuel Francis Collymore, "Examination of Witnesses Taken at the Bar of the House of Assembly . . . ," February 3 and 4, 1824, CO 28/93. The 1672 and 1770 laws were modified or repealed in 1829; see p. 101 of this volume.

immunity from arrest under the laws of 1672 and 1770 was undoubtedly of greater symbolic than real significance to most freedmen.)

Despite his free status, the vulnerability to which the freedman's racial characteristics exposed him, and his exclusion from legal testimony, made a mockery of his freedom. Whites, for example, could ignore debts, could cheat, rob, falsely accuse, and even assault freedmen with relative impunity. By the late eighteenth century, tensions were especially high between freedmen and lower-class whites. The latter, who were becoming increasingly depressed economically—as a result of conditions largely created by the slave system itself[26]—and who shared the racist attitudes of wealthier whites, were apparently not too hesitant to unleash their racism and frustrations against freedmen and slaves. William Dickson, who knew Barbados well and had lived on the island for about thirteen years in the 1770s and 1780s, remarked that "many of the poor whites are disposed to take, and too many of them do take, every advantage over the Negroes."[27] "The Negroes and mulattoes, both the slaves and those called Free," he later wrote, "daily suffer the most atrocious injuries."[28] Joshua Steele, a knowledgeable planter, offered a similar opinion,[29] and within the same general period Governor Seaforth observed that freedmen received "the most barbarous and insulting oppression . . . by the refuse of the whites."[30] Whites of all socioeconomic levels, however, were well aware that the racist attitudes of their peers sitting on juries or the bench would generally yield them the benefit of any doubt in legal cases; if nonwhites were the only witnesses to legal transgressions, there was even less of a chance that a victimized freedman could win redress. In sum, freedmen could not effectively bring charges against injustices nor defend themselves, because "Negroes or their descendants . . . [were] evidence in no case whatsoever, against white men."[31]

Although freedmen were not denied legal counsel, the disabilities they suffered were dramatically illustrated in a highly publicized and controversial incident that occurred in 1796. Joe Denny, a freedman resident of Speightstown, was accused of murdering his neighbor, John Stroud, a poor white with whom Denny was on relatively good terms. Evidence presented at the trial strongly indicated that Stroud's death was accidental and that Denny had fired his gun in order to protect his property: his garden, con-

---

[26]See pp. 123–24.

[27]William Dickson, *Letters on Slavery, to Which Are Added Addresses to the Whites and to the Free Negroes of Barbados* (London, 1789), p. 41.

[28]Dickson, *Mitigation of Slavery*, p. 356.

[29]Reply of Joshua Steele to Governor Parry, 1788, *PP*, 1789, vol. 26, p. 35.

[30]Seaforth to Camden, September 1, 1804, Seaforth Papers, 46/7/7.

[31]Reply of Joshua Steele to Governor Parry, 1788, *PP*, 1789, vol. 26, p. 34. "Without the power of giving evidence against ill disposed Whites, the Free Negroes . . . have, in truth, far less protection than the slaves of spirited and athletic White owners; . . . [Whites] scruple not to put in force the [law] . . . against men of their own complexion" (Dickson, *Mitigation of Slavery*, p. xxv).

taining food crops, had been robbed several times; Stroud appeared one night, and because of the darkness Denny mistook him for the thief and fired. Neither Denny nor other freedman witnesses could testify, and the prejudice and hostility of the white witnesses and jury made it difficult to determine whether the shooting had been premeditated. Denny was nonetheless judged guilty and sentenced to death. There was considerable pressure for his execution, especially among "the lower orders of white people," but because of ambiguities in the case Governor Ricketts suspended the execution. Denny was ultimately pardoned by the Crown, although he was permanently exiled from Barbados in order to pacify the white populace and avoid internal strife.[32]

During the slave period, there were a number of instances wherein slaves assaulted and sometimes murdered whites. Stroud's case, however, is the only known one that involved a white killed by a freedman. Freedman physical assaults on whites were apparently equally rare, and one must assume that, if they occurred, they were met with extreme harshness by white society. (The rarity of such cases is indicated not only by the lack of positive evidence, but also by the fact that the Barbadian plantocracy never created legislation specifically for freedmen who struck whites, legislation that did exist, for example, in the Leewards.)[33] However, white assaults on freedmen (and, of course, slaves) were much more common, and the island's legal code and judicial machinery functioned minimally to inhibit their occurrence. "The most shocking outrage and unprovoked mistreatment"[34] that freedmen experienced at the hands of whites sometimes led to murder.

"It is usual," Joshua Steele reported in 1788, "when a Negro is wantonly shot by some angry white man, in the neighborhood of Bridgetown, that the free Negroes and Mulattoes make a ceremonious funeral. . . . Many such wanton murders [of freedmen and slaves] happen in the country, but when distant from the towns are scarcely noticed, any more than the death of a cow."[35] In 1799 a freedwoman, Sarah Payne, was permanently crippled, and her infant son killed, by gunfire; not long afterward Solomon Sargeant, a

---

[32]A considerable number of documents on the Denny case and its repercussions are on file in CO 28/65. The case was also discussed by Robert H. Schomburgk (*The History of Barbados* [London, 1848], pp. 354–55), and, in more prejudicial fashion, by John Poyer (*The History of Barbados from the Discovery of the Island . . . till . . . 1801* [London, 1808], pp. 632–44). Governor Ricketts's behavior was severely criticized by many Barbadian whites who felt that his "strange partiality to people of colour" in general, and in the Denny case in particular, was a result of the influence exerted on him by his freedwoman mistress Betsey Goodwin; she had come to Barbados with him from Tobago in 1794. As far as can be determined, Ricketts was the only governor of Barbados who had a freedwoman mistress, and it is perhaps of more than passing interest to mention that he was a Jamaican creole. According to Poyer, Betsey Goodwin resided at the governor's mansion and "enjoyed all the privileges of a wife, except the honour of publicly presiding at his table" (*ibid.*, p. 639).

[33]Elsa Goveia, "The West Indian Slave Laws of the Eighteenth Century," *Revista de Ciencas Sociales*, 4 (1960): 85.

[34]Seaforth to Hobart, June 6, 1802, Seaforth Papers, 46/7/7.

[35]Reply of Joshua Steele to Governor Parry, 1788, *PP*, 1789, vol. 26, p. 35.

freedman, also was murdered. The two killings were unrelated and occurred in different parishes. In each case, however, a white man was held responsible, and the coroners' inquests "declared wilful murder." Apparently nothing was done in the Payne case, but the person accused of murdering Sargeant was arrested and brought to trial. Although the island's attorney general felt there was sufficient evidence to warrant an indictment, the accused was discharged and released from prison. The precise reason for this discharge is unclear, but freedmen evidently believed that it related to the inadmissibility of freedman testimony and the racism of the all-white jury.[36] A similar case occurred some three decades later, at a time when the right of testimony had been extended to certain, but not all, freedmen. W. G. Mandeville, a white man, was accused of murdering James Clarke, a freedman, and was arraigned before a magistrate. Various sworn depositions made it clear that Mandeville had deliberately fired at Clarke, but all the principal deponents were freedmen; they were later disqualified as competent witnesses under the existing law, and Mandeville was set free.[37]

Petitions by freedman groups to legislative bodies had become relatively common by the time the Mandeville-Clarke case took place, and private petitions were submitted throughout most of the slave period, but the 1799 murders precipitated what may have been the first group petition, in which freedmen called for their protection under the law and a change in their legal status. This petition apparently marked the beginning of a civil rights struggle which, despite many vicissitudes, frustrations, and the intransigence of a basically reactionary plantocracy, was to continue to the end of the slave period.

In a 1799 "memorial" addressed to Governor Ricketts and the Barbados Council, fifty-eight freedmen poignantly expressed their concerns and anxieties. Since the release of the accused murderer, they noted, "many profligate white persons have wantonly threatened to kill some of your Memorialists without the smallest provocation; and we not only walk abroad under apprehension of being assassinated, but we are continually in dread of being murdered in our houses; that we conceive from such threats, that we are not under the protection of the laws, and that we may at any time be deprived of our lives, without redress; if so, the condition of your Memorialists and their posterity must be deplorable indeed." Their identification as British subjects was stressed in their "unfeigned and inviolable attachment . . . to our King and Constitution" and in their "glory in being subjects under such a government." Nonetheless, the freedmen were aware of their

[36]These events are related in a petition signed by fifty-eight freedmen and addressed to the governor and the Council: "The Humble Memorial and Remonstrance of the Free Coloured People . . . ," October 14, 1799, Minutes of the Barbados Council, October 15, 1799, Lucas MSS, BPL.

[37]Musson to Lyon, January 12, 1831, CO 28/107; "Case of Mandeville for Murder, John Mayers, King's Solicitor," January 15, 1831, *ibid.*; "Address to Viscount Goderich from a Committee of Free Coloured Persons," July 3, 1832, CO 28/109.

"subordinate state" and were "convinced that it is our interest, as well as duty, to use our constant endeavors by every act of gratitude, obedience, and loyalty, to endear ourselves to all in authority." As British subjects, however, they were entitled to "enjoy the rights of freemen, and the protection of the laws," and their petition went to the heart of the matter when it pointed out the contradiction in their free status:

> Your Memorialists . . . have always been led to believe, and the opinions of the ablest lawyers support them in such belief, that unlawfully to kill, with malice of forethought, any free person, whether White or Coloured, is murder; and that the perpetrator of so horrid a deed, is both by the law of God, and the common law of the land, liable to be tried for a capital offence, and if convicted upon sufficient evidence, to suffer death. But if a white man may murder a Free Coloured man, and escape the punishment of such laws, then we have no security for our lives, and we are in a much worse condition than our slaves.[38]

The "memorialists" specifically requested the governor and the Council to "interpose in our behalf, and by such measures as they may think proper, to put our lives under the protection and security of the law." Implicit within this appeal was the right of legal testimony, a right which was of major significance (and the acquisition of which became a dominant issue in the civil rights struggle of the ensuing years). At this period, however, conditions were not yet ripe for so dramatic a move as ameliorating the status of freedmen; in fact, the plantocracy perceived that the problem lay in the freedmen's increasing numbers and wealth, and its response involved moves to slow the growth of the freedman population and to limit its ability to acquire property.

By the turn of the nineteenth century, the freedman community was becoming increasingly organized, the number of freedmen had grown considerably, and some had become—relative to local standards for nonwhites— noticeable in their wealth and property holdings. Concerned with the increase in the freedman population, the legislature passed an act in 1801 which significantly raised manumission fees and which, from its own perspective, was designed to inhibit population growth. John Poyer, an articulate ideologist for the racial stratification system that was the foundation of the Barbadian social order, applauded this act, but felt that it did not go far enough. He suggested additional legislation to limit the property holdings of freedmen: "That they should be allowed to exercise their talents and industry in procuring a comfortable subsistence for themselves and their families . . . is readily admitted. But that they should be prohibited from purchasing or acquiring lands or slaves is a measure of prudence inseparably connected with the safety of the country and perfectly congenial with

---

[38]"The Humble Memorial and Remonstrance of the Free Coloured People . . . ," October 14, 1799, Minutes of the Barbados Council, October 15, 1799, Lucas MSS.

the spirit of our constitution."[39] In a similar vein a wealthy planter, reflecting the views of many within his class, advised a friend that "we certainly ought to open the eyes of the legislature and convince them of the immediate necessity of checking by proper measures the growing . . . power of that class of people in our island, and more particularly in Bridgetown."[40]

In the plantocracy's thinking, property implied wealth, and wealth could create influence. It was also felt that both wealth and influence would exacerbate the freedmen's dissatisfaction with the restrictions under which they lived. This dissatisfaction might lead to a serious movement for an extension of civil rights, and thus threaten the status quo that was necessary for the preservation of a society based on a premise of white superiority. "Like the Baron in feudal times," John Poyer commented, "these coloured proprietors may become turbulent and dangerous."[41] Governor Seaforth also found political dangers inhering in the "strange inconsistency in our laws and customs," by which freedmen were denied "the shadow of any civil right," and yet were "allowed to acquire and possess land and other real property."[42] On a number of occasions he urged the legislature either to reform the laws, a move with which his own sentiments accorded, or to restrict the freedman's acquisition of property, a move which he felt would be necessary for the island's security if civil rights were not extended. In the first few years of the nineteenth century, views which stressed the political dangers of a wealthy freedman population were manifest in serious plantocratic efforts to restrict the property holdings of freedmen.

Concerned about these efforts, a group of freedmen petitioned the Assembly in October 1801; they expressed their anxieties and also requested reform in their status, particularly in the right to testify.[43] No action was taken on this request. Instead, about eleven months later, "an act to prevent the accumulation of real property by free Negroes and free persons descended from Negroes" was introduced in the Assembly by General Robert Haynes, a wealthy planter and attorney for a number of estates. The bill, which was rapidly passed and sent to the Council for approval, prohibited

---

[39][Poyer], *Letter*, pp. 25–26.

[40]Alleyne to Thorne, November 20, 1801, and February 1, 1802, Alleyne Letters, pp. 66, 138, WIC.

[41]John Poyer, *History of Barbados from 1801 to 1803, Inclusive: Comprising the First Part of the Administration of . . . Baron Seaforth* (Bridgetown, 1808), p. 29.

[42]Seaforth to Hobart, June 6, 1802, Seaforth Papers, 46/7/7.

[43]A copy of this petition could not be located. Evidence for its existence derives from Minutes of the House of Assembly, October 13, 1801, which briefly record that "the Humble Petition of the Free Coloured People, Inhabitants of this Island was presented, by order read, and ordered to lie on the table" (BDA). Evidence for the petition's substance is contained in a letter written by John Foster Alleyne while on a visit to England: "I shall be anxious to hear in what way the Assembly treated the petition . . . presented to them by the coloured people respecting the receiving of their oaths in courts of law, and their holding landed property" (Alleyne to Thorne, February 1, 1802, Alleyne Letters, p. 138).

freedmen from owning more than five slaves (they had to dispose of the excess if they held more than five) and prevented nonslaveowners from buying any; in addition, landownership was limited to less than ten acres and houseownership to houses whose annual taxable value was under £10— that is, the minimum property qualifications for freeholders. Freedmen were also prevented from bequeathing property, including slaves, to their kinsmen or other freedmen.[44]

The Council disagreed with some of the bill's wording and provisions, and returned it to the Assembly with modifications; major among these were the specifications that the bill neither affect those who already owned property nor dispossess freedmen in general of the right of bequeathal.[45] The Assembly formed a committee to consider the Council's amendments, and sometime between July and October 1803 it passed a new version of the bill. This version contained the earlier restrictions on slave-, house-, and landownership, but modified the question of inheritance. Displaying a shrewd sensitivity and callous awareness of a widespread social pattern among freedmen, the Assembly permitted them to bequeath their property, *but only to legal heirs*; if there was no legal heir, the property was then to escheat to the Crown and be sold at public auction.[46]

Deeply aroused by the Assembly's actions, "and overwhelmed with horror and dismay at the ruinous consequences of such a bill," freedmen again petitioned and directed their appeal to the Council in an effort to prevent the bill's final passage. The petition, signed "by upwards of three hundred" persons expressed their attitudes toward slave- and property-ownership, the society in which they lived, and their position in it:

> We humbly submit . . . whether such a law . . . can be considered as constitutional; for many of us, although we have children whom we dearly and tenderly love, . . . [have] never been lawfully married, and therefore [have] no legitimate heirs to whom our properties can descend, must be under the necessity of selling the greatest part of our landed property and houses and every slave . . . ; and although we have all our lives been accustomed to the assistance of slaves, we must immediately deprive ourselves of them and perform every menial office with our own hands, lest death . . . should come suddenly upon us, and then they will all escheat to the King. . . . Many of our children who are

[44]Minutes of the House of Assembly, November 9, 1802, BDA. The bill's text was not entered into these minutes, but its substance has been ascertained from subsequent Assembly Minutes, as well as from those of the Council.

[45]Message from the Council to the Assembly, Minutes of the House of Assembly, February 15, 1803, BDA.

[46]Barbados's archival repositories lack the Minutes of the House of Assembly for the period July 1803 through December 1804, and the Minutes of the Council from May 1801 through October 1803. Thus, reconstruction of the provisions of the bill in its different versions and of related legislative actions has been based on alternate use of the Assembly and Council minutes.

now grown almost to the years of maturity have from their earliest infancy been accustomed to be attended by slaves; if this bill should pass
into law, when we are no more, these children cannot possess a single
slave. What will then be the meaning of their condition? Surely death
would be preferable to such a situation! . . . [The law] will prevent our
children from enjoying every benefit arising from our industry, will
throw them upon the mercy of the wide world, and will make them feel
all the miseries attending upon want and wretchedness. . . . We are
aware that in a country like this it is necessary to make distinctions and
lay restraints. To such restrictions as have been already laid we have
always submitted . . . with cheerfulness, rejoicing that it has been our
lot to live under so free and happy a constitution; and as long as we have
conceived our lives and liberties and our properties to be secured by the
laws, we have been, and always shall be, ready to assist to the utmost of
our power to defend the country, and . . . lose our lives in the service of
our gracious Sovereigns. . . . But should we not only be prevented from
acquiring property, but even be bereaved of that which we have hon-
estly and lawfully acquired, what must be our state of wretchedness and
despondency, as well might we be reduced to a state of slavery for the
greatest blessing attending upon freedom is the acquirement and enjoyment of property, and without that liberty is but an empty name. . . .
Such a law would not only be oppressive in the highest degree, but
totally ruinous to us, and that it must utterly destroy that spirit of industry which we have always thought to be the wise policy of the governing power to encourage, as congenial to the good of the country and
beneficial to every civilized society, and that to deprive us of our property will remove the best security for our loyalty and fidelity.[47]

It is curious that the petition did not mention what surely must have
been another important consequence of preventing freedmen from purchasing or bequeathing slaves. As was discussed in Chapter 2, not only
were some of their slaves kinsmen whom they intended to manumit, but
also freedmen often attempted to buy their enslaved kinsmen for the
purpose of manumission; by being prevented from acquiring slaves, freedmen would be thwarted in liberating their kinsmen or mates. It may have
been that a small proportion of freedman-owned slaves were kinsmen, or
perhaps the appeal was omitted because freedmen felt it would hold little
or no attraction for a plantocracy that had already expressed, by increasing manumission fees, its interest in limiting their population growth. In
either event, freedmen clearly believed that stressing the concept of private property and their political loyalty were the most compelling arguments they could muster to defeat the bill in Council.

In fact, in the last sentence of the above petition, there is an indication
that freedmen believed the bill could be stopped if they emphasized that,

---

[47]"The Humble Petition of the Free Coloured People, Inhabitants of the Island," Minutes
of the Barbados Council, November 1, 1803, Lucas MSS.

as a group, they might well hold a crucial position in a confrontation between white slaveowner and slave. Barbadian whites (indeed, those throughout the West Indies) were well aware of the coalition between freedmen and slaves that had so transformed Haiti. Although it cannot be ascertained with certainty whether events in Haiti specifically influenced the Barbadian white community's thinking, John Alleyne Beckles, an influential member of the Council who opposed the Assembly's bill, certainly viewed the general situation in these terms:

> I am inclined to think that it will be politic to allow them to possess property; it will keep them at a greater distance from the slaves, and will keep up that jealousy which seems naturally to exist between the free coloured people and the slaves; it will tend to our security, for should the slaves at any time attempt to revolt, the free coloured persons for their own safety and the security of their own property, must join the whites and resist them. But if we reduce the free coloured people to a level with the slaves, they must unite with them, and will take every occasion of promoting and encouraging a revolt.[48]

However, Beckles's objections to the bill went further than its possible implications for internal security. He found the bill unconstitutional and wondered if the Crown would accept legislation that so violated the fundamental property rights of "free subjects." He also thought it "an absurdity and contradiction" to permit freedmen to acquire up to ten acres of land, on the one hand, but to prevent their buying any slaves, on the other; "for to what purpose should they purchase land," he asked, "if they cannot purchase a slave to cultivate it?" Beckles also agreed with the freedmen's sentiments on their, and their children's, dependency on slaves for personal comfort. The children, he argued, "have had good educations, and have been brought up with all the tenderness of white children; . . . as none but the heir at law can inherit, when the father dies, these children . . . cannot have one [slave] to attend them. . . . I can see no necessity for such a law as this which must destroy every motive to industry in the people of colour, and encourage idleness and profligacy."[49]

Beckles was the most elaborate in his objections, but he was not alone in his views in the Council. Although some members disagreed on specific points, they generally agreed that property rights, including the right of bequeathal, were fundamental to free status; furthermore, aside from the negative attitudes some members had toward freedmen, it was felt that the Crown was likely to disallow a bill which so blatantly infringed on these rights. The five Council members who were present when the bill was

[48] Minutes of the Barbados Council, November 1, 1803, *ibid.* It is likely that a 1795 revolt in Grenada, involving both freedmen and slaves, also had an impact on Barbadian whites (see Goveia, *Slave Society*, p. 252).

[49] Minutes of the Barbados Council, November 1, 1803, *ibid.*

debated disagreed with its wording, but only three voted against its second reading, and the bill was returned to the Assembly.[50] A joint committee of both legislative bodies was formed in November 1803 to prepare a compromise bill "to prevent free people of colour from holding real property beyond a certain extent"; however, other than an 1804 attempt in the House of Assembly to revive the bill, efforts to limit freedman property-holding were dropped, and there is no indication that such efforts were renewed in subsequent years in either chamber.[51]

In fact, the trend from this period onward was characterized by the struggle of freedmen to gain an extension of their civil rights and by the growing pressures for amelioration from the metropolitan power. As a consequence of these movements, plantocratic concerns and legislative actions were increasingly directed toward the maintenance and defense of the status quo rather than toward further curtailment of the freedman's civil rights and legal status.

---

[50] *Ibid.*

[51] *Ibid.*, November 29, 1803. The Council's Minutes for its next twelve meetings (until January 15, 1805) do not mention this bill. Neville Hall has suggested that these efforts "were overshadowed by the controversy then developing [in the legislature] over . . . the particularly vexed question of whether the murder of a slave . . . should be made a capital offense" ("The Judicial System of a Plantation Society—Barbados on the Eve of Emancipation," *Colloque d'Histoire Antillaise: Le Passage de la Société Esclavagiste a la Société post-Esclavagiste aux Antilles au XIXe Siècle* [Pointe-à-Pitre, Guadeloupe, 1969], p. 66). Although this issue did arouse considerable legislative debate, opinions were more strongly divided within the plantocracy on the issue of freedman property holdings, and legislative interest in curtailing these holdings may have been deflected by a graver problem that was looming on the horizon. By early 1805, and continuing for a number of months thereafter, the island feared a French invasion. There was considerable excitement, tension, and military activity as elaborate plans were laid for defense in the event the invasion materialized (see, for example, Seaforth Papers, 46/7/1 and 46/17/27, *passim*). With major concern focused on internal security, one can speculate that no measure would have been taken which had the potential of weakening that security; it may well have been felt that depriving freedmen of their property was an action that might have had this potential.

IV

THE POLITICO-JUDICIAL
SYSTEM: LEGAL STATUS
AND THE EXPANSION
OF CIVIL RIGHTS

THE RIGHT OF TESTIMONY AND REFORMIST TRENDS

By 1801, freedmen had explicitly made it known that they regarded a law giving them the right to testify as vital to their interests. Governor Seaforth also favored such a move and argued for it, "not only to the purposes of justice and humanity as far as the coloured people are concerned, but also [because it is] necessary to the administration of justice among the whites which is often rendered difficult, sometimes impossible, through the inadmissibility of black or coloured, and the want of, white evidence."[1] The governor finally concluded, however, that reform legislation would come only through strong directives from the imperial government, for, as he wrote from Barbados in 1804, "nothing can be expected to be effectually done on this side of the water. . . . I find it impossible either to rouse them [the legislature] from the torpor they are in, or to shake their barbarous and almost incomprehensible prejudices."[2] But at this early stage the imperial government made little effort to interfere with what it defined as the internal affairs of a colonial government, and home pressures were not yet sufficient to force it to take a firm position on the conditions under which nonwhites lived.[3] Thus, the intransigence of the Barbadian plantocracy on the issue of amelioration continued and was not easily to be moved.

The increasing economic success of freedmen, combined with widespread depression among lower-class whites,[4] continued to cause tensions between the two groups. Taking advantage of their racial characteristics and the freedman's lack of judicial protection, lower-class whites verbally

[1]Seaforth to Hobart, June 6, 1802, Seaforth Papers, 46/7/7, SRO.
[2]Seaforth to Camden, September 1, 1804, *ibid.*
[3]See D. J. Murray, *The West Indies and the Development of Colonial Government, 1801–1834* (London: Oxford University Press, 1965), pp. 33–37 and *passim.*
[4]See pp. 123–24.

and physically assaulted freedmen, thus heightening the latter's concern with bodily and property security. "The privilege of testimony," as 172 freedmen proclaimed in an 1811 petition, was regarded as essential to the protection of this "personal security."[5] In this petition, freedmen again requested the "privilege" and argued that, although there once may have been a need for restrictive legislation, there was now need for "laws most suitable to the present age," laws that would also place them "on the like footing of People of Colour in Jamaica, and the other sister colonies."[6] The Barbados Assembly refused to act on the petition, and when it decided to consider it, eight months later, only three members voted "for the measure, the others [being] decidedly against it."[7] With obvious and keen disappointment, the freedmen concluded that "their cause has fallen to the ground," and they appealed directly to Governor Beckwith to help them in petitioning the Crown for "relief of a grievance of such magnitude."[8] They also hoped to raise funds that would enable a group to travel to England to present the petition personally.[9] In their "memorial" to Beckwith they eloquently expressed their chagrin and anxiety: although "deeply impressed with a sense of their condition," the memorialists were seeking only "a participation of the British Constitution" that would permit them to share in a right that had already been granted to freedmen in other West Indian colonies. The "memorialists" were careful to emphasize that "in claiming a privilege so essentially necessary to their welfare and security . . . they totally disavow[ed] any attempt at parity of condition with the other [that is, white] orders of the community," but that the lack of this privilege denied them "the security of the slave" and "manifestly tend[ed] to brand their condition with infamy and contempt." They thus underscored the fact that denial of legal testimony weakened their status

[5]Minutes of the House of Assembly, February 19, 1811, BDA.

[6]*Ibid.* The first of Jamaica's ameliorative laws with respect to freedmen was passed in 1796, when those who could produce baptismal certificates were allowed to testify in the courts. Although a freedman could give evidence in a case involving himself and a white, he could not do so as a third party in a case involving a white and some other freedman. The latter right was extended to baptized freedmen in 1813, and in 1823 baptismal certificates were no longer required. See Sheila Duncker, "The Free Coloured and Their Fight for Civil Rights in Jamaica, 1800–1830," (M.A. thesis, University of London, [1960]), pp. 22–23, 32. In Barbados, the right to testify was first extended to some freedmen in 1817, but baptismal certificates were required until 1830.

[7]Beckwith to Liverpool, November 2, 1811, CO 28/80.

[8]"The Memorial of the Free People of Colour," October 7, 1811, *ibid.*

[9]Six freedmen, chosen by their peers, presented the "memorial" to the governor. He convinced them not to go to England, because he "did not conceive such a step could be of advantage to them"; instead, he sent the memorial and petition to England with a cover letter that objectively conveyed the freedmen's concerns (Beckwith to Liverpool, November 2, 1811, *ibid.*). The freedmen's anxiety over action on their petition caused them to address another "memorial" to the governor nine months later, asking if the documents sent to England were "likely to be productive of the effect so earnestly desired" ("The Memorial of the Free People of Colour," July 21, 1812, CO 28/81).

distinction from slaves, but, in delineating why, in everyday affairs, this right was of central importance, they emphasized protection of their persons and property:

> From being deprived of the privilege of testimony, [we] are exposed to the insults of any low bred or abandoned white person . . . and such persons may intrude themselves into [our] houses, there commit the most flagrant crimes (murder not excepted) and escape with impunity, and this even when [we] are occupied in the peaceable enjoyment of [our] families and friends. Instances have occurred where [our] wives have been insulted in [our] presence, and [we] could not obtain redress. And further, . . . many individuals of [our] class, have from habits of industry acquired moderate competencies which, from the incapacity above stated, they cannot enjoy the quiet possession of, through dread of the unlawful intrusion of the lower order of white persons, occasioned by envy and a knowledge of the protectless situation of the people of colour.[10]

The right to testify was especially crucial to the growing class of freedman shopkeepers and merchants, whose often small-scale business enterprises depended to a considerable degree upon the extension of credit; by being denied this right, such persons were unable to "prove their debts . . . both against white and coloured persons."[11] Thus, the issue of legal testimony went beyond concerns of security against bodily harm, and drove to the heart of an increasingly important part of the freedman community's economic life.

The importance of the right to testify in relation to the protection of economic interests and property was stressed earlier in 1811 by a pamphlet that defended the freedmen's petition to the Assembly and urged the Assembly to grant legal equality. Extending privileges to freedmen, the pamphleteer argued, would give whites a "faithful band of auxiliaries" in the event of a slave rebellion, since freedmen would have "rights which are worth defending." The right of legal testimony not only would help to secure the freedman in his property but also would encourage him to acquire more: "This acquisition of property is a powerful guarantee of the peaceful conduct of these unoffending people . . . [and] it is known by experience, how much possession of this nature acts as a counterbalance to revolutionary spirit; and that . . . they only are willing to hazard a change who have nothing to lose. . . . Oppression, and not liberality is the mother of sedition."[12]

---

[10]"The Memorial of the Free People of Colour," October 7, 1811, CO 28/80.

[11]Beckwith to Liverpool, November 2, 1811, *ibid.*

[12]*An Essay Attempting to Prove the Policy of Granting the Late Petition of the Free Coloured People of Barbadoes* [Barbados, 1811]. This work provoked a political furor, and attempts were made to prosecute its publisher; see Robert H. Schomburgk, *The History of Barbados* (London, 1848), p. 381.

Although the plantocracy in general was adverse to reforming the civil status of freedmen, freedmen kept the issue alive[13] and were assisted by growing pressures from abroad, as well as by a few members of the white community. "There are a few, and but a few, enlightened moderate men," Governor Beckwith wrote in 1811, who feel that extension of civil rights is not only morally just but also "politically wise" because a change in the freedmen's status would more effectively place them "as a barrier between the whites and the slaves."[14]

The force of this political argument came through a few years later when a slave revolt tipped the scales in favor of ameliorative legislation. The revolt, which broke out on the night of April 14, 1816, lasted no more than a day or two, and was suppressed by British military forces (including black troops of the First West India Regiment) and the island's militia. The white community almost universally attributed the general cause of the revolt to the "slave registry bill," which was impending in the British Parliament. Whites felt that the revolt actually occurred because some literate freedmen and slaves, who read English newspapers, misstated the intent of the bill and convinced the slave population that "the King of England had set them free, but that the people of this island would not give them their freedom."[15]

During the period of martial law, which was proclaimed early on the morning of April 15 and endured until July 12, 144 persons were executed for participation in the revolt in conformity with sentences passed by courts-martial.[16] Although information is not available on the total number of freedmen accused and convicted, it is clear that the number was very small. For example, during seven weeks of the period of martial law, 150

[13]For example, in February 1814, prior to Beckwith's departure from the island, freedmen addressed another petition to him, urging action in the right to testify: "We humbly conceive that it must appear very extraordinary in this enlightened age, . . . that there should exist, in any part of his Majesty's Dominions, statutes which deny to any portion of the subjects whatever may be their colour, who by those very statutes are allowed to be free, the common and natural right of protection for their properties, and security for their persons and lives; a right without the enjoyment of which, freedom is but an empty name; and life itself not worth preserving" (quoted in Neville Hall, "The Judicial System of a Plantation Society: Barbados on the Eve of Emancipation," *Colloque d'Histoire Antillaise: Le Passage de la Société Esclavagiste a la Société post-Esclavagiste aux Antilles au XIXe Siècle* [Pointe-à-Pitre, Guadeloupe, 1969], p. 64).

[14]Beckwith to Liverpool, November 2, 1811, CO 28/80.

[15]*The Report from a Select Committee of the House of Assembly Appointed to Inquire into the Origin, Causes, and Progress of the Late Insurrection* (Barbados, [1818]), p. 33 and *passim*. Elsewhere in the British West Indies, slaves responded to the registry bill in a similar manner (Eric Williams, *Capitalism and Slavery* [New York, 1961], p. 203). An 1826 investigation in Barbados into rumors of a possible slave revolt also revealed that slaves and freedmen gathered together while newspapers were read to them by literate freedmen (Minutes of the Barbados Council, March 22, 1826, CO 31/50).

[16]Leith to Bathurst, September 21, 1816, CO 28/85. About seventy more were under death sentence when martial law was lifted, and, as of Leith's writing, close to 100 persons were still awaiting trial.

persons, 4 of whom were freedmen, were tried in Saint Michael; of this number, 111 slaves and 3 freedmen were executed.[17] One of the freedmen was Joseph Pitt Washington Franklin.[18] Franklin lived on a plantation in Saint Philip, where much of the revolt raged, and was accused of being a principal in publicizing to the slaves that they had been freed, but that their freedom was being withheld by the planters; rumor had it that, if the revolt succeeded, Franklin "was to be Governor, and to live at Pilgrim," the governor's residence.[19]

Freedman participation in the revolt was very limited, and the conduct "of the most respectable of that class" was, as a House of Assembly investigating committee concluded, "with scarcely any exception . . . highly meritorious."[20] In addition, the fact that freedman companies of the island's militia, especially those in the Saint Michael and Christ Church regiments, carried out their assigned duties conscientiously and with dispatch helped considerably in strengthening the case for the freedman's loyalty and the removal of the legal disabilities that had been placed against him.[21]

A bill which permitted the testimony of freedmen in legal proceedings— the first of the reform laws and the one to which the freedmen themselves gave highest priority—was introduced in the Assembly on October 8, 1816. For the first few readings it could not get the support of the necessary minimum of twelve members, and it was not until January 7, 1817, that the bill, after considerable amendments involving some heated debates, passed the Assembly and was forwarded to the Council.[22] Those in the Assembly who favored amelioration in general, and this bill in particular, stressed the freedman's loyalty to white interests and his "respectability," as evidenced by his behavior during the slave revolt; in fact, the formal rationale behind the bill's passage, as expressed in its preamble, emphasized how "during the late calamitous insurrection" the freedman population had "evinced the greatest attachment and fidelity to the white inhabitants of the island."[23]

Yet, the Barbados Assembly was not prepared to extend its "favourable consideration" to all categories of freedmen, and it limited the law's

[17] *Report from a Select Committee*, pp. 56–57.
[18] See notice in *Barbados Mercury*, July 2, 1816.
[19] *Report from a Select Committee*, p. 30. The other two executed freedmen may have been Cain Davis, John Richard Sarjeant, or a man whose last name was Roach. These persons, as well as Franklin, are mentioned as fomenters in testimonies included in the Assembly's report on the revolt (*ibid.*, pp. 26, 27, 30, 33, 35).
[20] *Ibid.*, p. 11.
[21] See, for example, Moody to Bishop of Durham, July 4, 1816, CO 28/85.
[22] Journal of the Assembly of Barbados, October 8 and December 17, 1816, and January 7, 1817, CO 31/47; see also Schomburgk, *History of Barbados*, p. 401.
[23] "An Act Allowing the Testimony of Free Negroes and Free People of Colour to Be Taken in All Cases," copy in CO 28/86. The act was assented to by the president of the Council, acting for the governor, on February 5, 1817.

application to those who had been baptized,[24] who had been free for at least a year prior to being called upon to give testimony, and who, subsequent to the passage of the act, had been manumitted by the laws of Barbados. (That is, all persons who had been manumitted in England or other colonies prior to passage of the act were eligible to testify; newly manumitted slaves had to be freed in Barbados. Those who had been manumitted outside of the island subsequent to the act's passage were considered free, but the right to testify did not extend to them.) The last two provisions were not repealed until 1830.

Despite this law, there were some in the judiciary who, through accident or design, continued to deny freedmen the right to testify, or interpreted the law so as to mitigate the privilege they had won. When, in 1823, a justice of the peace refused to accept the testimony of a freedman who had been manumitted in England, the governor issued a proclamation which re-emphasized that only slaves manumitted in England *after* the act's passage were exempted from the right to testify.[25] In addition, although slaves were prohibited from testifying against whites, since 1739 they had been permitted to give evidence against freedmen. The 1817 law, however, implicitly prohibited slaves from testifying against freedmen who were eligible to testify, although slaves were sometimes permitted to do so. Investigating the island's legal and judicial system in 1823, a parliamentary commission reported that, by the 1817 act, freedmen have "the same privileges and liabilities as whites. Slave evidence is not admitted against them," but the commissioners were informed by the senior magistrate "that he had sometimes admitted slaves 'with strong corroborating circumstances to give evidence against free coloured people under Hall 180' [that is, the 1739 law]."[26]

However the 1817 law was interpreted in the years following its passage, it is clear that, when enacted, it was intended to apply to relatively few freedmen, and primarily to those whose demeanor and life style reflected the values that whites considered appropriate and nonthreatening. It can also be suggested that the bill was enacted mainly for reasons that

[24]One member, for example, in considering amending an early version of the law, said that he "would most willingly on this day give my vote . . . that evidence on oath be admitted to the enlightened class of the free people of colour, who ought to know the obligations of an oath; but . . . to extend the privilege to the vulgar class, many of whom have no idea of the nature or solemnity of an oath, would, I conceive, be not only profanation, but prove an alarming innovation in our jurisprudence, and be productive of great ferment and dangerous consequences in our country" (Journal of the Assembly of Barbados, October 8, 1816, CO 31/47).

[25]"A Proclamation by Governor Henry Warde," Minutes of the Barbados Council, May 31, 1823, CO 31/48.

[26]F. Dwarris, *Substance of Three Reports of the Commission of Inquiry into the Administration of Civil and Criminal Justice in the West Indies* (London, 1827), pp. 79–80; see also J. W. [I. W.] Orderson, *Cursory Remarks and Plain Facts Connected with the Question Produced by the Proposed Slave Registry Bill* (London, 1816), pp. 18–20.

would insure the protection of plantocratic interests (and, by extension, white ones in general). That is, the 1816 revolt had profoundly shaken the white population, and had effectively demonstrated that its traditional anxieties vis-à-vis the slaves were well founded. The fact that a few freedmen were accused and convicted of assuming leadership positions dramatically underscored the potential threat posed by any coalition between freedmen and slaves. The fact that most freedmen remained loyal to white interests during the revolt was good fortune, but how long this loyalty could be assured if the freedman's basic requests for civil rights were continuously denied was another matter. Apparently reasoning of this kind, which John Alleyne Beckles, among others, had effectively articulated in 1803 (when he noted, "if we reduce the free coloured people to a level with the slaves, they must unite with them, and will take every occasion of promoting and encouraging a revolt"),[27] and not primarily liberalism or humanitarian considerations, was instrumental in the passage of the bill. An additional intent of the bill may have been to discourage manumission in England, which at this time, as was discussed in Chapter 2, was the most prevalent mode by which persons gained their freedom. For example, from 1808 to August 18, 1816, about 98 percent of the manumissions reported were effected in England, and the Barbados Council, after an investigation in 1823, concluded that "at least nine-tenths of the slaves who have been emancipated during the last six years, have obtained their freedom by virtue of English manumissions."[28]

As the number of manumitted slaves increased, the number of freedmen was augmented, especially by those freed in England, who were disqualified from testifying under the 1817 law. (Others who might have been eligible could also be denied the right because they were unable to produce their baptismal certificates or sufficient proof of the date and mode of manumission—a form of status validation which apparently was frequently required in the courts, yet was difficult to achieve.) Thus, in any given year an increasing number of persons fell under the 1817 law's restrictions on testifying, and over the years removal of these restrictions became a vital political issue to a growing and considerable proportion of the freedman community.

Even in 1817, however, many freedmen were not members of the group to which the law applied. Yet, a few weeks after its passage, twelve of this group addressed the House of Assembly, expressing their gratitude for "the privilege of giving testimony on all occasions." Their letter is an interesting reflection of the ideology held by at least some of the freedmen to whom the law was primarily directed:

[27]Minutes of the Barbados Council, November 1, 1803, Lucas MSS, BPL.
[28]A Report of a Committee of the Council of Barbadoes Appointed to Inquire into the Actual Condition of the Slaves in this Island (London, 1824), pp. 82–83.

This inestimable privilege we are free to confess we were anxious to enjoy for without it we conceived that our lives and properties were not secure and that our condition was little if any thing better than that of slaves. We are sensible that in a country like this where slavery exists, there must necessarily be a distinction between the white and free coloured inhabitants, and that there are privileges which the latter do not expect to enjoy. The right of giving testimony was all we wished for, having through the justice and wisdom of the legislature obtained that we are perfectly satisfied and contented. . . . We hope that there never will be found amongst us any capable of abusing this invaluable gift, but if there should be any such it is our wish that they may receive the most severe and exemplary punishment. It affords us a great satisfaction to find that our conduct upon a late unfortunate occasion has met with the approbation of the legislature and has been thought to render us worthy of their consideration and attention. We assure your worships that we shall be ready at all times to give proofs of our loyalty and sincere attachment to the king and constitution and to risk our lives in the defence and protection of our country, and its laws.[29]

Regardless of the sentiments expressed in this letter, the ameliorative door had been opened, and increasing pressures from Britain to reform slave codes intensified the movement to push that door open farther. Although these pressures were primarily directed in favor of the slave, they implicitly affected the freedman; it was felt that, if breaks could be made in colonial laws respecting slaves, an extension of liberal measures to freedmen could follow more easily.[30] In January 1817 the Barbadian plantocracy had been all but compelled by the British government to pass its own "slave registry act."[31] The controversy surrounding its passage had exacerbated traditional plantocratic sensitivity concerning its own definition of colonial political rights, which, the Assembly noted, "can never be safely or advantageously exercised by those who are utter strangers to these colonies," and individual rights over private property.[32] The irritation and tension of local whites were also compounded, especially in the early 1820s, by external events.

Briefly, these events included the following. The antislavery movement in Britain had influenced the formation of a parliamentary commission in 1822 to investigate the judicial and legal system of the colonies, and the

[29]"To the Honorable John Beckles, Speaker of the House of Assembly and the Rest of the Honorable and Worshipful Members," March 4, 1817, CO 28/86.

[30]For a summary of the imperial government's position, see Murray, *West Indies*, pp. 214–15.

[31]CO 30/20, no. 343. For background to this bill and colonial responses in general, see Murray, *West Indies*, pp. 95–98.

[32]"Resolutions of the House of Assembly of Barbados . . . January 17, 1816," *Report from a Select Committee*, pp. 57–58; see also Gibbes W. Jordan, *An Examination of the Principles of the Slave Registry Bill, and of the Means of Emancipation, Proposed by the Authors of the Bill* (London, 1816), *passim*.

commission arrived in Barbados in late 1823. By this year, the movement had coalesced into the Anti-Slavery Society, whose avowed goal was ultimate emancipation, with a determined effort to seek reform measures as a means to that end. The influence of the Anti-Slavery Society was considerable and, during 1823, official governmental policy was declared in favor of slave amelioration. Buxton's resolution to the House of Commons in May of that year called for gradual emancipation; although officially withdrawn, it nonetheless was distributed in the colonies, as were Canning's resolutions, which passed the House and which placed the government on record as favoring amelioration and the ultimate granting of civil rights. In July the colonies were sent the circular dispatch of the secretary of state for the colonies, which effected the government's stance by calling for specific reform measures.[33] Also in 1823, events within the colonies themselves influenced developments in Barbados—particularly the large-scale slave revolt in Demerara and the acceding to many of the demands for full civil rights of the freedmen of Grenada.[34]

EVENTS OF 1823–24 AND DIVISIONS IN THE FREEDMAN COMMUNITY

In the West Indies, wrote Barbados's Governor Combermere in 1819, "the public mind is ever tremblingly alive to the dangers of insurrection," and in Barbados during the early 1820s there was considerable apprehension that the events of 1816 would be repeated.[35] Apprehensions about a slave revolt reached a peak in June 1823, when rumors were circulated among the slaves that their emancipation was imminent as a result of events in the British Parliament. The rumors were nurtured in an atmosphere wherein the topic of emancipation was continuously discussed among the white population, and the situation became so tense that Governor Warde was forced to issue a proclamation assuring the slaves that "the rumour of a speedy emancipation is false."[36] Anxieties had not yet abated when, in late August, word reached Barbados of the large-scale slave revolt in Demerara, causing a resurgence of apprehension among whites.[37] By late September a group of Barbadian freedmen, spurred on by the reform movement in England and the granting of civil rights to

[33]For details, see Murray, *West Indies*, pp. 107, 109, 126–29.

[34]Warde to Bathurst, August 27, 1823, CO 28/92; H. A. Vaughan, "Samuel Prescod: The Birth of a Hero," *New World Quarterly*, 3 (1966): 55.

[35]Combermere to Bathurst, January 15, 1819, quoted in Williams, *Capitalism and Slavery*, p. 202. See also Haynes to Lane, June 23, 1820, Newton Estate Papers, 523/831, ULL; Reece to Lane, June 25, 1823, *ibid.*, 523/897; Warde to Clinton, October 10, 1821, Rhodes House Library, Oxford University; Warde to Bathurst, June 14, July 2, and August 27, 1823, CO 28/92, nos. 24, 25, 41; and Schomburgk, *History of Barbados*, pp. 416–17.

[36]Warde, *Proclamation*, June 10, 1823, CO 28/92.

[37]Warde to Bathurst, August 27, 1823, *ibid.*

freedmen in Grenada, began talking about petitioning the island's legislature to grant them their own "rights and privileges," which included the
right to elect and hold office.[38]

The freedman community, however, rapidly divided over the petition,
and a small group began formulating its own "loyal address to the legislature," feeling that "in the then agitated state of the country" it was not
propitious to request ameliorative legislation. On October 20, 1823, while
this "loyal address" was being formulated, a white mob destroyed the
Methodist chapel in Bridgetown and forced the departure of the missionary.[39] Aside from reflecting tensions within the white community and its
animosity toward Methodist missionaries (who some felt were inciting the
slaves—an action the missionaries had been accused of in 1816), the
Methodist church was of some significance to the freedman population.

Tensions rose between whites and freedmen, and a few days after the
chapel's destruction the governor, impelled by his personal alarm, notified
the home government "that great apprehension is entertained here that a
conflict may take place between the white inhabitants and the free people
of colour, the horrible consequence of which would be beyond all power of
calculation."[40] Shortly before this letter, and but a day after the chapel
was destroyed, a group of twenty freedmen, led by Jacob Belgrave, Jr.,[41]

[38]See "Examination of Witnesses Taken at the Bar of the House of Assembly . . . ,"
February 3 and 4, 1824, CO 28/93.

[39]The Methodist chapel incident, and its repercussions, became a *cause célèbre*, the
source of a bitter controversy, and ultimately the subject of a lengthy debate in the British
Parliament. See *An Authentic Report of the Debate in the House of Commons, June 23,
1825, on Mr. Buxton's Motion Relative to the Demolition of the Methodist Chapel and
Mission House in Barbadoes* (London, 1825).

[40]Warde to Bathurst, October 25, 1823, CO 28/92.

[41]Belgrave was probably the island's wealthiest freedman at this time, and one of a
handful who owned sugar plantations during the entire slave period (see p. 121). Belgrave
was "colored," and he was considered one "of the most respectable of that class" by the
plantocracy when the Assembly solicited his deposition concerning the 1816 revolt. In his
deposition, Belgrave reported that, on his way home to his plantation in Saint Philip before
the revolt, he was accosted by slaves who "were very abusive towards him, complaining they
were free, and that he was one who prevented them from having it" (*Report from a Select
Committee*, pp. 11, 38–39).

For reasons that are unclear, Belgrave went (or intended to go) to London in 1825 and
attempted to solicit an interview with the Colonial Office. It is not known whether the interview actually took place, but, in a letter to the undersecretary for state, the colonial agent for
Barbados wrote that Belgrave was "of the highest respectability of character and possessing
considerable landed property. . . . [He] has signified his kindness to answer any questions
that may be put to him with reference to his class of the community. . . . The opportunity
of a conference with a . . . [freedman] who possesses so much information does not often
occur at least from Barbados, and at any rate I considered it my duty to convey to you the
wish he expressed to me" (Carrington to Horton, July 10, 1825, CO 28/96). As reformist
pressures in England increased, Carrington, who represented plantocratic interests, was interested in demonstrating to the Colonial Office that Barbados's freedmen were "neither so
degraded nor discontented as has been asserted" (Carrington to Horton, April 16, 1826, CO
28/99), and it is highly unlikely that he would have supported any freedman in directly approaching the Colonial Office, whose views were not generally acceptable to the plantocracy.

submitted its "loyal address" to the Assembly, Council, and governor. This address was to arouse further controversy and to lay bare growing antagonisms and divisions within the freedman community itself.

The addressors expressed their distress and regret at current events and the "alarming crisis which appears to be approaching." As with many Barbadian whites, they attributed this "crisis" to British emancipationists, those "few mistaken individuals, who, in their exuberant zeal to effect a theoretical reform in institutions and customs of which they have obtained but a very superficial and imperfect knowledge, would run the risk of involving impractical and lamentable ruin in the property and even the lives of thousands of their fellow subjects." Noting that Barbadian slaves were treated better than in earlier years (an argument frequently offered by the plantocracy), they supported the current efforts of Anglican missionaries among the slaves, for Christianity would teach them "to be contented and happy with their present highly improved position." The addressors strongly affirmed their fidelity to the "land of our nativity and to the institutions and form of government under which we have hitherto had the happiest of lives." They asserted their willingness to oppose any radical innovation in the social order, such as emancipation, and declared their readiness to "assist with all their power in the maintenance of subordination and good order." Although they strenuously denied a rumor that freedmen intended to take advantage of the unsettled state of the country and to request "certain rights and privileges of which they are at present deprived," there were indeed "certain legal disabilities" which they hoped would be removed in the near future. "However, their removal," the address concluded, "unless by the general conviction of their injustice and inexpediency, would only have the affect of increasing the prejudice already in operation against us by white people."[42]

This address was greeted positively by the Assembly, which found it "loyal and dutiful" in its expression of "grateful appreciation of the protection enjoyed by the Free Coloured Body"; in fact, the House exclaimed its "most pleasurable feeling" in giving its "approbation of the conduct of those individuals whose intentions were happily guaranteed by the selection of Mr. Belgrave, as a leader—a person whose fidelity and attachment to the local interests of the community, so justly entitle him to the favorable consideration of this House."[43]

Regardless of the plantocracy's reactions, however, the Belgrave address did not represent a consensus of Barbadian freedmen. It had been formulated by a small group which claimed to represent the views "of all the enlightened, respectable and wealthy part of their body." However,

[42]For a copy of the Belgrave address, see Minutes of the Barbados Council, October 21, 1823, BDA.

[43]Resolutions passed by the House of Assembly, February 18, 1824, printed in *Barbadian*, February 25, 1824.

although they had been approached to sign the "loyal address," a few "respectable" freedmen had refused to do so, and the opinions of hundreds more outside this elitist group had not been solicited. Displeased and annoyed by the Belgrave address, another freedman group began to contemplate forwarding a counteraddress to Governor Warde.[44] Rumors, which ultimately incensed the House of Assembly, quickly spread in the freedman community that the governor (who was relatively "liberal") had objected to the Belgrave address because it cast derogatory innuendoes upon Englishmen; the governor's rumored displeasure was used to support the plan to submit a counteraddress.

Among the freedmen there were a number of objections to the Belgrave address, but they seem to have clustered around two central issues which, in themselves, reflected further divisions within the dissident group. One issue related to the fact that a handful of men had selected themselves to be spokesmen without consulting or gaining the consent of the freedman community. That is, the disagreement was not so much with the sentiments of the address itself, but rather with "the manner in which that address was got up"; the Belgrave group, it was felt, had behaved with "impropriety . . . sending in an address without the sanction of the whole body." Here it is important to mention that in June 1819, at a public meeting of between four and five hundred freedmen, a committee had been chosen to lead the struggle against the "alien bill," which was then awaiting the governor's assent.[45] The committee, which numbered between sixteen and twenty persons, was elected unanimously, for no candidates ran against those who were nominated. This committee was specifically formed to draft a petition against the "alien bill," but it was understood

[44]Information in this section dealing with the background to the Belgrave address and the counteraddress, as well as subsequent events related to these addresses, is derived, unless otherwise noted, from the two-day investigation conducted by the House of Assembly and reported in "Examination of Witnesses Taken at the Bar of the House of Assembly Relative to a Publication Which Appeared in the Globe Newspaper of the 22 Ultimo . . . ," February 3 and 4, 1824, CO 28/93.

[45]The short-lived struggle proved to be futile, for the act passed the Assembly and the Council in May and was signed by the governor on June 29, 1819. A distrust of foreigners in general, and particularly of freedmen from former French colonies, resulted in passage of the "alien bill." "Much danger arises to this colony," the preamble to the bill briefly states, "from the admission of aliens and disaffected free Negroes and Persons of Colour who are not natives of this island." The act established an "Alien Office" and a variety of administrative procedures and penalties governing the admission to Barbados of "all persons, not being natural born subjects of His Majesty, and all free Negroes and all free persons of colour, not natives of this island." Barbadian freedmen, however, particularly objected to clause 12, which not only permitted the governor to deport, "whenever he shall deem it necessary for the public safety," any alien freedman who had been in jail, but also permitted the jailing and subsequent expulsion "for life" of any freedman, "whether the same be natives of this island, or who shall appear to be a person of dangerous and suspicious character." Anyone who returned after being deported was considered a felon and was subject to the death penalty. See "An Act for Establishing an Alien Office . . . ," CO 30/20, no. 474, italics added. Similar fears of alien freedmen existed in Jamaica (see Duncker, "Free Coloured," pp. 12–14).

that it would also function more generally as a leadership group for the whole freedman community in the drive for reform legislation. Sixteen members of the 1819 committee were still members in 1823, and, although some had signed the Belgrave address, others were leaders in the group that formulated the counteraddress. Some of the latter persons, as well as others, felt that the Belgrave group had violated an organizational agreement within the freedman community by taking autonomous action.

But the more militant individuals had deeper objections, and the second major area of disagreement with the Belgrave address concerned the "sentiments contained in it." Objections to these "sentiments" focused on three major points: that freedmen did not in fact live under British law, but rather under the constraints of a "colonial code," and thus redress would have to be sought from the imperial government; that the Belgrave group should not have entered into wider political issues, particularly criticism of the English emancipationists (some also felt that the Belgrave group had exaggerated with respect to the slaves, and that "there was no improvement in their condition"); and, finally, in what was probably the major unifying issue of the dissidents, that claims for specific civil rights should have been made—that is, the Belgrave address "was a foolish address as nothing had been asked for, they had not demanded their rights and privileges." Some of those who most forcefully urged ameliorative legislation, particularly the younger men, felt that "the few who had signed the address to the legislature had something and therefore looked down upon the others," and thus charged that the Belgrave group comprised men of property and wealth whose socioeconomic level not only placed them above the mass of the freedman community but also influenced their general conservatism.

The controversy provoked a mass meeting attended by from three to four hundred freedmen at which a committee was elected to draft the counteraddress. Tensions on the island increased again as rumors circulated that, in fact, the freedmen were plotting a revolt for the night of November 5; however, despite attempts at intimidation, by December 17, 1823, the counteraddress had been formulated and signed by 373 persons. On January 22, 1824, the counteraddress, specifically addressed to Governor Warde, was published in the *Globe*:[46]

> The approbation of our conduct, we humbly conceive would have exempted us from entering into any political question, unconnected with our situation, that might tend to involve us in unpleasant discussions, and which impels our objecting to certain passages in those addresses

---

[46] The *Globe* was first published in 1818 and represented the interests of whites who were critical of the "aristocracy and their exalted notions"; in 1819 the House of Assembly brought charges against its publisher, Michael Ryan, for libeling the House and the colonial government in general—charges from which he was later exonerated (Schomburgk, *History of Barbados*, pp. 404–6).

presented . . . as the united sentiments of our body which, previous to their presentation, were known only to a few persons. . . . there are certain parts of our Colonial Code which [exempt] us from participating with our white brethren in certain privileges, and to which, as British subjects, we humbly conceive we have a claim; and that it is our intention, in a less agitated state of the Colony, to pray for a removal of such parts which . . . materially affect us. . . . Politically situated as we are, it is our ardent wish to pursue that peaceable demeanour and strict neutrality which has ever been the characteristic of the Free Coloured inhabitants . . . nor do we conceive an exposition of our sentiments on any political question by any means necessary. But should it be requisite to remove any unfavourable impression which might arise . . . from our neutrality . . . we will endeavor to prove . . . our unshaken attachment to his Majesty's Government and the interests of our Country, and that we are worthy of that kind consideration which we shall solicit at a future period.[47]

Although the counteraddress did not express the mood of the more militant freedmen, it did explicitly avoid entering into the emancipation controversy and stated the intention of freedmen to petition for complete legal equality. Most important, the counteraddress legitimized the freedmen's claims to civil rights on the basis of their being British subjects and not, as had the Belgrave address, with an appeal to the moral principles and discretion of the plantocracy. Consequently, the counteraddress succeeded only in infuriating the Assembly, which viewed "with the greatest indignation" the group of "dangerous and designing persons . . . who signed the address . . . disseminating doctrines injurious in the extreme to the best interests of the Colony, and in direct opposition to the loyal and dutiful address" presented by the Belgrave group.[48] An angered Assembly decided to investigate the reasons for the counteraddress and its implications for political stability, and to determine who was ultimately responsible for the rumor that Governor Warde had been displeased with the Belgrave statement.[49] The hearing took place on February 3 and 4, 1824, and a number of freedman witnesses, including members of both factions, were summoned to testify. In a particularly tense and hostile examination, Samuel Francis Collymore, a leader in the counteraddress group, was asked to elaborate on various points to which the House particularly objected:

Questioner: What do you mean by rights and privileges?
Collymore: I mean our franchises.
Questioner: Do you mean by that the right to elect and be elected?
Collymore: I do.

[47]"The Humble Address of the Undersigned Free Coloured Inhabitants of the Island Aforesaid," December 17, 1823, printed in *Barbadian*, February 25, 1824.
[48]Resolutions passed by the House of Assembly, February 18, 1824, printed in *ibid.*
[49]See "Examination of Witnesses Taken at the Bar of the House of Assembly . . . ," February 3 and 4, 1824, CO 28/93.

Questioner: What do you mean by certain privileges alluded to in the counter-address?

Collymore: We meant the removal of restrictions upon our giving evidence in requiring the production of our manumissions and certificates; and also to be exempt from arrests when possessed of property sufficient to exempt other persons.[50]

Questioner: Are you aware of any rights and privileges enjoyed by your forefathers which you do not now enjoy?

Collymore: Certainly not.

Questioner: Then you are fully sensible that you have not been deprived of any rights and privileges?

Collymore: We have not been deprived of any.

Questioner: Do you mean to say that you have a natural and reasonable claim to those rights and privileges, at present, or when?

Collymore: We intended to have petitioned for them in a less agitated state of the country, but of course should have left it to the legislature to fix the time when we should have them.

Questioner: Do you not enjoy your freedom and the privileges you have solely from the liberality of the colony?

Collymore: We certainly do.

The Assembly objected not only to the counteraddress's political intentions but also to the fact that it was addressed to the governor. The counteraddress was thus a direct affront to the Assembly on an issue about which it became increasingly adamant as pressures from Britain increased to reform the island's slave code—that is, its right to determine the island's internal affairs. "Were you not aware," one House member exhorted Collymore, "that the governor alone could not afford you relief were he willing to do so?" In one of its resolutions on the counteraddress, the Assembly emphatically asserted "that this House in the most positive and unequivocal manner, denies that the free coloured inhabitants of this island are entitled to any rights and privileges, except those granted to them by the Colonial Legislature; the continuance of which must depend entirely on their good conduct."[51]

The testimony presented to the House of Assembly during February 1824 made it abundantly clear that the freedman community was not uni-

[50]On exemption from arrest, see the discussion on pp. 72–73. "Manumissions and certificates" refers to proof that the person was freed under Barbadian law, had been free for at least a year, and was baptized—restrictions that applied to giving testimony during this period.

[51]Resolutions passed by the House of Assembly, February 18, 1824, printed in *Barbadian*, February 25, 1824. On the basis of evidence presented at its hearing, the Assembly requested Governor Warde to deport (under clause 12 of the "alien bill") John Thomas Calliard and Frederick Dottin. Dottin, a principal in the counteraddress group, was judged the originator of the rumor that Warde was displeased with the Belgrave address. As far as can be ascertained, Dottin was a Barbadian, but Calliard, who was considered to hold ultramilitant views on the issue of civil rights for freedmen, was a native of either Saint Vincent or Grenada (see "Examination of Witnesses Taken at the Bar . . . ," February 3 and 4, 1824, CO 28/93; and

fied. Although ideological differences were mitigated during the reform struggle of later years, at this period the Belgrave group was not only wealthier but more conservative, and for this reason it was viewed with greater approbation by the plantocracy. While the dissident group also contained some freedmen of wealth and achievement, it comprised many individuals of more modest circumstances and persons who were still denied legal testimony because of restrictions in the 1817 law; in addition, this group contained younger and, relative to the period, more militant individuals. The conflict between the two groups involved disagreements on the timeliness and means for achieving expansion of civil rights, as well as disagreements on the nature of the rights sought. There also were disagreements on who could legitimately represent the views of the community and how its corporate authority should be delegated, differences on the question of slave emancipation and amelioration and whether freedmen should publicly take a stand on this issue, and differences in opinion as to whether liberalization of the freedman's status would come from the colonial legislature or from the imperial government.

There were, however, freedmen who did not sign either address. Some were prompted to express their position after the Speaker of the Assembly announced that freedmen who did "not publicly come forward and declare their concurrence" with the Belgrave address would "be considered as approving" the counteraddress. This pressure, as well as their own inclinations, caused a group of twenty freedmen to publish a statement stressing their "entire approbation and concurrence in the sentiments" of the Belgrave address and expressing their willingness to have signed it "had the short time allowed for its preparation admitted of our being called up."[52]

THE "SLAVE CONSOLIDATION ACT"

Despite "conservative" elements in the freedman community, and beyond its reactions to the counteraddress, the plantocracy was increasingly placed in a defensive position; circumstances continued to favor ameliorating the condition of the slaves and, by extension, the freedmen. Yet the Assembly often delayed reform legislation, enacted it in piecemeal fashion, and frequently on the minimal level it thought it could get away with and still comply with directives from the Colonial Office. This policy of legislative procrastination was clearly reflected in the "slave consolidation act," the most comprehensive and lengthy slave law in Barbados's history. The act repealed or modified dormant laws, removed inconsistencies, and intro-

Address of the House of Assembly to Governor Warde, February 17, 1824, *ibid.*). It is not known whether any other freedmen were ever deported under the "alien bill," which remained in force until late 1827 or early 1828, when it was disallowed by the Crown (Schomburgk, *History of Barbados*, p. 425).

[52]*Barbadian*, February 25, 1824.

duced new measures. An early version of this law passed the Assembly and the Council in March 1825,[53] but it did not include a number of changes desired by the Colonial Office. A new version passed the legislature, and was assented to by the governor, in October 1826.[54] The law was approved by the Crown one year later,[55] but the approval was a qualified one, and the island's government was warned that, "unless a further and more decisive progress be made in the improvement of the slave code of the Colony, His Majesty's expectations will not be satisfied."[56]

The "slave consolidation act" was not specifically intended to apply to freedmen, but they found three clauses in it particularly offensive and potentially debilitating. Clauses 27 and 42 applied sanctions against slaves found guilty of using "insolent language or gestures to or of any white person," and who "shall wilfully strike or assault any white person." Thus, freedmen were denied protection they had possessed up to that time under laws, passed in 1688 and 1749, which made it a crime for slaves to "offer any violence to any Christian, by striking or the like," or to use "any insolent language or gesture to any white or free person."[57] Denial of such protection by the "slave consolidation act" eliminated, as the freedmen stated in a late 1827 (or early 1828) petition to the president of the Council, "all legal remedy against personal assaults, and other behaviour tending to provoke a breach of the peace, committed by the largest class of the population of the island. . . . any turbulent slave, who, instigated by his own malignant suggestions, or those of an unprincipled master, may be disposed to insult or injure your petitioners, may, under particular circumstances, escape with impunity."[58] The complaint expressed here reflected not only a long-standing theme in the freedman's drive for amelioration—that is, a maximization of the status difference between himself and the slave—but also the actuality of often tense relations between the two groups. In 1823, for

[53]See CO 30/20–21, no. 446.

[54]For a copy of the "slave consolidation act," see *PP*, 1826–27, vol. 25, unnumbered rept., pp. 205–30 of Barbados section.

[55]It is well to remember that all Barbadian (and colonial) laws required the ultimate sanction of the Crown. In most cases, when the governor assented to a law, it went into force and continued until, or unless, it was disallowed by the Crown (see, for example, Dwarris, *Substance of Three Reports*, p. 3). Some laws, however, contained suspending clauses, which specified that the laws were to remain inactive until approved by the Crown. The lengthy and often cumbersome process involved in acquiring this approval meant that the status quo could endure for a relatively long period beyond the date of the governor's assent. For example, the "slave consolidation act" and the important "brown privilege bill" (see p. 102) contained these suspending clauses; although the former received the Crown's approval in one year, the latter required about seventeen months. Thus, although the enactment of a reform measure may have lifted the freedmen's morale, the status quo remained until word was received from England that the act had met with the Crown's approval.

[56]Huskisson to Skeete, October 18, 1827, *PP*, 1828, vol. 27, unnumbered rept., pp. 37–41.

[57]Richard Hall, *Acts, Passed in the Island of Barbados. From 1643 to 1762, Inclusive* (London, 1764), pp. 114, 355.

[58]"To the Honourable John Brathwaite . . . the Humble Petition of the Undersigned Free Coloured Inhabitants . . . ," *PP*, 1828, vol. 27, unnumbered rept., pp. 42–44. This petition

example, the senior justice of the peace in Bridgetown informed the British parliamentary commission that he had "received 2,500 complaints in fifteen months in breaches of the peace and misdemeanors, most of them complaints by free coloured persons against slaves and against each other"; freedmen, the island's attorney general remarked, were "very litigious."[59]

In their petition the freedmen suggested that the racial limitations of the two clauses were an oversight caused by the massive chore involved in consolidating the island's slave laws. (Despite the petition's willingness to accept as accidental the abrogation of privileges formerly held, it is not too difficult to assume that the clauses were intentionally worded as such, the plantocracy knowing how extremely sensitive many freedmen were to emphasizing their status differences from the slaves.) But they could not "attribute to the same cause" a restriction against them in the act's twenty-fourth clause.

This clause removed restrictions on the cultivation and marketing of cotton and aloes by slaves. Relative to sugar, these crops were of secondary importance to the island's economy, but they were prominent among a group of minor export crops (including, as well, arrowroot and ginger) which, although produced by some plantations, were also cultivated by slaves, poor whites, and freedmen on small land units; these minor export crops were the major cash crops produced by the island's small-scale agriculturalists.[60] In order to protect the "industrious and honest" slave producers of aloes and cotton and to insure that the crops that were marketed belonged to the producer and had not been stolen, the clause provided that they be harvested "under the immediate inspection of some white person" resident on the plantation or "place" (that is, a small freehold of around ten acres—often less, sometimes more) to which the slave belonged; but, "if there shall be no white person" on the land unit, the reaping was to be done "under the inspection of some other fit and proper white person." These whites were to make declarations on oath that the crops had been reaped under their supervision from the slaves' gardens, and a cotton inspector (a role defined and provided for by earlier laws that applied only to free producers) was to issue certificates which permitted the marketing of the crops and served as legal proof that they were the property of the producer.

If, indeed, this clause was intentionally worded to exclude freedmen (as claimed in their petition) from authenticating the produce of their own

was signed by "526 free coloured and free black persons." No date is given for the petition in the *PP* source, but the Council president forwarded it to the colonial secretary on January 22, 1828. Another petition formulated during the same period contained similar objections to clauses in the "slave consolidation act" and was signed by 880 freedmen. This petition is referred to in the Minutes of the Board of Legislative Council, January 8, 1828, CO 31/50.

[59]Dwarris, *Substance of Three Reports*, pp. 71, 106.

[60]See Jerome S. Handler, "The History of Arrowroot and the Origin of Peasantries in the British West Indies," *Journal of Caribbean History*, 2 (1971): 70–73, 78–81. A number of

slaves, the motivation underlying this exclusion is ambiguous. However, it is possible that the plantocracy was mistrustful of potential collusion between freedmen and slaves in the marketing of stolen goods. That is, the plantocracy may have felt that freedmen would encourage their slaves to steal such crops and then authenticate them as having been legally produced. Aloes and cotton were easily disposable on the internal market, and it is known that a variety of stolen commodities often turned up in the marketing transactions that took place between freedmen (as well as whites) and slaves. The freedman petitioners stated that the clause "operates with peculiar hardship" on those "who own landed property." The small-scale agricultural freeholders who worked their land with the assistance of a handful of slaves were unable to dispose of their own produce unless it was harvested in the presence of a white person. As they put it, "Your petitioners fondly anticipated rather a removal of previous disqualifications, than the addition of new ones." In general, the petitioners concluded that by the "slave consolidation act" they were "divested of certain privileges and advantages hitherto enjoyed by them in common with their white fellow subjects [and that] their interests [were] slighted." Although they called for "such relief . . . as will exonerate them from these new and unmerited grievances and disabilities," they were also chagrined that there was no change in their status and that "the ban of political exclusion pronounced against them by former legislatures [is] reiterated and confirmed."

Although the plantocracy was not yet prepared to expand the freedman's civil status by permitting him to vote, the climate of the times (which was greatly contributed to by continual reform pressures from Great Britain) made it difficult for even the Barbadian legislature to continue the objectionable clauses in the "slave consolidation act." On January 8, 1828, the Assembly passed a new act which received rapid approval from the Council and the governor. This new act extended the protective clauses of the "slave consolidation act" to freedmen so that they "shall enjoy the like protection against the insults, assaults, and aggressions of slaves, as is secured to white persons," and authorized freedmen "to inspect the cotton and aloes of their own slaves and of any other slaves under their lawful charge."[61]

THE GROWING REFORM MOVEMENT

By now the ameliorative trend had become firmly established and, although the Barbadian legislature was still reluctant to move too fast, freedmen were becoming bolder in their stance on the extension of civil

---

nineteenth-century laws were designed to encourage the production of aloes, cotton, and ginger and to protect both their plantation and small-scale producers (see CO 30/19, nos. 299, 322; and CO 30/20, nos. 421, 434).

[61]CO 31/21, no. 505.

rights. On July 14, 1829, after months of discussion and public meetings, a group of eighteen men, representing the freedman community, forwarded a petition to the legislature. These petitioners, as H. A. Vaughan has recently written, requested "admission to the elective franchise and the right to be tried by an equal number of their peers. They stressed the fact that the free colored people contributed indiscriminately with their white fellow subjects to the internal support of the colony by the payment of all taxes and expressed the hope that in view of their loyalty in the anxious and critical moments of emergency and danger the House would, in its wisdom and justice, deem it expedient to establish that unity of interest where a unity of action might be essentially requisite."[62] The "critical moments" referred to were the movements toward slave emancipation. "Six years earlier," Vaughan remarks, "such language would have been regarded as containing a veiled threat"; however, despite rapidly changing conditions on the island, "the Assembly was not to be hurried."[63] And, rather than grant full legal equality at one time, the Assembly continued to enact civil rights legislation in piecemeal fashion.

For example, in July 1829 the House of Assembly modified (or repealed) laws of 1672 and 1770 which exempted debtors from arrest if they owned ten or more acres of land. These laws had not applied to females, Jews, and freedmen—that is, to persons ineligible to vote under the island's electoral laws. "Several instances occurred where such persons were actually arrested and held to bail upon contracts," however, and thus legislative action in 1829 was designed "to remedy these defects."[64] Although "exemption from arrests when possessed of property sufficient to exempt other persons" was a privilege freedmen wanted and had alluded to in their 1823 counteraddress, the legislature still made no significant move to meet the major demands of their 1829 petition. Thus, in July 1830 the freedmen again petitioned, but this time directly to Governor Lyon. They implored him to influence the Assembly and the Council to grant them civil rights "in common with their white fellow subjects. . . . Claims which we conceive ourselves justly entitled to as British, Christian, faithful and loyal subjects"; although they stressed their "natural desire" to have all legal disabilities removed "by the legislature of our country," their increased militancy emphasized that failure with the legislature would cause them to request the governor's "powerful influence and support, in enabling us . . . to lay our grievances at the foot of the throne"[65]—a phraseology which, in earlier years, could have done little more than insure hostility and inaction from the plantocracy.

[62]Vaughan, "Samuel Prescod," pp. 55, 58–59.
[63]Ibid., pp. 58–59.
[64]Schomburgk, *History of Barbados*, p. 429.
[65]"We . . . the Undersigned Free Coloured Inhabitants of this Island," July 15, 1830, Minutes of the House of Assembly, July 27, 1830, printed in *Barbadian*, April 22, 1831.

Yet these were different times, and in a relatively short span of years the island's political atmosphere had rapidly altered; internal changes were reflected in the increased activity in reform legislation. On October 6, 1830, the Assembly passed a law (assented to by the governor on December 3) which extended the "benefit of testimony" by eliminating the 1817 restrictions that had denied it to persons who had been free for less than a year and/or had not been manumitted under Barbadian law; in addition, freedmen were permitted to testify "without being obliged or compellable to produce any certificate of baptism."[66] It thus took more than thirteen years, or three decades since the issue had first been collectively raised by freedmen, for the plantocracy to grant all of them the legal right they had considered most vital and regarded as a fundamental element of their free status. On May 25, 1831, an act repealed all legal disabilities "on white persons . . . professing the Hebrew religion";[67] on June 1, all restrictions were removed from slaves' testifying in the courts;[68] and on June 9 manumission fees were eliminated.[69] Also on June 9, 1831, the governor assented to a bill which granted full legal equality to freedmen.

THE "BROWN PRIVILEGE BILL" AND LEGAL EQUALITY

Popularly known as the "brown privilege bill," the law repealed "all acts and such parts of acts as impose any restraints or disabilities whatsoever on His Majesty's Free Coloured and Free Black subjects . . . to which His Majesty's white subjects . . . are not liable."[70] Furthermore, it specifically provided that all free males were eligible to vote, to be elected to public office, and to serve on juries, subject only to age and property qualifications.[71] Although the law technically removed racial prerequisites from the definition of a freeholder, even at this late date the Barbadian legislature could not bring itself to maximize the number of eligible freedmen, nor could it resist the opportunity to render their legal victory incomplete. Property qualifications were specified in two areas: ownership of ten or more acres of land; or ownership of a house or houses in town whose an-

---

[66]CO 31/21, no. 528. On October 17, 1826, the Assembly and the Council passed a law which permitted slaves who had been manumitted outside of Barbados to testify, but the one-year freedom proviso and the clause requiring baptism were retained (see *PP*, 1826–27, vol. 25, unnumbered rept., p. 272). Because of a legislative technicality, however, the governor refused to assent to the bill (see Huskisson to Skeete, October 18, 1827, *ibid.*, 1828, vol. 27, unnumbered rept., pp. 37–41).

[67]CO 30/21, no. 530.

[68]*Ibid.*, no. 531.

[69]*Ibid.*, no. 542.

[70]*Ibid.*, no. 538.

[71]Schomburgk wrote that the act applied to "all the inhabitants who professed the Christian religion" (*History of Barbados*, p. 432), but he was clearly mistaken. The "brown privilege bill" explicitly repealed clause 8 of the 1721 law, which mentioned Christianity in the definition of a freeholder, and specified only free status, age, sex, and property. In addition, as mentioned above, a May 1831 law removed all legal disabilities of Jews.

nual taxable value was at least £30. Thus, land qualifications remained the same as they had been in 1721, but all new freeholders, if they did not possess the ten or more acres (a luxury few freedmen had) were required to have a house or houses whose value was three times higher than that required in the 1721 law. Equally important, however, was the fact that the "brown privilege bill" retained undisturbed the 1721 property requirements for all existing freeholders—that is, whites. Its crucial sixth clause specified that "nothing in this act contained shall in any way affect or be construed to affect the freehold rights of any person who may at the time of the passing of this act be really and bona fide a freeholder . . . agreeably to the laws of this island now in force, but all such freehold rights shall be and they are hereby expressly reserved."[72]

Thus, while white freeholders continued to be eligible under previous criteria, new freeholders were subjected to an increase in their property qualifications. It is of more than passing interest that the increase in property qualifications applied only to houses, these being the major form of property which wealthier freedmen possessed. Although the law also affected whites, it was, despite the legislature's formal denials, specifically designed to curtail the potential voting power of freedmen. As Governor Smith noted, "A coloured person in Bridge-town of the age of thirty is living in a ten pound freehold between two white persons of the same age and similar property, and all paying the same taxes; yet the two whites have the privilege of voting for their representatives, by whom they are taxed, and the coloured man has not. They may all live perhaps for thirty years more, and so long will that coloured person be excluded from one of the dearest privileges of a free man."[73]

Yet, even if the householding clause had been deleted, relatively few freedmen would have been enfranchised. The "brown privilege bill" actually went into effect on November 22, 1832, and close to a year later the governor reported that of the island's freedman population "there are in St. Michael's (and the other parishes have scarcely any free holders) about one hundred and twenty-five persons whose rents are from £10 and upwards, and who would enjoy the privilege of voters, if they were white; and there are only seventy-five voters by the present law of £30 qualifications."[74] At this time the island's total electorate was 1,016 persons, 446 of whom resided in Saint Michael alone.[75] Therefore, on the eve of emancipation, freedmen constituted only about 7 percent of the Barbadian electorate, although they comprised 33.1 percent of the island's nonslave population.

Many freedmen initially misunderstood the full implications of the "brown privilege bill." Soon after its passage they "hailed the apparent enfranchise-

[72]CO 31/21, no. 538.
[73]Smith to the House of Assembly, April 10, 1834, CO 28/113.
[74]Smith to Stanley, October 29, 1833, CO 28/111.
[75]Schomburgk, *History of Barbados*, p. 455.

ment, and held a public rejoicing on the occasion," but various persons, including Samuel Jackman Prescod (who was on his way to becoming a prominent leader in the freedman community), "succeeded . . . in convincing [their] brethren that the new provision was a mockery of their wrongs, and that the Assembly had only added insult to past injuries."[76] Through public discussions freedmen became convinced that the bill was "a perfect delusion, calculated to debar them from those privileges which are reserved for whites."[77]

As a result of the freedmen's complaints and prodding, Governor Smith, who was sympathetic to their plight, had on a number of occasions urged the legislature to modify the "brown privilege bill" so as to remove the disputed clause; he claimed no disagreement with "the good policy which raised the household vote to £30, had it embraced all free classes," but expressed the view that the law was patently discriminatory.[78] The Council and the Assembly repeatedly denied that the increased houseowning qualifications were intended to specifically discriminate against and disenfranchise freedmen, and were reluctant to change the wording of the bill.[79] Although aware of the legislature's behavior in the years prior to his arrival (in April 1833) and frustrated by "the blind bigotry with which they have resisted every practical relief to the free coloured caste,"[80] Governor Smith became optimistic that plantocratic sentiments were "gradually yielding to the liberal spirit of the times."[81] But even as late as April 1834 he could report that only one member of the Assembly was willing to introduce a bill to reduce the £30 householding qualification.[82] Not until 1840 was the electoral law changed,[83] but, as the era of slavery drew to a close, Barbados

[76]J. A. Thome and J. H. Kimball, *Emancipation in the West Indies* (New York, 1838), p. 74. Prescod related these events to the authors in 1837. Prescod's first formal step toward a position of leadership in the freedman community was taken in a speech he made at a public meeting on February 23, 1829, when he was twenty-two years old; the meeting had been convened to draft a petition calling for the extension of the franchise and the right to sit on juries. In April 1836 the *New Times*, the island's first freedman newspaper, was founded with Prescod as its editor, and in 1843 he became the first "coloured" man in the island's history to sit in the House of Assembly. For details on Prescod's life and career, see Thome and Kimball, *Emancipation in the West Indies*, pp. 74–75; Vaughan, "Samuel Prescod," pp. 55–60; and F. A. Hoyos, *Our Common Heritage* (Barbados, 1953), pp. 34–39.

[77]Smith to Stanley, September 27, 1833, CO 28/111.

[78]Smith to the House of Assembly, April 10, 1834, CO 28/113; see also "Governor's Message to Assembly and Council on Conveying the Act of Parliament for the Abolition of Slavery," October 15, 1833, CO 28/111.

[79]See, for example, Council to Smith, October 22, 1833, CO 28/111; Assembly to Smith, April 29, 1834, CO 28/113; Smith to Assembly, April 10, 1834, *ibid.*

[80]Smith to Stanley, July 2, 1833, CO 28/111.

[81]Smith to "Thomas Griffith, Esq., and the Free Colored Gentlemen Who Have Addressed the Governor," April 9, 1834, CO 28/113.

[82]Smith to Stanley, April 30, 1834, *ibid.*; see also House of Assembly to Smith, April 29, 1834, *ibid.*

[83]The new law, assented to by the Crown in 1842, established Bridgetown as a separate constituency and thereby increased the House of Assembly's membership to twenty-four. The

Figure 2. Samuel Jackman Prescod at the Age of Thirty-Four.
Detail from "The Anti-Slavery Society Convention, 1840,"
a painting by B. R. Haydon, courtesy of
the National Portrait Gallery, London.

remained, in the words of its governor, "the only island in the whole arch-
ipelago which keeps up any distinction amongst the King's free subjects."[84]

---

first election held under this law brought Samuel Prescod into the House as one of the representatives from Bridgetown, which in 1844 had 422 voters out of an island-wide electorate
of 1,103 (see Schomburgk, *History of Barbados*, pp. 208, 487–88, 494, 497–98).

[84]Smith to House of Assembly, April 10, 1834, CO 28/113.

THE STRUGGLE AGAINST SOCIAL DISCRIMINATION

The distinction that Governor Smith had in mind went beyond the legis-lature's blatant attempt to limit the number of enfranchised freedmen. It included an uneasiness and disapproval of the plantocracy's refusal to nominate enfranchised and eligible freedmen to positions of prestige, such as commissions in the militia and magistracies. This refusal became in-creasingly galling to freedmen, and, after Thomas J. Cummins, a leading and respected member of their community, was refused a position for which he had applied (and was insulted for being so presumptious as to apply for it), a public meeting of freedmen was held "to show their sense of an insult that had been publicly offered to one of their body" and to present their grievances directly to Governor Smith, who had recently arrived on the island.

The "numerous and respectable public meeting" of May 6, 1833, was reported in the *Barbadian*.[85] Although the newspaper's regular reporter was absent and at times it was difficult for his substitute to take notes, the excitement, animation, and vocal reactions to the proceedings are apparent in the account; freedmen were actively participating in a public meeting and exuberantly responding to the actions and words of their leaders. Foremost among these leaders was Samuel Prescod, who had been elected chairman of the meeting. In his opening and militant speech, he stated his conviction that "without great exertions on their part the benefits resulting from [the "brown privilege bill"] would never be any more than minimal. So long as [freedmen] continued to look up to the subordinate officials of the island for patronage, they would find themselves in the scale of Barba-dian society, just where they then were, at a vast distance below whites!" The audience responded with "cheers." It was only "with difficulty," Prescod continued, that freedmen "had obtained from the 'Elect' [that is, the plantocracy] an acknowledgement of their equality—and that coloured man who could believe that they would, without a struggle, admit Free Coloured and Black men into public situations must have very little knowl-edge of human nature." Freedmen must, Prescod exhorted the crowd, "take their cause out of the hands of these 'exclusives' and carry it to head-quarters"—that is, the Governor. When Prescod related in detail what had happened to Thomas Cummins, the noise in William Earle's house, where the meeting was being held, became so great that the *Barbadian* reporter was unable to take notes.

Prescod concluded his address by submitting four resolutions he and some others had prepared. The first noted "that so long as worthy individ-uals of our body are excluded from participating with their equals of the other free class in the enjoyment of those benefits which should result from

---

[85]Information on this meeting is taken from the account in the *Barbadian*, May 15, 1833.

an equality of rights, the legislative enactment which acknowledges that equality is but a dead letter." The second resolution unequivocally stressed "that the continued exclusion of our body from places of public trust, honor, and emolument is, in consequence of that legislative enactment, rendered more offensive to us, and more disgraceful to the community, than it was before that enactment took place, in as much as it furnishes an indubitable proof that the concession of our rights was more a matter of *necessity* [that is, pressures from Britain] than from a conviction of the *justice* of our claims." The third resolution pointed out how "certain worthy individuals of our body" had applied for vacant positions and were not only refused but also insulted. The fourth resolution stressed the necessity of forwarding grievances directly to the governor because no Barbadian white would recommend to him a freedman for a prestigious post.

Some freedmen felt that the resolutions were too strongly worded and they proposed amendments to tone down the language, but the overwhelming majority enthusiastically agreed with the original wording and the resolutions were unanimously passed—the second, especially, was adopted "amidst loud cheering." The meeting appointed Prescod, Thomas J. Cummins, and four others to present the address to the governor, and authorized this delegation to sign the address on behalf of the entire freedman community.

On May 13, 1833, the governor received the approved address. Although it was somewhat milder in tone than the resolutions upon which it was based, and did not give vent to the full range of sentiments and attitudes held by the freedman community, the address nonetheless contained what freedmen considered to be their essential grievances:

Your Excellency's predecessors in government invariably found, on their arrival here, two classes of free subjects, not more distinguished by complexion than by political enactments and social customs . . . during the administration of your Excellency's immediate predecessor . . . the political struggle of the free coloured and black inhabitants to obtain an acknowledgement of equal rights with the other free class, was crowned with success. As far as legislative enactments could remove the unnatural and impolitic distinctions between us and our white fellow-subjects, those distinctions have been removed. . . . [However] the distinctions are, in reality, still kept up; and are now rendered, in consequence of that enactment, more obviously invidious, and more galling to those to whose prejudice they operate. . . . We are aware that, owing in part to the political disadvantages under which we have hitherto laboured, there are, comparatively, but few of our body who can reasonably expect to participate, with the other free class, in the fruition of those social and political advantages which should result from an acknowledged equality of rights. All, therefore, that we ask—all that we expect—and we hope reasonably—is that the few who are qualified, will be admitted to participate with their equals of the other side. *The ex-*

altation of these must indirectly tend to the exaltation of our whole body.[86]

The address requested Governor Smith to appoint freedmen to "places of public trust, honor, and emolument," and assured him "that only the certainty that no individual of our body will ever be officially recommended to your Excellency for public situations, could have induced us to bring our claims before your Excellency."[87]

Although Governor Smith was favorably disposed to appointing freedmen magistrates and commissioned officers, little action was taken, largely because of plantocratic intransigence.[88] As a group, the plantocracy had resisted as long as it could the granting of civil rights to freedmen. The Barbados legislature was the last and most reluctant in the West Indies to grant freedmen legal equality;[89] even its final action, the "brown privilege bill," which was passed in the twilight of slavery when emancipation was already imminent, reflected its traditional intransigence and intractibility. These qualities had been primarily mollified by continued pressure from Britain, as well as by the organized efforts freedmen made on their own behalf. However, as the freedmen's petitions emphasized, the profound racism of white society did not disappear with the granting of legal equality, and to many their new status was empty so long as they continued to suffer from personal indignities and social discrimination. As

[86]"The Humble Loyal Address of His Majesty's Free Coloured and Free Black Subjects . . . ," May 6, 1833, printed in *Barbadian*, May 15, 1833, italics added.

[87]*Ibid.*

[88]See "Reply by Governor Smith to the Address of the Free Coloured . . . ," May 13, 1833, CO 28/111; and Smith to Stanley, May 23, 1833, *ibid.*

In various letters to the Colonial Office, Smith proclaimed his sympathy with the freedmen, but Joseph Sturge and Thomas Harvey, who undoubtedly derived their information from discussions with freedmen, gained a different picture of the governor's behavior:

> Sir Lionel Smith's professions of impartiality and freedom from prejudice excited great hopes in the minds of the colored people. They expected at least that some of their number, men of wealth, education and superior qualifications, would receive commissions in the magistracy. In this they were disappointed; the only attempt made by the Governor in their favor was, by inviting a colored gentleman to his table. One of his white guests manifested his offence by leaving the room, which created so much alarm that the Governor immediately relinquished his aggressive policy and fell back upon conciliation. . . . Sir Lionel Smith embarked for Jamaica amidst the execrations of the crowds of free blacks and apprentices assembled on the beach.

The West Indies in 1837 (London, 1838), app., p. xxxiv, italics in the original.

Smith was certainly subjected to opposing pressures from the plantocracy, on the one hand, and the Colonial Office (as well as his own predispositions), on the other, and this was not an unusual predicament for the governor of Barbados. The very positive acclaim that Smith received from the Council, the Assembly, and the white merchants of Bridgetown upon his departure from the island (see Schomburgk, *History of Barbados*, pp. 473–75) suggests that, in his actions, he ultimately capitulated to the plantocracy and compromised the rights of freedmen he had so often professed.

[89]See letter from Downing Street to Howick, March 15, 1831, CO 28/108; Smith to Stanley, May 23 and July 2, 1833, CO 28/111; and Smith to Stanley, April 10, 1834, CO 28/113. Barbados was also the last colony to pass the act to abolish slavery, as required by the imperial government.

the day of slave emancipation rapidly approached, freedmen were still surrounded by a variety of customary prohibitions that emphasized their subordinate status and excluded them from "public situations of honour and profit." Attempts to influence the plantocracy through the governor had for all intents and purposes failed. In what was probably the freedmen's last petition during the period of slavery, they made another attempt to appeal directly to the legislature for the social rights to which they felt legitimately entitled as free British subjects:

> Your petitioners . . . impelled by an imperious sense of duty to themselves, which renders it impossible for them to rest satisfied until they are placed on an equal footing with the present class of freeholders in all respects . . . again venture to approach your Honorable Board in the language of complaint and petition. . . . Your petitioners, though relieved from some of the most grievous disabilities under which they formerly labored . . . though fully aware that it is not in the power of any legislature, by its fiat, to change or annihilate feelings and opinions which have existed for a great length of time, and that from the restrictions under which they formerly labored, and which debarring them the acquisition of land, drove them for support to the handicraft trades and mechanical occupations, they cannot boast an equality of wealth or territorial influence. Yet feeling that they do comprise a large and rapidly increasing portion of the general body of freemen, having among them individuals fitted by education and gentlemanly habits, if not by equal wealth, to be entitled to participate with their white fellow subjects in the advantages derivable from their being elevated to posts of honor or emolument, they do complain of the manifest disposition evinced by many of the authorities to give permanence as matter of custom to those distinctions which have been abrogated as matter of law, thereby violating the principle and spirit of the measure passed for the relief of the free colored population, and exposing themselves to a charge of bad faith, in attempting to withdraw with one hand, that which they had offered as a boon with the other.[90]

However, the second-class citizenship of nonwhites was to continue beyond the emancipation period, and the integration of all classes of freedmen into the larger society of freemen remained limited by the status that had been historically ascribed to them on the basis of their racial characteristics. Not only did the freedman's racially defined status restrict his participation in the island's political and judicial institutions throughout the period of slavery, but it also governed the nature and degree of his involvement in other areas of the Barbadian social order. The following chapters review various of the island's national institutions and the participation of freedmen within them.

---

[90]"Address of the Free Coloured and Free Black Inhabitants of Bridgetown" to the Council and the Assembly, April 2, 1834, CO 28/113.

V

THE MILITIA OF BARBADOS

The freedman's participation in Barbadian political and judicial institutions was very limited, but "he possessed one privilege of citizenship," an American noted in 1814, "which the same class of men do not have in the United States."[1] That is, throughout slavery, freedmen were expected to serve in the island's militia, and it may be argued that this service constituted an important and positive aspect of their self-image as freemen and citizens. There is no evidence that freedmen were reluctant to assume their military responsibilities; in fact, "enrolling themselves in the parochial militia units where they reside" was one of the first steps taken by manumitted slaves in establishing their new identity.[2]

The militia had been organized on a parochial basis in the seventeenth century for protection against external attack and slave revolts. From the seventeenth century onward, all laws governing the militia noted the obligation of free adult (often specified between the ages of sixteen and sixty) males without referring to racial origins. These laws did not confine freedmen to noncombatant roles, nor did they prohibit freedmen from bearing firearms.[3] (From the seventeenth century to the early nineteenth, various militia acts or governors' proclamations implicitly or explicitly acknowledged "that many Negroes and slaves are worthy of great trust and confidence," and permitted the arming of a certain proportion of slaves in times

---

[1][Benjamin Browne], *The Yarn of a Yankee Privateer*, ed. Nathaniel Hawthorne (New York, 1926), p. 103. In 1792 the U.S. Congress "organized the militia and restricted enrollment to able-bodied white male citizens," although Negroes were not debarred from serving in the Army, Navy, and Marines; the laws of various states also prevented freedmen from joining their militias (Leon F. Litwack, *North of Slavery: The Negro in the Free States, 1790–1860* [Chicago, 1965], pp. 31, 32, 35; see also Lorenzo J. Greene, *The Negro in Colonial New England* [New York, 1968], pp. 127–28).

[2]J. W. [I. W.] Orderson, *Cursory Remarks and Plain Facts Connected with the Question Produced by the Proposed Slave Registry Bill* (London, 1816), p. 15.

[3]See, for example, the laws of 1799 (Samuel Moore, *The Public Acts in Force, Passed by the Legislature of Barbados, from May 11th, 1762, to April 8th, 1800, Inclusive* [London, 1801], pp. 381–408); 1805 (CO 30/17, no. 249); 1809 (CO 30/18, no. 277); and 1812 (CO 30/19, no. 321).

of emergency; these arms, however, were restricted to lances, pikes, bills, and the like, and never included firearms.)[4] In addition, the militia laws did not discriminate in the provision of benefits for militiamen severely injured during the course of battle. For example, the militia act of 1805 included a clause that applied "*to all such freemen* as shall cheerfully and boldly oppose the common enemy," and provided an annual pension for "*any poor freeman*" disabled in defense of the island (if killed, the person's wife received the pension).[5]

Although the bearing of firearms and eligibility for a pension might point toward an equality of status between the white and freed militiaman, the fundamentally subordinate position of the latter was emphasized in more crucial and recurring areas of the militia organization, such as the racial composition of units and the occupancy of important leadership positions.

During monthly drills and times of mobilization, freedmen were confined to companies composed solely of men of their own status group. This segregation pattern was apparently well established by at least 1805 (and persisted for the remainder of the slave period), when the island feared a French invasion. Reflecting on military preparations during this period, J. P. Mayers, a member of the House of Assembly, reported that "no part of the [Saint Michael] regiment assembled more readily than the free coloured companies."[6] The practice of segregating militia units was legally first made explicit in an 1809 militia act which stipulated that each parochial regiment was to be formed of companies "of not fewer than forty men each, except the free people of colour who may be formed into companies of fewer than forty men each, according to their numbers [in each parish]."[7] The same American referred to above witnessed the Bridgetown militia training on a number of occasions in 1814; he observed that freedmen "were enrolled in companies by themselves, officered by men of colour, but parading at the same time with the white militia."[8] His observation offers the only indication that freedmen were permitted some leadership roles in at least the Bridgetown units; however, the officers he referred to were certainly noncommissioned ones—for freedmen were debarred from holding commissions in all units, including their own.

[4]William Rawlin, *The Laws of Barbados* (London, 1699), pp. 223–24. See also *CSPCS, 1707*, pp. 618–20; Richard Hall, *A General Account of the First Settlement and of the Trade and Constitution of the Island of Barbados, Written in the Year 1755, with a Foreword by E. M. Shilstone* (Barbados, 1924), pp. 22–24; CO 30/17, no. 249; and William Dickson, *Mitigation of Slavery in Two Parts* (London, 1814), p. 362.

[5]CO 30/17, no. 240, italics added. The essence of this clause was continued in later militia acts—for example, in 1809 (CO 30/18, no. 277) and 1812 (CO 30/19, no. 321).

[6]Journal of the Assembly of Barbados, October 8, 1816, CO 31/47. William Dickson alluded to this pattern in the 1770s, when freed militiamen "made a far better appearance than any white corps in the island" (*Mitigation of Slavery*, p. 362).

[7]CO 30/18, no. 277. This clause was continued in subsequent acts.

[8][Browne], *Yarn of a Yankee Privateer*, p. 103.

Militia officers, especially the colonels in command of each parish, were required by law to be wealthy property owners, but even the relatively few freedmen who were eligible to hold commissions were prevented from doing so by the racial prejudice expressed against them. The governor was empowered to appoint all officers, but he customarily appointed only the colonels, leaving them to nominate the rest; colonels, in turn, with the support and encouragement of their fellow planters and merchants, would not appoint freedmen. Although it was unthinkable to Barbadian whites that nonwhites should command white regiments, an attempt to open up prestigious positions to freedmen was made by the governor in 1833. Prodded by the freedmen themselves, Lionel Smith urged "that all militia companies *wholly composed* of free men of colour, or of free blacks, ought in the first instance to be commanded by commissioned officers of their own caste."[9] He suggested a law to effect this change, emphasizing that "the surest way of securing the faith and loyalty of all subjects, is by giving them an interest in the institutions of the country they belong to and by removing every mark . . . tending to bind their energies and intelligence to a degraded or limited scene of action." Even though the issue did not go beyond freedmen commanding their own companies, the Barbados Assembly refused to consider such a law and explained its reluctance by noting that it

> is not a legislative concern. . . . In an unpaid military association, whose avowed object is to protect the holders of real property . . . some personal or collateral interest in their preservation is surely necessary to qualify an individual to command, and that a stake in the country and character in society are indispensably requisite. When these pretensions are united in any one, we are certain that the shades of complexion would necessarily be forgotten, without an extension of the prerogative on the part of your Excellency.[10]

The plantocracy had commonly relied on the concept of private property to rationalize its refusal to elevate the freedman's status. However, Governor Smith assured the freedmen that, if necessary, he would approach the British government for aid in improving their status, a move for which he was criticized by the Council.[11] Supported by the liberalizing pressures from Britain and moved by freedman requests, Smith followed his personal inclinations and "appointed one free coloured young gentleman to an Ensigncy" (the lowest commissioned rank), while "ordering the colonels to recommend one for a brown and one for a black company."[12] (This is the only suggestion I found that freedman companies may have

[9]"Speech on the Opening of the Legislature of Barbados," May 7, 1833, CO 28/111, italics added.

[10]"Reply of the House of Assembly to the Governor-General's Speech," [1833], CO 28/111.

[11]Smith to Stanley, July 2, 1833, *ibid.*

[12]Smith to Stanley, May 23, 1833, *ibid.*

been further segregated by phenotypic characteristics.) It is not certain that this appointment went into effect before emancipation, for, by his "Royal Instructions, the Governor was required to obtain the concurrence of the Council to military and civil appointments,"[13] but in July 1833 Smith reported that "the Lt. Genl. of Militia has at length promised me to recommend gentlemen of colour for commissions in the militia, as vacancies may offer."[14]

In his efforts to appoint freedman officers, Smith emphasized to the colonial secretary the importance of "bringing these castes forward. They are a sober, active, and energetic and loyal race and I could equally depend on them if need came, against either slaves or white militia."[15] Smith thus reiterated a point concerning freedman "loyalty" which had been made by others on earlier occasions; that is, in terms of his behavior as a militiaman, all accounts indicate that the freedman was obedient and compliant. In the late eighteenth century, for example, William Dickson found that freedmen "made a far better appearance, and were far better disciplined (being much more susceptible of discipline) than any white corps in the island,"[16] and about three decades later another observer opined that freedmen comprised "the most effective part" of the island's militia.[17] In general, there is no evidence that the freedman's military behavior was ever seriously called into question, and observers who commented on this issue invariably emphasized his conscientiousness during training and mobilization—for example, in the 1770s and in 1805, when the island feared French invasions, and especially during the 1816 slave revolt. In fact, as was discussed in Chapter 4, the freedman's behavior during the revolt helped considerably to effect passage of the island's first law expanding his civil rights. The commander of the Christ Church regiment, for example, lauded the "admirable" behavior of freedman militia units: "Have they not been side by side with the whites," he proclaimed to the House of Assembly, "sharing their toil and thus their danger. . . . In the limited sphere of my movements, I had a portion of coloured soldiers, and I can assure the House, the conduct of both whites and coloured people was so conspicuously good that it is hardly possible to make any discrimination; if there was a difference, I think the coloured soldiers took rather more than their share of the laborious duty in guarding prisoners."[18] In a similar vein, the com-

[13]Claude Levy, "Barbados: The Last Years of Slavery, 1823–1833," *Journal of Negro History*, 44 (1959): 325, n. 53.

[14]Smith to Stanley, July 2, 1833, CO 28/111.

[15]Smith to Stanley, May 23, 1833, *ibid.*

[16]Dickson, *Mitigation of Slavery*, p. 362. "I may defy any man," Dickson added, "to produce a single instance of either slaves or free Negroes manifesting the least sign of insubordination. On the contrary, a spirit of attachment to their country, and of loyalty to 'Grandy Massa,' . . . animated the Blacks and Mulattoes, both slaves and free . . . during the whole of the American war" (*ibid.*).

[17][Browne], *Yarn of a Yankee Privateer*, p. 103.

[18]Speech of J. Best, Journal of the Assembly of Barbados, October 8, 1816, CO 31/47.

mander of Saint Michael noted that, during the "late unfortunate insurrection," freedmen "repaired with . . . alacrity to their alarm-post, and
performed the most fatiguing and important duties in a zealous and highly
commendable manner"; "whenever opportunities have offered," he emphasized, "they have manifested a determination to do their duty by the
country, and a devotion to the interest of the whites."[19]

In the rural areas, some freedmen performed their militia service in the
role of "militia tenant." Plantations were obliged to send to their parochial
units one militiaman for every thirty to fifty acres of plantation land; the
acreage fluctuated by law, and could be reduced in contingencies, but, in
return for these services, the plantation allotted two or three acres to each
tenant for the cultivating of provisions and minor cash crops and the raising of small livestock.[20] These "militia tenants," the majority of whom
were poor whites throughout most, if not all, of the slave period, made up
a considerable proportion of the militia's noncommissioned men. Freedmen, however, were performing this role by the late eighteenth century,[21]
presumably because plantations could not find a sufficient number of poor
whites to meet their quotas.[22] Washington Franklin, a freedman who was
executed because of his leadership role in the 1816 slave revolt, had lived
at the Vineyard plantation in Saint Philip,[23] and may have been a "militia
tenant" on the estate. He, or others like him, may have been the reason
behind a provision in an early draft of the 1819 militia bill which specified
that "only white men shall be received in future as [militia] tenants."[24]
This provision was deleted in the bill's final version, however, and in subsequent years the number and proportion of freedmen "militia tenants"
probably increased over those of earlier periods. Not all freedmen in the
militia were tenants, but lack of data prevents an estimate of how many
were, or of what percentage of all freedmen in the militia they comprised.

In fact, information is generally lacking on the number of freedmen in
the militia, but, judging from their total population (or the number of
adult males), it is clear that at all times they were a minority. In 1802, for
example, the militia comprised 3,218 officers and men,[25] but the freedman
population of adult males was about 400;[26] as a rough estimate, then,
freedmen in the militia were no more, and probably less, than the latter

[19]Speech of J. P. Mayers, *ibid.*; see also Barbados Council to Warde, April 3, 1827, CO
28/100.

[20]Jerome S. Handler, "The History of Arrowroot and the Origin of Peasantries in the
British West Indies," *Journal of Caribbean History*, 2 (1971): 71–73.

[21]See reply of Joshua Steele to Governor Parry, 1788, *PP*, 1789, vol. 26, p. 33.

[22]"The disasterous emigration of the lower class . . . has tended considerably to the de-
cline of the militia, by diminishing our numbers" ([John Poyer], *A Letter Addressed to His
Excellency . . . Francis Lord Seaforth, by a Barbadian* [Bridgetown, 1801], pp. 20–21).

[23]Robert H. Schomburgk, *The History of Barbados* (London, 1848), p. 395.

[24]Minutes of the House of Assembly, March 2, 1819, printed in *Barbados Mercury and
Bridgetown Gazette*, April 20, 1819.

[25]Grinfield to Seaforth, November 6, 1802, CO 28/69.

[26]"Returns of Free Coloured People in the Island of Barbados, May 1802," CO 28/72.

number. As both the size of the militia and the island's total freedman population increased, it can be assumed that the number of freedmen in the militia increased as well. In 1823, the militia comprised 3,379 officers and men,[27] and by 1833 there were 4,255 on the militia rolls.[28] However, the number of effective fighting men—that is, those who were "armed and accoutred" and in good health—was less than the number on the militia rolls, and in 1833 the "effective" part of the militia was limited to 2,560 men, including 1,883 whites and 677 freedmen.[29] In this year the total freedman population was larger than it had ever been before, and it can thus be assumed that the number of freedmen militiamen was also greater than in previous years. (It can also be assumed, on the basis of population distributions, that Saint Michael—including Bridgetown—contained the largest number of freedmen in its militia units, the remainder being scattered throughout the ten other parishes.)

The numerical significance of freed militiamen at this time, as well as the greater number the impending slave emancipation would add, caused the legislature to pass the island's first act (in July 1833) that was designed to limit the number of nonwhites;[30] the law prohibited anyone "who may hereafter become free" from serving in the militia unless they owned at least two acres of land or a house whose annual value was placed at £10 island currency.[31] Finding even these restrictions insufficient, in July 1834 (two months after the island's own slave emancipation act was passed) the legislature raised the qualifications for serving in the militia to five or more acres of land or a house with a minimum annual value of £20.[32]

Although these restrictions were specified in terms of property-holding rather than racial ancestry, new freedmen were now debarred from what they had traditionally defined as a privilege of citizenship. That is, not only was the militia a national institution of considerable importance, but participation in it figured prominently in the freedman's image of himself as a freeman. This self-image had been consistently supported by earlier requirements that all freemen serve in the militia. The importance of these requirements was underscored in 1833, when freedmen petitioned Governor Smith to do what he could so that "the few who are qualified" would be permitted to hold commissions "along with their equals of the other side" (that is, whites); the petition did not challenge property qualifications, and it emphasized that "the exaltation of these [qualified persons] must indirectly tend to the exaltation of our whole body."[33]

---

[27]"Return of the Militia of the Island of Barbados . . . ," *JBMHS*, 13 (1946): 180–82.

[28]Smith to Stanley, July 29, 1833, CO 28/111.

[29]*Ibid.* In addition to the "effective" portion, there were 904 "unaccoutred" men and 791 "invalids," but racial breakdowns were not reported in these figures.

[30]Levy, "Barbados," pp. 336–37.

[31]CO 30/21, no. 545.

[32]*Ibid.*, no. 561.

[33]"The Humble Loyal Address of His Majesty's Free Coloured and Free Black Subjects . . . ," May 6, 1833, printed in *Barbadian*, May 15, 1833.

If participation in the militia had not played a role in the freedmen's self-image, it is doubtful that they would have been so concerned about achieving commissions in it or have behaved with such conscientiousness in the performance of their military obligations. In fact, given their exclusion from the judicial and political systems for much of the slave period, the militia was an especially important national institution because participation in it was a function of free status rather than racial ancestry. Thus, the significance of the militia to freedmen can be viewed in terms of its confirming their free status (thereby throwing into stronger contradiction their exclusion from the politico-judicial system), despite the discriminatory practices to which they were subjected.

VI

THE ECONOMIC SYSTEM: OCCUPATIONS, WEALTH, AND PROPERTY

AGRICULTURE AND LANDHOLDING

Barbadian freedmen engaged in a relative diversity of economic activities, but, above all, they shunned agricultural wage labor on the plantations. On occasion they could have found employment on plantations whose slave contingents were low, but their freedom, if it meant nothing else, meant that they were not compelled to engage in work that was the hallmark of slave status or to subject themselves to the control and arbitrary discipline of the plantation.[1] "It is a known fact," wrote a leading member of the plantocracy, "that without compulsion . . . [manumitted slaves] will not engage in agricultural labour. Wages will not induce them to undertake it. . . . A state of slavery alone can ensure such labour from them."[2] The dislike for plantation field labor was especially evident during the Apprenticeship period among those who were able to achieve their manumissions. Although economic and geographical circumstances compelled most former field slaves to continue working on the sugar plantations, they avoided it whenever alternative choices were available. Women in particular, as a stipendiary magistrate observed in 1836, "generally shun field-labour. . . . They consider it a degradation to work in the field." "In no instance," another remarked, "will [parents] entertain the idea of agriculture as a pursuit" for their free children; "the thought appears humiliating to them," he added, "and it is rejected with ridicule."[3] Sturge and Harvey, the English emancipationists, were also impressed with the

[1]See, for example, reply of Joshua Steele to Governor Parry, 1788, *PP*, 1789, vol. 26, p. 33; William Dickson, *Mitigation of Slavery in Two Parts* (London, 1814), p. 429.

[2]Haynes to Warde, October 23, 1826, *PP*, 1826–27, vol. 25, unnumbered rept., Barbados section. See also *Report of a Committee of the General Assembly upon the Several Heads of Enquiry, etc., Relative to the Slave Trade* (London, 1790), p. 7; and J. A. Thome and J. H. Kimball, *Emancipation in the West Indies* (New York, 1838), p. 64.

[3]"Papers . . . in Explanation of the Measures Adopted . . . for Giving Effect to the Act for the Abolition of Slavery . . . ," pt. 4, *PP*, 1837, vol. 53, rept. 521–I, pp. 397, 414; see also *ibid.*, pp. 387, 389, 403–4.

way in which the apprenticeship system "continues and increases the character of degradation which is attached to field labor."[4]

During the slave period, critics would attribute the freedman's reluctance to "labour in the field" to his pride and indolence,[5] but he was apparently not adverse to agricultural work when there were opportunities in which he had some control over his own time and labor.[6] Thus, by the late eighteenth century, some freedmen engaged in small-scale agriculture by working the small acreage they were allotted as plantation "militia tenants"; Joshua Steele observed that, in general, freedman "militia tenants . . . cultivate their tenements industriously," and he approvingly cited two of his tenants, "a mason and carpenter," who "labour on their tenements with their own hands."[7] Other freedmen rented small plots of agricultural land,[8] and there were some individuals who, "by their industry, have been able to purchase little freeholds, and build good habitations on them."[9]

Although there were no legal restrictions on the ownership or rental of land, freedmen had limited opportunities to become owners or renters. Most freedmen did not own agricultural land, and few were able to acquire more than a very small number of acres (even this acreage, it can be assumed, largely comprised land that plantation managements considered agriculturally marginal[10]). Among forty-five non-plantation-owning freedmen for whom information on the size of landholdings is available, thirty-three (73.3 percent) individuals owned less than three-fourths of an acre of land, which was occasionally divided into two or three separate parcels, but most of these holdings were less than one-eighth of an acre, and many were considerably smaller than this; virtually all of the holdings were housespots located in the towns, primarily Bridgetown. Nine individuals (19.9 percent) owned from one to ten acres, and only three (6.6

---

[4]Joseph Sturge and Thomas Harvey, *The West Indies in 1837* (London, 1838), p. 124.

[5]See, for example, replies of Parry, Brathwaite, and the Council of Barbados to queries 5, 37, and 38, in "Report of the Lords of the Committee of Council . . . ; Submitting . . . the Evidence . . . concerning the Present State of the . . . Trade in Slaves; and . . . the Effects and Consequences of this Trade, . . . in Africa and the West Indies . . . ," pt. 3, Barbados section, *PP*, 1789, vol. 26; and *Report of a Committee of the General Assembly*, p. 7.

[6]Similar comments were made with respect to the slaves when their work performance in plantation fields was contrasted with that in their garden plots. See, for example, [Benjamin Browne], *The Yarn of a Yankee Privateer*, ed. Nathaniel Hawthorne (New York, 1926), p. 112; Joseph Boromé, ed., "William Bell and His Second Visit to Barbados, 1829–1830," *JBMHS*, 30 (1962): 34; Beilby Porteus, *An Essay towards a Plan for the More Effectual Civilization and Conversion of the Negroe Slaves, on the Trust Estate in Barbados Belonging to the Society for the Propagation of the Gospel in Foreign Parts* (London, 1807), pp. 195–96.

[7]Reply of Joshua Steele to Governor Parry, 1788, *PP*, 1789, vol. 26, p. 33.

[8]*Ibid.*; and reply of Parry to query 38, "Report of the Lords."

[9]Reply of Joshua Steele to Governor Parry, 1788, *PP*, 1789, vol. 26, p. 33.

[10]F. Dwarris, *Substance of Three Reports of the Commission of Inquiry into the Administration of Civil and Criminal Justice in the West Indies* (London, 1827), pp. 59–60.

percent) had above ten acres; the forty-five acres of the largest landholding were divided into three separate parcels of five, fifteen, and twenty-five acres in 1833 (Table 9).[11] Most of the land between one and six acres, and all of it in excess of seven acres, was located in rural areas, and was presumably largely utilized for agriculture. The landowning distribution ex-

[11]Unless specified otherwise, statistical information on freedman property in the tables and text of this chapter has been calculated from the property inventories of fifty-four individuals and the wills of twenty-seven others—a total sample of eighty-one individuals. The documents span the period from 1789 to 1833, and all are located in the BDA.

The inventories include monetary appraisals of property held by deceased persons at the time their wills were probated. In the BDA, there are a total of 2,114 inventories, and these date from 1780 to 1834. Each inventory was checked, but only 54 were definitely identifiable as those of freedmen (the earliest freedman inventory is dated 1789 and the latest ones are from 1831). Freedmen were either specified as such on the inventories themselves, or were identified by cross-checking known freedman wills with inventories bearing the same names and dates.

There are thousands of wills in the BDA, so a systematic search of all of them was impractical. However, a sampling of volumes for a number of years from the late eighteenth century to 1834 yielded twenty-seven cases for which no inventories could be found. The twenty-seven wills were thus added to the fifty-four inventories so as to provide an expanded sample of eighty-one from which statistical information on property holdings could be derived.

Eighty-one individual property-owners is a small number, but, more important, it is not known to what extent these owners were numerically representative of all freedmen, or even of those who left wills. It is assumed that many freedmen died intestate and that wealthier persons were more prone to leave wills; thus the eighty-one cases are probably much more representative of wealthier property-holders than they are of poorer ones, including those who died intestate and/or did not own major property such as houses, land, or slaves.

Although qualitative evidence indicates an increase in the freedmen's wealth and property-ownership from the late eighteenth century to emancipation, the eighty-one cases (which derive from thirty-two different years over a forty-four-year period) do not manifest significant periodic differences in property value, the amount and type of property owned, and similar topics discussed in this chapter. The statistics are thus employed without reference to specific periods of time, although one might assume that, if a larger number of cases were available, quantitative changes over the entire period would be more evident.

Finally, it must be noted that complete information on all topics is lacking in a number of cases; for this reason the sample referred to in the text and tables varies, and is often less than the total number of eighty-one cases.

In order to illustrate the relative position of wealth and property-ownership among freedmen, the freedman sample is contrasted with a white one in this chapter. For comparative purposes, property information was tabulated from all white inventories for the years 1815, 1825, and 1830. These years were arbitrarily selected, but they fall within a time period when the freedman population was wealthier and larger than in previous years. The white inventories included thirty-two individuals in 1815 and forty-nine each in 1825 and 1830. It must be understood that, unless otherwise specified in the text or tables, the statistics employed for freedmen range over the period between 1789 and the early 1830s, while those for whites derive only from 1815, 1825, and 1830. This is one reason why the white and freedman samples are not strictly comparable. Other reasons include the fact that the freedman community was larger and wealthier by emancipation than it had been in earlier years, and that the representativeness of each of the samples is not known. It is assumed, however, that the white sample is probably more representative of the white community (because whites had a greater tendency to leave wills) than the freedman sample is of all freedmen. These and other limitations in the samples and in their selection mean that the statistical data alone cannot be considered as conclusive evidence, but rather as suggestive of the differences and similarities between propertied whites and freedmen (as well as among the freedmen themselves).

pressed in these figures clearly supports the qualitative evidence, which stresses the limited amount of freedman-owned land that was of sufficient acreage to provide for even small-scale agriculture.

Many of the island's whites were small-scale agriculturalists,[12] and they were also more heavily represented among small landowners with larger land units. For example, among fifty-two non-plantation-owning whites, only 19.2 percent owned less than one acre of land, but 34.6 percent owned from one to ten acres; 46.1 percent held over ten acres, contrasted with the 6.6 percent among freedmen (Table 9). Freedmen were prevented from

Table 9. Freedman and White Landowners (Nonplantation) by Number of Acres Owned

Number of Acres Owned	Freedmen		Whites	
	No.	%	No.	%
less than 1	33	73.3	10	19.2
(less than 1/8)	(26)	(57.8)		
(1/8 to less than 1/4)	(5)	(11.1)		
(1/4 to less than 1/2)	(0)	(0.0)		
(1/2 to less than 3/4)	(2)	(4.4)		
(3/4 to less than 1)	(0)	(0.0)		
1–2	4	8.9	2	3.8
3–4	1	2.2	6	11.5
5–6	2	4.4	4	7.7
7–8	1	2.2	3	5.8
9–10	1	2.2	3	5.8
11–20	1	2.2	14	26.9
21–30	1	2.2	7	13.5
31–40	0	0.0	2	3.8
41–50	1	2.2	0	0.0
51–60	0	0.0	1	1.9

Sources: Compiled from materials discussed in Chapter 6, note 11.

[12]William Dickson found that this agricultural involvement was compelling proof against the argument "that white men cannot stand . . . labour, in the open fields. . . . The fact is, that, in Barbadoes many whites of both sexes, till the ground, without any assistance from Negroes, and poor white-women often walk many miles loaded with the produce of their little spots" (*Letters on Slavery, to Which Are Added Addresses to the Whites and to the Free Negroes of Barbados* [London, 1789], p. 41).

acquiring small landholdings of sufficient size for growing cash crops because of their limited financial resources, the fact that land was generally scarce and largely controlled by whites, and because of the racial discrimination exercised against them. In addition, with few exceptions, white society effectively excluded wealthier freedmen from larger landholdings.

There is clear evidence of only four freedman plantation-owners from 1780 to 1834, and three of them were members of the same "colored" family, the Belgraves. In 1803, the inventory of Jacob Belgrave, Sr., recorded his ownership of the Adventure (today known as Summervale[13]) in the parish of Saint Philip, which comprised over 98 acres and included 94 slaves. The plantation descended to one of his sons, John Thomas Belgrave, who by 1811 had increased its acreage to 144 and the number of slaves to 99. John Thomas's brother, Jacob Belgrave, Jr., whose name figured so prominently in early freedman petitions and political events of the mid-1820s, owned two plantations in 1828: Graeme Hall in Christ Church and Sterling in Saint Philip. The plantations had a combined acreage of about 480 and included 306 slaves, 10 of whom were designated for manumission upon Belgrave's death. The fourth plantation-owner was Robert Collymore, a member of a wealthy "colored" family that was also prominent in the struggle for civil rights; in 1825, Collymore owned Haggatt Hall in Saint Michael, a plantation of 368 acres and 90 slaves.[14] Amaryllis Collymore was possibly a fifth plantation-owner. In her 1829 will she mentioned Robert as her "late friend," and her bequests to the eleven children she had by him indicate a considerable amount of wealth, including 62 slaves (all of whom were bequeathed to members of her family) and a "place called Lightfoots," which she directed be sold with the "land, dwelling house and buildings thereon"; the will, however, did not mention acreage or the location of Lightfoots. There was a plantation by that name in Saint John parish in the middle of the nineteenth century (and the large number of slaves owned by Amaryllis suggests a plantation), but it may have been that, at the time she owned it, Lightfoots was a large town property, perhaps a subdivision of a former plantation.[15] Whether or not Lightfoots was a plantation at the time of Amaryllis Collymore's death, it is doubtful that many more than the above-mentioned plantations were owned by freedmen during the pre-emancipation decades of the nineteenth century.

[13]Michael J. Chandler, *A Guide to Records in Barbados* (Oxford: Basil Blackwell, 1965), p. 175.

[14]Inventories, Original, 1803, 1811, 1825, 1828, BDA.

[15]The possible nature of Lightfoots was suggested by Michael J. Chandler (personal communication); see will of Amaryllis Collymore, January 5, 1829, RB 4/65, BDA. Quite a few members of her family and their relationships can be reconstructed from her will; among her children were Samuel Francis Collymore, Jackson Brown Collymore, and Renn Philip Collymore, all of whom were active in the civil rights struggle.

Thus, with respect to land use in general, some of the housespots owned by freedmen were used for the cultivation of kitchen gardens, but the vast majority of freedmen did not have the land resources to permit full-time engagement in agricultural activities or to depend on agriculture for a livelihood. When freedmen engaged in agricultural activities, they were largely involved in the small-scale production of food crops, for home consumption and sale on the internal market, and to some extent in the production of minor cash-export crops such as cotton, aloes, and arrowroot. As an economic enterprise, then, agricultural production appears to have played a relatively minor role in the life of the freedman population as a whole, and it certainly contributed less than other activities to the wealth of most individuals. It may be, however, that agricultural activities were somewhat more significant, albeit still of secondary importance, than is assumed here. This is suggested by the objections freedmen raised against a clause in the 1826 "slave consolidation act" which frustrated their harvesting of aloes and cotton,[16] and it is likely that a number of rural freedmen, particularly "militia tenants," combined small-scale agriculture with other occupational or economic pursuits. In general, however, the freedmen's occupational emphasis was clearly in areas other than agriculture. As they wrote in an 1834 petition (which only partially explained the economic niche they occupied), "the restrictions under which [we] formerly labored . . . debar[red us] from the acquisition of land, [and] drove [us] for support to the handicraft trades and mechanical occupations."[17]

THE SKILLED TRADES

In the towns during the eighteenth century, freedmen occasionally found employment in unskilled tasks such as loading sugar or doing similar kinds of waterfront work.[18] But such labor was traditionally and largely performed by slaves, and thus, not only were opportunities limited, but, more important, the social context of the labor was not fundamentally different from plantation work; in addition, skilled labor paid more than unskilled work, had a higher prestige value, and provided greater personal autonomy. Thus, if the freedman did not already possess a skill upon being manumitted, he attempted to learn one, and he gravitated toward the skilled trades. By the late eighteenth century, "Many of the men work[ed] at the various trades of smiths, carpenters, and masons";[19] others hired themselves out as domestic servants, and some even made a living as

[16]See pp. 98–100.

[17]"Address of the Free Coloured and Free Black Inhabitants of Bridgetown," April 2, 1834, CO 28/113.

[18]Testimony of Joseph Woodward, PP, 1791, vol. 34, p. 237.

[19]Reply of Joshua Steele to Governor Parry, 1788, ibid., 1789, vol. 26, p. 33; see also reply of Parry to query 38, "Report of the Lords."

musicians, playing for white audiences and probably at slave dances as well.[20]

Working-class whites had traditionally performed many skilled mechanical jobs, but, as early as the seventeenth century, plantation-owners, for reasons of economy, convenience, and an assured labor supply, encouraged the training of slaves in a variety of skilled occupations.[21] As the years progressed, these slaves became especially valuable to plantation-owners, as well as to landless whites in towns, "for the great profit which their labour brings in, and the hire which they fetch when let out to work."[22] Throughout the eighteenth century, slaves continued to learn skills, often from one another; as in earlier years, this process resulted in considerable pressures upon the job market for the white working class. "So many blacks are now bred to all kinds of trades," William Dickson observed in the 1770s and 1780s, "that the poor white artificers often find it difficult to get bread."[23] The "Society for the Encouragement of Arts, Manufactures, and Commerce in Barbados" was founded in 1781 and its objectives included the promotion of small-scale industries in which poor whites could find employment.[24] The Society played an important role in encouraging the legislature to create a number of incentives whereby white artisans, in particular, would return to, or enter new types of, skilled occupations. Passed in 1783, the law noted the "many thousands" of poor whites who lacked "profitable employment" and who were "sunk with despair and consequent indolence into a state of profligate and vagrant beggary."[25] Even though the law was minimally applied, the conditions it was designed to mitigate were too strong, and many whites lost their initiative or emigrated. "In no other colony is the same number of unemployed whites to be met with as in Barbados," observed a colonial official visiting the island at the turn of the nineteenth century.[26] At about the same time, John Poyer, who was especially sympathetic to the plight of the white working class, noted how "many slaves are employed as trades-

---

[20]Reply of Parry to query 38, "Report of the Lords"; and Jerome S. Handler and Charlotte Frisbie, "Aspects of Slave Life in Barbados: Music and Its Cultural Context," *Caribbean Studies*, 9 (1972): 26–31.

[21]See, for example, "Some Observations on the Island Barbadoes," [1667], CO 1/21, no. 170. In 1680 the Assembly even tried, but failed, to pass a law prohibiting slaves from learning "arts or trades" (see Journal of the Barbados Assembly, February 18 and August 31, 1680, CO 31/2; and Minutes of the Barbados Council, September 28, 1680, *ibid.*).

[22]John A. Waller, *A Voyage in the West Indies* (London, 1820), pp. 92–93.

[23]Dickson, *Letters on Slavery*, p. 26.

[24]See Society for the Encouragement of Arts, Manufactures, and Commerce in Barbados, *Institution and First Proceedings of the Society . . . Established in Barbados, 1781* (Barbados, [1784]), *passim*; letter from Joshua Steele, July 14, 1781, quoted in D. G. C. Allan, "Joshua Steele and the Royal Society of Arts," *JBMHS*, 22 (1954): 84–86.

[25]Samuel Moore, *The Public Acts in Force, Passed by the Legislature of Barbados, from May 11th, 1762, to April 8th, 1800, Inclusive* (London, 1801), pp. 226–27.

[26]*Sketches and Recollections of the West Indies* (London, 1828), p. 27; see also Dickson, *Mitigation of Slavery*, p. xx, n.

men . . . while the industrious white mechanic is destitute of employment; or if he work[s], is ill treated, and finds great difficulty in obtaining payment of his hard earned wages. No wonder that under such discouragements he is compell'd to forgo his fond attachment to his native soil, and emigrate to the neighboring colonies, where his skill and diligence are better rewarded."[27] By 1811–12, economic "distress among the poor inhabitants . . . was so great," having been exacerbated by a drought which particularly affected small-scale farmers, that the legislature passed a bill which provided for the distribution of relief funds.[28]

In general, however, the unemployment of poor whites was a condition created by the slave system itself, and this condition provided increased opportunities for freedmen to gain employment in skilled occupations, occupations they had often learned while they were still slaves. An American who had lived in Bridgetown wrote that in 1814 "Free Negroes carried on all the lighter mechanical trades, such as tailors, shoemakers, jewellers, etc., and were expert workmen."[29] A little more than a decade later, a Barbadian, alarmed at the number of poor and unemployed whites, observed that freedmen "have usurped and now successfully rival" whites in trades such as joinery, carpentry, masonry, painting, shoemaking, and the like.[30] The "mechanical trades and occupations which are so profitable when exercised with skill and application," remarked the Ladies Society for the Promotion and Encouragement of Arts, Manufacturers, and General Society, an organization of upper-class women, "are now almost extinct among our white population."[31] And, shortly before emancipation, the archdeacon of Barbados summarized the island-wide situation in the following words: "The free blacks have, by their superior industry, driven the lower order of whites from almost every trade requiring skill and continued exertion. I believe that not one in twenty of the working shoemakers in Barbados is a white man. The working carpenters, masons, tailors, smiths, etc. are for the most part men of colour; and this at a time when a large white population are in the lowest state of poverty and wretchedness."[32] The Colonial Charity School, formed in 1819 for the

---

[27][John Poyer], *A Letter Addressed to His Excellency . . . Francis Lord Seaforth, by a Barbadian* (Bridgetown, 1801), pp. 20–21. See also J. W. [I. W.] Orderson, *Leisure Hours at the Pier: Or, a Treatise on the Education of the Poor of Barbados* (Liverpool, 1827), *passim*; Dickson, *Letters on Slavery*, p. 42.

[28]Robert H. Schomburgk, *The History of Barbados* (London, 1848), p. 382.

[29][Browne], *Yarn of a Yankee Privateer*, p. 103. See also remarks of J. Best, Journal of the Assembly of Barbados, October 8, 1816, CO 31/47; and J. W. [I. W.] Orderson, *Cursory Remarks and Plain Facts Connected with the Question Produced by the Proposed Slave Registry Bill* (London, 1816), pp. 13–14.

[30]Orderson, *Leisure Hours*, pp. 11–13.

[31]Quoted in *ibid.*, p. 53.

[32]Edward Eliot, *Christianity and Slavery; in a Course of Lectures Preached at the Cathedral and Parish Church of St. Michael, Barbados* (London, 1833), pp. 225–26. By this period some of the island's potters may have been freedmen (Jerome S. Handler, "A Historical Sketch of Pottery Manufacture in Barbados," *JBMHS*, 30 (1963): 142–44.

children of poor freedmen and slaves, also contributed to the flow of freedmen into the skilled trades. For example, in 1830–32, after completing their studies, fifty-eight boys went into the following occupations: thirty-nine into carpentering, seven into tailoring, five into shoemaking, and two into cabinetmaking; two became sailors, and one each became a cooper, turner, and domestic.[33] These trades not only indicate the range and types of occupations available to freedmen but also suggest which were the most popular and in greatest demand.

During the Apprenticeship period, freedmen cemented their monopolization of trades as their ranks were augmented by manumitted apprentices who invariably continued the skilled occupations they had performed while in bondage. Some of these tradesmen became self-employed, while others found employment in established enterprises. "Some of the most respectable mechanics in Bridgetown," observed a visitor between 1835 and 1837, "are Negroes who own large establishments and employ only workmen of their own color."[34] Women discharged from apprenticeship either engaged in domestic work in their own houses or hired themselves out as servants or washerwomen; quite often, however, they took "to trafficking, commonly called huckstering."[35] By becoming hucksters, or hawkers, these women continued a well-estabished pattern that for many years had formed a vital element in the freedman's economic life. Although men were prominent in the trades, they, as well as women, had traditionally been active participants in the island's internal marketing system.

THE INTERNAL MARKETING SYSTEM

Many of the traders within this system, whose roots went deep into the seventeenth century, were slaves who sold or bartered their own food crops and small livestock, as well as goods stolen from their masters' properties. A number of seventeenth- and early-eighteenth-century laws attempted to arrest or circumscribe the slaves' marketing activities,[36] and quite often slaves found it more convenient and safer to deal with white hucksters, "who, in fact, are often worse than the Negroes, by receiving all stolen goods."[37] By the middle of the eighteenth century, freedmen (many of whom, it can be assumed, were continuing the marketing activities they

[33]"Report of the Society for the Education of the Coloured Poor," *Christian Remembrancer*, 15 (1833): 53–55.

[34]Sylvester Hovey, *Letters from the West Indies* (New York, 1838), p. 205.

[35]"Papers . . . in Explanation of the Measures Adopted . . . for Giving Effect to the Act for the Abolition of Slavery . . . ," pt. 4, *PP*, 1837, vol. 53, rept. 521-1, p. 402; see also *ibid.*, pp. 389, 397, 403–4, 412.

[36]See, for example, John Jennings, *Acts and Statutes of the Island of Barbados*, 2nd ed. (London, 1656), p. 17; William Rawlin, *The Laws of Barbados* (London, 1699), pp. 26, 71; and Richard Hall, *Acts, Passed in the Island of Barbados. From 1643 to 1762, Inclusive* (London, 1764), pp. 185–88, 295–99, 496.

[37]Alleyne to SPGFP, December 9, 1741, Letter Books, vol. B8, no. 51, USPGA.

had engaged in as slaves) had assumed this "receivership" role as well. As early as 1739, a law permitting slaves to testify in legal proceedings against freedmen took note of freedmen trading with slaves in stolen goods, and complained that they were "enticing and corrupting . . . slaves to steal and rob their owners."[38] "Many of them," Governor Parry reported in 1788, "clandestinely offend against the laws," and the Barbados Council more forcefully complained that "Free Negroes are the pests of our society, the receivers of stolen goods, and the encouragers of slaves in every kind of vice."[39]

How much of the freedman's trading activities actually depended on the disposition of stolen goods is difficult to ascertain, despite the complaints made against him. Although there is little doubt that trade in such commodities was important, it is also apparent that the freedman trader, especially in the eighteenth century, frequently acted as an agent for white shopkeepers or hucksters, who themselves encouraged the slaves "to plunder their owners of everything that is portable."[40] In 1788, for example, Joshua Steele, a plantation-owner who was more charitable in his assessment of freedmen than most of his peers, admitted that their shops were "generally receptacles of all sorts of stolen property"; but, he emphasized, "the Free Blacks and Mulattoes in this trade are only few, otherwise than as the servants and sub agents of the white hucksters (some of whom denominate themselves merchants in the capital towns) [who appoint freedmen] to collect stolen property . . . out of the plantations; knowing that under the disqualification of Negro evidence the crime of being *receivers of stolen property*, cannot be proven against them."[41]

In general, the trading activities of freedman hucksters were similar to those of the white and slave hucksters. Vegetables, meat, fish, poultry, and so forth, were sold by plying the countryside, and the "Huckster Negroes," as they were commonly referred to by white society, often met incoming ships and sold fresh foods to their passengers and crews. In towns, they sold from door to door, sometimes using handcarts, established them-

---

[38]Hall, *Acts*, pp. 323–25. Slaves often acquired necessities and luxuries by this means and viewed their activities from a different perspective. For example, as Thome and Kimball noted in 1837, "For a slave to steal from his master was never considered wrong, but rather a meritorious act. . . . The blacks in several of the islands have a proverb, that for a thief to steal from a thief makes God laugh" (*Emancipation in the West Indies*, p. 56). George Pinckard, visiting Barbados in 1796, made a similar observation and recorded, in more colloquial terms, "an expression very common among [the slaves] viz. 'me no tief him; me take him from massa' " (*Notes on the West Indies*, 3 vols. [London, 1806], 2: 118). Especially among recently emancipated slaves it might be expected that such a perspective would continue and be applied to the property of whites in general.

[39]Reply to query 38, "Report of the Lords."

[40]Dickson, *Letters on Slavery*, p. 42.

[41]Reply of Joshua Steele to Governor Parry, 1788, *PP*, 1789, vol. 26, p. 33, italics in the original; see also John Poyer, *The History of Barbados, from the Discovery of the Island, . . . till . . . 1801* (London, 1808), pp. 581–83.

selves at set locations in the streets or alleys, or set up stalls in front of their houses. In Bridgetown, especially on weekends and holidays, many hucksters sat at "the great market" with their trays or baskets, while others wandered about hawking their wares. Hucksters sometimes sold goods they had produced, or they acquired vendibles from plantation slaves or free small-scale agriculturalists, from whom they purchased goods, or with whom they exchanged items (such as food delicacies) they brought from town. Sometimes vendibles were acquired by going directly to the plantations or rural producers; at other times slaves and others were met on the roads while on their way to town markets. A favorite practice of the "Huckster Negroes" involved boarding incoming vessels and purchasing livestock for resale, or going into the country districts "to meet such persons as bring in stock, fruit, roots, and other produce"; in so doing, "Huckster Negroes" were able to "buy up and engross" livestock and vegetable products which resulted in increased prices to free townsmen, most of whom were white.[42]

Because of such practices and in order to protect the white consumer and seller, as well as to curtail the movements of slaves, a number of late-eighteenth- and early-nineteenth-century laws contained provisions designed to inhibit or eliminate various types of trading activities.[43] These laws, however, generally had limited effect; in most cases the practices they were designed to control continued, and the laws were later repealed or modified.[44]

In 1779 the legislature capitulated to its ineffectiveness in restricting freedman hawkers and at the same time contrived to gain additional revenues for the public treasury from huckstering activities in general. A law was passed which made it mandatory for all hucksters to carry licenses, and which authorized the island's treasurer to license any freedman "desiring the same . . . to carry on the usual trade of a huckster."[45] The license was to be valid for a year, but it cost £10, in addition to a 25s. fee to the treasurer. By this law the plantocracy in effect officially condoned huckstering as a legitimate enterprise for freedmen and probably further stimulated their involvement in it. Although the law also attempted to "put a stop to the traffic carried on by slaves who pass under the denomination of Huckster Negroes," slaves continued their participation in the internal marketing system, and undoubtedly many freedmen carried on their huckstering activities without licenses.

[42]Moore, *Public Acts*, pp. 166–67. Trading practices described in this paragraph have largely been reconstructed from the laws referred to in notes 43 and 44 below.

[43]See, for example, acts passed in 1774 (Moore, *Public Acts*, pp. 154–71), 1809 (CO 30/18, no. 285), 1811 (CO 30/19, no. 301), and 1819 (CO 30/20, no. 381).

[44]See acts passed in 1779 (Moore, *Public Acts*, pp. 212–17), 1811 (CO 30/19, no. 301), 1819 (CO 30/20, no. 393), and 1828 (CO 30/21, no. 512).

[45]Moore, *Public Acts*, pp. 215–16.

Figure 3. "The Barbadoes Mulatto Girl."
Print by A. Brunias, *ca.* 1790, courtesy of
the Barbados Museum and Historical Society.

Whether licensed or not, freedman hucksters continued to create economic opportunities and to avail themselves of those that occurred. Not only was huckstering deeply embedded in the cultural system of non-whites, but it was also one of the few ways in which women, in particular, could meet household and familial responsibilities, enjoy personal independence and autonomy, and make a living. It is thus understandable why, during the Apprenticeship period, so many freedwomen, especially those who had been plantation field laborers, took to huckstering as a major economic activity. But equally important to the continuing, and often uninhibited, marketing operations of freedmen and slaves was the fact that the internal marketing system, which rested upon the services of hucksters, was essential to the distribution of foodstuffs, and those who lived in the towns were especially dependent upon it. Thus, the marketing system directly impinged on the everyday life of Barbados's white population. In 1796, for example, George Pinckard described the marketing of provisions that slaves had raised in their garden plots or received from plantations, and he stressed "that the markets of the island depend almost wholly upon this mode of supply. They are all held weekly, and upon the Sunday."[46]

The Sunday market was thus an institution of fundamental importance to all segments of Barbadian society, and the role of slaves and freedmen in it was crucial to its operation. (One visitor to the Bridgetown market in 1830 even reported that the "major proportion" of produce sellers were "free coloured people . . . and not slaves.")[47] An 1826 law, popularly known as the "Sunday and marriage act," effectively banned Sunday markets,[48] but it was not intended to eliminate marketing activities, and within a relatively short period of time Saturday became the island's main market day. J. A. Thome and J. H. Kimball left what is perhaps the most detailed and vivid description of the flow of rural people into town for Saturday marketing activities. Although their observations were made in 1837, there is every reason to assume they were equally applicable to at least the later years of the slave period.

> We left Bridgetown after breakfast, and as it chanced to be Saturday, we had a fine opportunity of seeing the people coming into market. They were strung all along the road for six miles, so closely that there was scarcely a minute at any time in which we did not pass them. As far as the eye could reach there were files of men and women, moving peaceably forward. From the cross paths leading through the estates, the busy marketers were pouring into the high way. To their heads as usual was committed the safe conveyance of the various commodities. It was amusing to observe the almost infinite diversity of products which loaded them. There were sweet potatoes, yams, eddoes, Guinea and Indian corn, various fruits and berries, vegetables, nuts, cakes, bottled

[46]Pinckard, *Notes on the West Indies*, 1: 369–70; see also Porteus, *An Essay*, p. 186.

[47]"Notes on Slavery, Made during a Recent Visit to Barbadoes," *Negro's Friend*, no. 18 (London, [1830]), p. 6.

[48]For a copy of this law, see *PP*, 1826–27, vol. 25, unnumbered rept., pp. 277–78 of Barbados section. The "Sunday and marriage act" was passed at a time when efforts to Christianize the slaves were increasing; "the due observance" of Sunday was "essentially necessary to the furtherance of this object" (*ibid.*). The act also attempted to "encourage" baptism and church marriage among slaves, although neither rite had ever been prohibited by law.

beer and empty bottles, bundles of sugar cane, bundles of fire wood, etc. etc. Here was one woman (the majority were females, as usual with the marketers in these islands) with a small black pig doubled up under her arm. Another girl had a brood of young chickens, with nest coop, and all, on her head. Further along the road we were especially attracted by a woman who was trudging with an immense turkey elevated on her head. . . . Of the hundreds whom we past, there were very few who were not well dressed, healthy, and apparently in good spirits. . . . About four miles from town, we observed on the side of the road a small grove of shade trees. Numbers of the marketers were seated there, or lying in the cool shade with their trays beside them. It seemed to be a sort of rendezvous place, where those going to, and those returning from town, occasionally halt for a time for the purpose of resting, and to tell and hear news concerning the state of the market.[49]

SHOPKEEPERS AND MERCHANTS

During slavery, the proceeds saved from marketing activities, as well as monies earned in the trades, permitted some freedmen to acquire the necessary capital to open shops. Freedman shopkeepers were already fairly common in the late eighteenth century, but over the years their numbers increased substantially. In Bridgetown in 1814, as one observer remarked, "many of them were shop keepers; indeed, I should think that the largest number of shops were kept by them";[50] by 1825 the freedman population in Speightstown was considerably augmented by those coming "from other parishes, for the purpose of carrying on a small retail trade which is now almost entirely in their hands."[51]

Although freedmen continued to open shops throughout the slave period, relatively few were able to develop small-scale businesses into mercantile establishments that, in effect, competed with the larger enterprises of wealthier whites. In the late eighteenth century, "and for many years subsequently," a white creole explained, "no man . . . ranked as a merchant who was not his own general importer"; because merchants invariably refrained from "retail traffic with the inferior dealers, their sales being always made on an extensive scale, . . . a sort of middle-man [was created], who purchasing in larger quantity, retailed them in smaller lots to the petty hucksters."[52] The more successful freedman shopkeepers undoubtedly functioned as the kind of middleman described here. They were supplied by large-scale merchant-importers, who also catered to the sugar-

[49]Thome and Kimball, *Emancipation in the West Indies*, p. 66.
[50][Browne], *Yarn of a Yankee Privateer*, p. 103.
[51]Hinds to Husbands, November 21, 1825, *PP*, 1826, vol. 26, rept. 350.
[52]J. W. [I. W.] Orderson, *Creoleana: Or, Social and Domestic Scenes and Incidents in Barbados in Days of Yore* (London, 1842), p. 2. Although written in the late 1830s, this novel is set against the background of Barbados in the last quarter of the eighteenth century and it provides a variety of details on the society of this period.

planter; the planter "never thought of importing his plantation stores, or of shipping his [sugar] crop, these being considered the exclusive rights of the merchant; and thus a reciprocal interest . . . was established between the landed and commercial interests."[53] Freedmen were by and large excluded from this mercantile system, not only because whites made a conscious effort to maintain their dominance in large businesses, but also because of the freedmen's lack of capital (the small scale of their shopkeeping activities, combined with the extension of credit to customers, inhibited its accumulation), credit, and internal and overseas business and social connections, within whose framework large-scale enterprises operated.

The relegation of freedmen to small businesses was especially pronounced during the eighteenth century. An outstanding exception, and even more remarkable because of the early date, was Joseph Rachell, "a black merchant in Bridgetown, who had large and extensive concerns." Rachell was born a slave, but he died around 1758 "possessed of a good deal of property." In the later years of his life he apparently lost some of his wealth, but in the earlier days he had developed "what is called a dry-good shop" into a business enterprise whose trading activities extended to the Leewards and Guianas. He employed some whites, lent money "to poor, industrious men, in order to enable them to begin their trade," and even helped planters and merchants out of financial difficulties. Rachell was reported to have been "so fair and complaisant in business, that in a town filled with little peddling shops, his doors were thronged with customers," and "whenever the captains of vessels arrived with a cargo, J. R. was one of the first persons waited upon, and one of the first to whom the cargo was offered."[54]

Joseph Rachell was certainly not typical for his period, but, by the early nineteenth century and throughout the remaining years of slavery, more freedmen became relatively wealthy merchants, most of them presumably by extending their initial shopkeeping activities, others, perhaps, by building up small businesses that were inherited from kinsmen. Few details are available on these men and the nature of their businesses, but some illustrations can be given. Samuel Frances Collymore, who was a leader in the movement for civil rights legislation in the 1820s, owned at least one vessel which traded in Barbados, Martinique, Saint Lucia, Tobago, and perhaps Saint Vincent and Antigua.[55] When Thome and Kimball visited

[53] *Ibid.*

[54] Biographical details on Rachell have been compiled from: Dickson, *Letters on Slavery*, pp. 180–82; James Ramsay, *An Essay on the Treatment and Conversion of African Slaves in the British Sugar Colonies* (London, 1784), pp. 254–59; and testimony of the Reverend Robert B. Nicholls, *PP*, 1790, vol. 30, p. 333. More details on Rachell's personal life and business activities can be found in these sources.

[55] "Examination of Witnesses Taken at the Bar of the House of Assembly . . . ," February 3 and 4, 1824, CO 28/93. Some of the apprenticed Africans who won their freedom in Barba-

Barbados, they conversed at length with men who were among the wealthier members of the freedman community. Some of these men also had been active participants in the drive for civil rights during the slave period. Thomas J. Cummins, "a colored gentleman," was a Bridgetown merchant and also held what was an unusual position for a freedman—he was the agent for the Edgecombe plantation, owned by a white planter. Thomas Harris, another prominent merchant, was a slave until he was seventeen years old; after his manumission "he engaged as a clerk in a mercantile establishment, and soon attracted attention by his business talents."[56] (During slavery, Thome and Kimball reported, white merchants "were compelled to make clerks of [freedmen] for want of better, that is, *whiter* ones.")[57]

"One of the wealthiest merchants in Bridgetown" was London Bourne, who did "extensive business at home and abroad." Bourne was a slave until he was twenty-three years old, when his father, a freedman, purchased and then manumitted him, his mother, and four brothers for a total sum of $3,000. The senior Bourne was undoubtedly in some form of business, but London,

> by industry, honesty, and close attention to business . . . has now become a wealthy merchant. . . . He has his mercantile agents in England, English clerks in his employ, a branch establishment in the City, and superintends the concerns of an extensive and complicated business with distinguished ability and success. . . . He owns three stores in Bridgetown, lives in a very genteel style in his own house, and is worth from twenty to thirty thousand dollars. He is highly respected by the merchants of Bridgetown for his integrity and business talents.[58]

As "respected" as Bourne might have been, and despite the fact that, in 1837, freedmen "comprise[d] some of the first merchants of the island,"[59] Bourne and his colleagues were still excluded "as far as was practicable . . . from all business connections. . . . Colored merchants of wealth were shut out of the merchants' exchange, though possessed of untarnished integrity, while white men were admitted as subscribers with-

---

dos served "in mercantile shipping," from which they earned "a fair livelihood" (Aberdein to Skeete, February 14, 1828, CO 28/102); these persons may have been sailors on vessels owned by freedmen, such as Collymore, as well as on those owned by whites. Through the trading ventures of freedmen, liaisons were established with freedman communities in other islands; these liaisons were sources of information on political changes and ameliorative trends elsewhere, information which had an impact on Barbadian freedmen in their own struggle for civil rights (see "Examination of Witnesses Taken at the Bar of the House of Assembly . . . ," February 3 and 4, 1824, CO 28/93).

[56]Thome and Kimball, *Emancipation in the West Indies*, pp. 64, 72–73.

[57]*Ibid.*, p. 79.

[58]*Ibid.*, p. 75.

[59]Sturge and Harvey, *The West Indies in 1837*, pp. 141–42; see also Thome and Kimball, *Emancipation in the West Indies*, p. 75.

out regard to character." One of the ironies in Bourne's case was the fact that the merchants' exchange, which excluded him from membership, rented the upstairs rooms in the building which he owned and in which he operated a store and lived with his family.[60]

There is no evidence that freedwomen (indeed, women in general, regardless of racial ancestry) ever became merchants of wealth and position comparable to men such as London Bourne; with few exceptions, women who traded beyond the huckstering level were largely confined to the operation of small shops. The case of Phoebe Forde is illustrative. "In the early part of her life," she had been a slave, but "by her industry she earned and saved a sum of money with which she purchased her freedom from her owner"; after her manumission, Forde "kept a retail shop" in Holetown, in the parish of Saint James, and was able to save enough money to purchase and then manumit her enslaved children. At her death in 1823, she owned a house (in which she probably had kept shop), valued at about £500, "two slaves, and some furniture of small value, and [she was] also entitled to outstanding debts to the amount of about 80 pounds."[61] Other freedwomen shopkeepers were far more successful than Phoebe Forde. Susanna Ostrehan, for example, owned, among other property, two houses in Bridgetown, one of which also included her store, valued at £2,850, and twelve slaves. In 1809 the total value of her estate was appraised at £3,956, a considerable sum of money for the period.[62]

TAVERNS AND PROSTITUTION

By the late eighteenth century and throughout the remainder of the slave period, the hotel-taverns, or inns, in Bridgetown were the enterprises of freedwomen. Apparently no more than two or three of these inns were maintained during any one period, but they provided important services in the form of meals and lodging to island visitors and in-transit ship passengers. The taverns were, as Waller observed in 1807–8, "generally filled with strangers, who must submit to the most exorbitant charges for every article of eating and drinking, as well as for the accommodation of

---

[60]Thome and Kimball, *Emancipation in the West Indies*, p. 79.

[61]"Petition of Samuel Gabriel, Catherine Abel Duke, and William Collins Ford, Coloured Persons Inhabitants of this Island of Barbados," March 8, 1823, CO 28/92, no. 16x. Unless specified otherwise, all currency figures are quoted in Barbadian pounds. The exchange rate of Barbadian currency fluctuated. In 1802, for example, £120–£135 local currency was worth £100 British sterling; in 1816 the rate was about £139 currency to £100 sterling; and from 1823 to 1833 the rate fluctuated between £147 and £157 local currency per £100 sterling. See Seaforth to Bishop of London, March 8, 1802, Seaforth Papers, 46/7/4, SRO; Gibbes W. Jordan, *Copies of a Letter Containing Queries Respecting the State of the Silver and Copper Coins in Barbados* (London, 1816), p. 25; and [Samuel Yearwood], *The Barbados Pocket-Book . . . for . . . [1833] . . . by a Barbadian* ([London, 1832]), p. 48.

[62]Inventories, Original, 1809, BDA.

lodging and washing."[63] The taverns were also popular rendezvous for white creoles and British military and naval personnel, and tavern owners sponsored "dignity balls" (or "quality balls")—formally organized supper dances which required an admission fee—which were largely attended by "colored" females, and "to which only white men were admitted."[64] The hotel-taverns were usually successful business enterprises, and their owners were able to become relatively wealthy and to acquire "considerable property, both in houses and slaves."[65] Visitors often commented not only on the resourcefulness of the proprietresses in their business dealings but also on their independent spirit, assertiveness, and managerial abilities. Some of these women had been "the favoured enamorata" of a white man from whom they gained manumission,[66] while others had been tavern slaves who were manumitted by their freedwoman mistresses.

The first of the Bridgetown taverns owned by a freedwoman appears to have begun operating in the early 1780s and to have belonged to Rachael Pringle Polgreen, the daughter of a Scottish schoolteacher and shopkeeper and an "African woman whom he had purchased."[67] Rachael was bought from her father, and then manumitted, by a British naval officer whose mistress she had become; the house he provided for her in Bridgetown ultimately became her celebrated "Royal Naval Hotel." It was given this name because Prince William Henry (later King William IV) was a frequent visitor when the naval vessel he commanded docked in Barbados. One legendary episode in the hotel's life took place on a night in 1786 when the prince, while at a party, "commenced a royal frolic by breaking the furniture"; joined by his fellow officers, they "carried on the sport with such activity, that in a couple of hours every article [in the hotel] was completely demolished." While this drunken spree and wanton destruction was going on, Rachael Pringle was reported to have "sat quite passive in her great arm chair at the entrance door of the hotel," but on the following

[63]Waller, *Voyage in the West Indies*, p. 6. See also Pinckard, *Notes on the West Indies*, 1: 244–49; and R. R. Madden, *A Twelvemonth's Residence in the West Indies during the Transition from Slavery to Apprenticeship*, 2 vols. (London, 1835), 1: 22–24. A white creole who emigrated from Barbados in 1812 wrote that all of Bridgetown's taverns were owned by freedwomen and "were all situated in one particular part of the town, the most lonesome and unfrequented . . . near the wharf on the sea shore" (Joseph D. Husbands, *An Answer to the Charge of Immorality against the Inhabitants of Barbadoes* [Cooperstown, N.Y., 1831], p. 8).

[64][Browne], *Yarn of a Yankee Privateer*, p. 104. It was also reported that "the British naval and military officers were great frequenters of these balls" (*ibid.*). One such officer, who attended a ball in 1807, wrote that "the ladies were all splendidly dressed and they danced uncommonly well. The ballroom was brilliantly lighted and highly perfumed" ([Major Richard A. Wyvill], "Memoirs of an Old Officer," [1814], p. 385, Manuscript Division, Library of Congress, Washington, D.C.). The most detailed, albeit racist and ethnocentric, description of a "Dignity Ball" is contained in chapter 31 of Frederick Marryat's novel *Peter Simple* (London, 1834); as an officer in the British navy, Marryat had actually attended such a ball when he visited Barbados around 1813.

[65]Waller, *Voyage in the West Indies*, p. 6.

[66]Pinckard, *Notes on the West Indies*, 1: 245.

[67]Orderson, *Creoleana*, p. 95.

morning she sent the prince an itemized bill for the damage, "which was duly paid, and 'Miss Rachael' thereby enabled to furnish the 'Royal Naval Hotel' with more splendour than ever!"[68] At her death in 1791, Rachael owned "houses and lands" and nineteen slaves, six of whom were to be manumitted by the terms of her will.[69]

Figure 4. "Rachel Pringle of Barbadoes."
Print by T. Rowlandson from a drawing by an unknown artist, 1796,
courtesy of the Barbados Museum and Historical Society.

[68]*Ibid.*, pp. 100–102.
[69]Will of Rachael Pringle Polgreen, July 21, 1791, RB 6/19, BDA.

Rachael Pringle's hotel was taken over by Nancy Clarke, whose "noted tavern" during the 1790s was one of the two "most frequented" ones in Bridgetown, the other being the property of Mary Bella Green.[70] In 1796, Betsy Lemon, "a respectable mulatto" slave and "the leading support of the bar at Mary Bella Green's," was manumitted and opened her own tavern, which competed with that of her former mistress; "should any more of your friends follow us to Barbados," Pinckard wrote, "you may assure them of attention and good treatment at the house of Betsy Lemon."[71] In 1806 or 1807 Bridgetown's two hotels were owned by Nancy Clarke and Betsy Austin; although Clarke's apparently ceased operations in 1812, when it may have been destroyed by fire, Austin's was still in business in 1846.[72] By the early 1830s Betsy Austin had been joined by Hannah Lewis, and both women engaged in an active competition for customers.[73] William Lloyd, a British emancipationist who arrived in Barbados in 1836, described how customers were solicited at the Bridgetown harbor: "Boats came from two different hotels with black rowers, each with a Negro woman as steerer, to deliver their cards of recommendation. The women came on board and politely invited us to the shore. We had previously made up our minds to go to one of the most retired, and therefore took the cards of H. Lewis, who had been recommended as very respectable."[74] Sturge and Harvey also stayed at Lewis's hotel because of its "notions of propriety. The other principal hotels in Bridgetown are reported to be a standing reproach to the morals of the colony."[75]

Sturge and Harvey were suggesting that the hotels still functioned, as they had in earlier days, as "houses of debauchery, a number of young women of colour being always procurable in them for the purposes of prostitution."[76] Indeed, this function was a major attraction of the taverns, and, as Pinckard observed in 1796, it was to the proprietress's "advantage that the female [slave] attendants of her family should be as handsome as

[70]William Young, "A Tour through the Several Islands of Barbadoes, St. Vincent, Antigua, Tobago, and Grenada, in the Years 1791 and 1792," in Bryan Edwards, *An Historical Survey of the Island of Santo Domingo* (London, 1801), pp. 261–62; Pinckard, *Notes on the West Indies*, 1: 249.

[71]Pinckard, *Notes on the West Indies*, 1: 393, 244.

[72]Thomas S. St. Clair, *A Residence in the West Indies and America*, 2 vols. (London, 1834), 1: 373–74; A. Aspinall, "Rachael Pringle of Barbadoes," *JBMHS*, 9 (1942): 119; Charles W. Day, *Five Years Residence in the West Indies*, 2 vols. (London, 1852), 1: 37; Trelawney Wentworth, *The West India Sketch Book*, 2 vols. (London, 1834), 2: 282.

[73]Madden, *A Twelvemonth's Residence*, 1: 16, 22–24.

[74]William Lloyd, *Letters from the West Indies during a Visit in the Autumn of 1836 and the Spring of 1837* (London, [1837]), pp. 6–7.

[75]Sturge and Harvey, *The West Indies in 1837*, p. 1.

[76]Waller, *Voyage in the West Indies*, pp. 6, 103. Husbands, whose pamphlet was primarily designed as a rebuttal to Waller, agreed that the taverns functioned for purposes of prostitution, but claimed that they were largely frequented by foreign whites; "were a tavern visited by any regular inhabitant for any impure purpose," he added, "the visit was generally made under the cover of darkness" (Husbands, *Answer*, pp. 8–9).

she can procure them."[77] "One privilege," he wrote, "is allowed them, . . . that of tenderly disposing of their persons; and this offers the only hope they have of procurring a sum of money, wherewith to purchase their freedom; and the resource among them is so common, that neither shame nor disgrace attaches to it; but, on the contrary, she who is most sought, becomes an object of envy, and is proud of the distinction shewn her."[78]

Aside from the hotel-tavern proprietresses, other owners also used their slave women as prostitutes. "It was a very common practice in the towns," observed a British military officer who, in 1780 and 1781, visited Barbados and other islands, "for female slaves to be let out for . . . [prostitution], or at least by paying themselves so much weekly to their owners . . . to have leave to go on board ships of war for that purpose. . . . I have known a Negro girl severely punished on her return home to her owner without the full wages of her prostitution."[79] In fact, the increased numbers of British military and naval personnel stationed in, or visiting, Barbados in the late eighteenth century probably stimulated the growth of the hotel-taverns and prostitution— the latter as a source of livelihood not only for freedwomen but also for slaveowners who depended on slave earnings for their own sustenance. Some of the slaves who worked in taverns, as well as those who were compelled or permitted to sell themselves to white men, continued to support themselves by prostitution after they were manumitted. In 1788, Joshua Steele described the occupations of freedwomen, and reported that "the younger ones, besides needlework, probably derive some profits by gallantry."[80] Governor Parry, however, was less uncertain, and noted that, while some freedwomen "are good housewives, and conduct the business of their families within doors, others support themselves by the prostitution of their persons."[81]

The sources often do not clearly distinguish between prostitutes and women who lived in more or less stable relationships as the mistresses of white men; although there was some prostitution, as an occupational category, more freedwomen apparently supported themselves by becoming the mistresses of military officers, civilian bachelors from abroad, or creole married and unmarried whites.[82] These sexual liaisons not only provided

---

[77]Pinckard, *Notes on the West Indies*, 1: 245.

[78]*Ibid.*, pp. 244–45.

[79]Testimony of Captain Cook, *PP*, 1791, vol. 34, p. 202; see also Waller, *Voyage in the West Indies*, pp. 20–21. Defending the behavior of white creoles, Husbands denied that owners forced their slaves into prostitution, but he noted that, when a slave was permitted to seek outside work, she was required to pay her owner a certain amount of money each week, and that some slaves engaged in prostitution, "but it was their own voluntary choice" (*Answer*, p. 13).

[80]Reply of Joshua Steele to Governor Parry, 1788, *PP*, 1789, vol. 26, p. 33.

[81]Reply of Governor Parry to query 38, "Report of the Lords."

[82]See, for example, [Browne], *Yarn of a Yankee Privateer*, p. 104; Waller, *Voyage in the West Indies*, pp. 20, 96–97; [Poyer], *Letter*, pp. 24–25; Husbands, *Answer*, pp. 12–14; and Thome and Kimball, *Emancipation in the West Indies*, p. 79.

material security for the women involved but also sometimes resulted in the acquisition of capital or property which permitted them to enter other business ventures. In 1836, for example, J. B. Colthurst, a stipendiary magistrate, described "a coloured lady" who "was bred in slavery" and for seventeen years had been the mistress of a wealthy planter; at his death she inherited property that included eight or nine slaves. By the time Colthurst encountered the woman she was no longer young, but she was still "handsome"; she kept a "liquor store" near the garrison where the British military personnel were stationed, and she "was very intimate with the officers."[83]

WEALTH AND PROPERTY

In general, huckstering, shopkeeping, and work in the skilled trades were the major activities by which most freedmen elevated their standard of living. Despite the economic success of some individuals, toward the end of the eighteenth century many freedmen were living a marginal economic existence and others lived in extreme poverty. It is difficult, however, to achieve an accurate assessment of their standard of living at this period. For example, in the late 1780s, Governor Parry, among other critics, reported that "the Free Negroes are so proud and indolent that many of them will not labour for their own maintenance, but become beggars, and are frequently supported by the parish they belong to."[84] At the same time, an opposite evaluation was given by Joshua Steele: "It is in general obvious to any person of observation, that Free Negroes and Mulattoes must apply themselves to some kind of industry, as they are never seen begging, either males or females; whereas the island in general is pestered with white beggars, of both sexes, and of all ages, covered with only filthy rags; while the Free Negroes and mulattoes are well clothed and appear to be well fed."[85] Other comparisons between the standard of living of freedmen and that of poor whites also varied in emphasis (some writers finding poor whites generally worse off than freedmen, others finding them slightly better off), but the sources generally give the impression that many freedmen were quite poor.[86]

By the early nineteenth century, when the plantocracy was attempting to curtail the freedman's acquisition of property, a growing minority,

---

[83]John B. Colthurst, "Journal as a Special Magistrate in the Islands of Barbados and St. Vincent, July 1835—August 1838," entry for November 1836, pp. 87–89, Boston Public Library MSS.

[84]Reply of Governor Parry to query 37, "Report of the Lords."

[85]Reply of Joshua Steele to Governor Parry, 1788, *PP*, 1789, vol. 26, p. 33.

[86]There are considerable references to the standard of living and poverty of the island's lower-class whites, but only some of these materials compare their standard of living with that of the slaves, and a few offer comparisons with the freedmen. See testimony of A. Campell, *PP*, 1790, vol. 29, p. 149; *Sketches and Recollections*, p. 27; Pinckard, *Notes on the West Indies*, 2: 109–10, 132; and Dickson, *Letters on Slavery*, pp. 40–43.

especially in Bridgetown, was increasing its wealth. Governor Seaforth, among others, took note of this increased wealth and reported how "already not only the needy but other whites crowd around the opulent coloured people and accept dinners and favours from them."[87] While the evidence does indicate a growth in property-holding and financial resources, contemporary observations on this growth probably reflect less the absolute wealth of the freedman community than the unusual situation of nonwhites achieving a standard of living traditionally enjoyed exclusively by whites; adjectives such as opulent, wealthy, and so on, used in the sources, must therefore be understood within the context of Barbadian slave society at this period, and even in this qualified sense they applied to relatively few individuals. Waller, in 1807–8, provided what appears to be a balanced perspective for the period when he observed that "the great bulk" of freedmen "are far indeed from being in a comfortable condition. Many of these, however, having learned some useful trade, and being brought up in habits of industry, accumulate a comfortable independence"; he noticed that "colored" freedwomen, in particular, were "often . . . seen very expensively dressed after the European fashion, parading the streets, attended by their slaves, with no small dignity."[88]

As the years progressed, more freedmen came to live under "comfortable circumstances . . . some of them possessing a good deal of wealth."[89] This increased wealth, especially in commercial ventures and property holding in Bridgetown, was reflected in the priority that freedmen gave to legal testimony in their drive for ameliorative legislation (their early petitions, for example, often emphasized the security of property rights). In 1830, William Bell, commenting on changes that had occurred on the island since his visit twenty years earlier, noted a "very perceptible change in the manners & habits of the Coloured People. Property is becoming more general amongst them. One meets them driving their carriages & riding their horses, the same as white persons."[90] Such changes were evident and observed mainly in Bridgetown, and, although the freedmen themselves acknowledged in 1834 that they "cannot boast an equality of wealth or territorial influence" with the island's whites, they did assert their having "among them individuals" of "equal wealth."[91] In 1833, however, only 75 freedmen, virtually all of whom lived in Saint Michael, were able to satisfy the property qualifications for en-

[87]Seaforth to Camden, May 4, 1805, Seaforth Papers, 46/7/12; see also Alleyne to Thorne, November 20, 1801, Alleyne Letters, p. 66, WIC.

[88]Waller, *Voyage in the West Indies*, pp. 4, 95.

[89][Browne], *Yarn of a Yankee Privateer*, p. 103. See also Orderson, *Cursory Remarks*, p. 30; *An Essay Attempting to Prove the Policy of Granting the Late Petition of the Free Coloured People of Barbadoes* [Barbados, 1811], p. 10.

[90]Boromé, "William Bell," p. 23.

[91]"Address of the Free Coloured and Free Black Inhabitants of Bridgetown," April 2, 1834, CO 28/113.

franchisement (out of an island-wide electorate of 1,016 persons), a fact which provides a reasonable indication of the approximate number of *males* who, by Barbadian standards, could be considered relatively wealthy; had the property qualifications been reduced to those in effect just a few years earlier, 50–125 freedmen would have been added to the electoral rolls.[92]

The relative wealth of freedmen and whites can also be seen in the monetary value of their property, including houses, land, and slaves. *Excluding* plantation-owners, the property inventories of 114 whites during the years 1815, 1825, and 1830 show an average £1,095 value; 14 freedmen about whom information was recovered during the same years were valued at an average of £386—that is, £709 less than the whites. By increasing the number of freedmen to 29, a figure which includes all individuals for whom information on property value is available for the period 1815–30, the average is also increased to £675 per person, but this is still £420 less than the white average. Among whites, 18.4 percent owned property valued at £2,000 or more, but only 6.9 percent of the freedmen were in this category; the property of 45.6 percent of the whites, but 65.5 percent of the freedmen, was valued at less than £500 (Table 10). Although these figures cannot be considered precise indicators of wealth differences between freedmen and whites, they do give concrete expression to these differences. They also support the more general conclusion, based on

Table 10. Freedman and White Property Values (Nonplantation), 1815–30

Property Value (Barbadian Currency)	Freedmen		Whites	
	No.	%	No.	%
£3,000 and above	0	0.0	12	10.5
£2,500–£2,999	0	0.0	4	3.5
£2,000–£2,499	2	6.9	5	4.4
£1,500–£1,999	4	13.8	7	6.1
£1,000–£1,499	1	3.4	17	14.9
£500–£999	3	10.3	17	14.9
£499 and less	19	65.5	52	45.6

Sources: Compiled from materials discussed in Chapter 6, note 11. The freedman sample is from the period 1815–30, and the white one is from the years 1815, 1825, and 1830.

[92]Smith to Stanley, October 29, 1833, CO 28/111.

qualitative evidence, that, despite the presence of freedmen whose wealth and property exceeded that of whites, freedmen were—on the average and as a group—a poorer population.

As the period of slavery drew to a close, one can surmise that many freedmen, including the majority of those who lived in the rural areas, had a generally modest standard of living which placed them at the lower end of the wealth spectrum among the island's free population. Nonetheless, as a group, the freedman's wealth and standard of living had steadily increased over the years. The relative success and mobility he experienced in the economic system sharply contrasted with the arduous and lengthy struggle involved in achieving legal equality and removing social discrimination. And one might suppose that the contradiction between economic success and mobility, on the one hand, and sociolegal restrictions, on the other, contributed to the tension that made freedmen increasingly unwilling to acquiesce to their subordinate legal position.

Wealth, however, was not evenly distributed within the freedman community. Although economic strata cannot be defined with statistical precision, the fact that only 75 were electors in 1833 gives an indication of the small number of relatively wealthy males. Other figures also provide an idea of how wealth was distributed among freedmen. Although there is no information on merchants, among individuals for whom there is information on the total value of property holdings, the wealthiest were plantation-owners. The average value of their plantations was around £18,000 (compared to approximately £20,000 for white-owned plantations in 1815, 1825, and 1830). In 1828, the two plantations owned by Jacob Belgrave, Jr., were worth approximately £16,500 and £21,500 (only six of the eighteen white-owned plantations in 1825 and 1830 exceeded the latter amount), and there is little doubt that his wealth surpassed that of most, if not all, freedmen during this period.

The vast majority of propertied freedmen were much less wealthy than the plantation-owners, and there were probably many adults who did not own a major form of property such as a house, land, or slaves. No statistics are available on the number or proportion of propertyless freedmen, but information on fifty-two nonplantation property-holders gives some idea of wealth variations. Three of these persons owned property worth more than £3,000. The wealthiest was John Straker Thomas, a "colored" carpenter in Saint Michael who in 1808 owned two houses, an unspecified amount of land, fourteen slaves, and an assortment of other personal property; the total value of his estate was £4,583. The property of most freedmen, however, was worth much less. For example, thirty-two persons owned property valued at less than £500 (Table 11), but nineteen of these fell below £200. The average property value of the fifty-two freedmen was £873, but a mean value of £394 more accurately reflects the distribution of wealth. Although these figures probably give a greater indication of wealth variations among propertied freedmen than within the freedman community as a whole,[93] they provide concrete examples of wealth differences and support qualitative evidence that the freedman community was economically stratified—as, indeed, the white one was.

Other than revealing that the few freedman plantation-owners were the wealthiest of the freedman group, the data are insufficient to show a meaningful statistical correlation between property and wealth, on the one hand, and occupational status or major economic activity, on the other; however, available statistics do suggest correlations between wealth, as indicated by value of property holdings, and phenotype and sex. In the above-mentioned sample of fifty-two freedmen, phenotype appears to have been the most significant correlative of property value, and "colored" persons were, on the average, significantly wealthier than blacks. The average property value of the former was £1,146, while that of the latter was £311; 40 percent of the "colored" sample and 5.9 percent of the black owned property valued in excess of £1,000 (Table 11), and all four of the known plantation-owners were "colored." Of the eighty-one freedmen for whom wills or inventories were recovered, phenotype is known in seventy-seven cases; 66.2 percent of the individuals were "colored," and 33.8 percent were black, which again suggests that a greater percentage of wealthier property-holders were "colored" rather than black. In all of these cases, the percentage of "colored" persons was greater than their apparent percentage in the total freedman population (see Table 3), and this also supports the conclusion that "colored" freedmen tended to be disproportionately wealthy.

Sex was another important correlative of wealth. Although the sexual ratio among the freed population was roughly equal (see Table 4), the average property value of males, exclusive of plantation-owners, was £1,106, while that of females was £716; "colored" males had an average property value of £1,706, but £854 was the average for "colored" females. The average difference between black males and black females was not so great—£305 for the latter, and £318 for the former—but 38.1 percent of the male, and 22.6 percent of the female, sample owned property valued in excess of £1,000 (Table 11). Despite limitations in the statistical data and the small number of cases from which they are derived, these figures strengthen the qualitative evidence, which suggests that "colored" males were, by-and-large, among the wealthier members of the freedman community. As noted in Table 11 and elsewhere, however, females could achieve positions of relative wealth and acquire property of some consequence.

The most valuable types of property were houses, land (including housespots), and slaves, and most propertied freedmen appear to have

[93]See note 11 above.

Table 11. Freedman Property Values (Nonplantation) by Sex and Phenotype of Owner

Property Value (Barbadian Currency)	Males				Females				Both Sexes			
	"Colored"		Black		"Colored"		Black		"Colored"		Black	
	No.	%	No.	%	No.	%	No.	%	No.	%	No.	%
£3,000 and above	2	16.7	0	0.0	1	4.3	0	0.0	3	8.6	0	0.0
£2,500–£2,999	0	0.0	0	0.0	1	4.3	0	0.0	1	2.9	0	0.0
£2,000–£2,499	3	25.0	0	0.0	1	4.3	0	0.0	4	11.4	0	0.0
£1,500–£1,999	1	8.3	0	0.0	3	13.0	0	0.0	4	11.4	0	0.0
£1,000–£1,499	1	8.3	1	11.1	1	4.3	0	0.0	2	5.7	1	5.9
£500–£999	1	8.3	0	0.0	3	13.0	1	12.5	4	11.4	1	5.9
£499 and less	4	33.3	8	88.9	13	56.5	7	87.5	17	48.6	15	88.2

Sources: Compiled from materials discussed in Chapter 6, note 11.

owned at least two of these types. Of seventy-one non-plantation-owners for whom there is information on types of property, 80.3 percent owned at least two of the three types, and 62.0 percent owned all three (Table 12).

As was discussed earlier, most of the landholdings were small house-spots and were primarily located in Bridgetown and its environs. Because ownership of ten or more acres of land was one of the qualifications for voting eligibility, it can easily be seen why, even had there been no racial barriers, very few freedmen would have qualified on the basis of their landholdings.

Freedman houseownership (which included dwellings used for shop-keeping) was most noticeable in Bridgetown, where, as Orderson observed in 1816, "many of the best houses belong to them; and I am well persuaded that at least one-twelfth of the whole town is the actual free-hold property of the coloured people."[94] Orderson was arguing that freedmen were generally well off, but, although he was knowledgeable about local conditions, his estimate could have been, by accident or design, an inflated one; nevertheless, it supports the limited statistical evidence, which indicates that houses were an important form of property to freedmen. This importance is also reflected in the 1831 "brown privilege bill," by which freedmen were enfranchised. As was discussed in Chapter 4, this law, despite its formal elimination of racial barriers to voting, holding elective office, and serving on juries, was still designed to minimize the number of eligible freedmen. It did so by increasing property qualifications, but only those with respect to houses. Ownership of at least ten acres of land, a qualification that had been in force for more than a hundred years, was retained, but the annual taxable value of a house was tripled. By not raising the minimal land requirements for enfranchisement, the Barbados legislature in effect asserted that houses, not land, were the most significant form of real property held by wealthier freedmen. In 1833, as noted earlier, Governor Smith reported that only 75 freedmen could meet the minimum £30 qualification on the taxable value of houses; there were, however, 50 to 125 additional persons, virtually all of whom lived in Saint Michael, whose taxes were at least £10 and who thus would have been enfranchised if earlier qualifications on houseownership had been retained.[95]

Yet, references to enfranchisement can be misleading in assessing the value of houses among all freedmen; only males were eligible voters, but many houseowners were females, and there is every indication that the property of some was of comparable value to that of the men. For example, among the fifty-seven houseowners listed in Table 12, thirty-five were women, and a number of their houses had a relatively high value in rela-

---

[94]Orderson, *Cursory Remarks*, p. 30.
[95]Smith to Stanley, October 29, 1833, CO 28/111.

Table 12. Freedman Property-Owners (Nonplantation) by Type of Property Owned

Type of Property	Owners	
	No.	%
House, land, and slave	44	62.0
House and land	9	12.7
Slave and land	4	5.6
Slave only	10	14.1
House only	4	5.6
Land only	0	0.0

Sources: Compiled from materials discussed in Chapter 6, note 11.

tion to the total sample; in fact, females owned the three houses that were worth the most. The range and variation in house values is illustrated in the following cases of houses owned in the urban areas: from 1808 to 1810, James Bosden owned an "old house" valued at only £2, the "boarded and shingled" house of Rachel Carter was worth £60, and one of Susanna Ostrehan's three houses was appraised at £1,750; in 1824, Joseph Leacock owned a "boarded and shingled" house valued at £10, as well as a "wooden" house whose value was £40. All of the above cases excluded land values.[96]

Freedmen increased their ownership of houses of quality as the years progressed. Although Orderson may have exaggerated in his 1816 observation that "many of the best houses" in Bridgetown were owned by freedmen,[97] all evidence indicates that some lived in houses that were comparable to the houses of wealthier whites. However, it is equally clear that many freedmen lived under poor housing conditions and that the dwellings they owned and/or inhabited were very small and dilapidated. Houses, such as those owned, but not necessarily inhabited, by James Bosden, Susanna Ostrehan, Romeo Clark, Thomas Griffith, and Joseph Leacock, were all appraised at less than £10, and these houses could not have been more than small shacks. A visitor to Barbados in 1802 felt that one of the major reasons why West Indian towns in general, and Bridgetown in particular, had such "an air of poverty and filth [was] the great proportion of houses with which they are crowded, belonging to people of colour and emancipated slaves, whose means will rarely enable them to

[96]Inventories, Original, BDA.
[97]Orderson, *Cursory Remarks*, p. 30.

build anything better than a shed; and who . . . take possession of and patch up the wrecks of houses that otherwise would be deserted."[98] Although this observation was made at an early date, there appears to be little reason why it cannot generally be applied to later years as well.

A number of houses inhabited by freedmen were not owned by their occupants, and it appears that many freedmen, probably including a consequential number of recently manumitted slaves, rented their dwellings. These dwellings were owned by whites and freedmen, and there is little doubt that freedmen, in particular, sought to acquire income property. There appears to be no other reasonable explanation to account for many of the cases in which persons owned more than one house. Among the 57 houseowners listed in Table 12, 27, or 47 percent, possessed two or more houses: 18 persons owned 2 dwellings; 2 each owned 3, 4, and 5 houses; and 3 individuals owned 6 houses. Phrased another way, 27 individuals owned 78 of the total 108 houses, an average of 2.9 houses per owner. These statistics, as with others presented in this chapter, involve relatively few cases whose representativeness cannot be determined, but they offer positive evidence suggesting that multiple houseownership was a common occurrence; furthermore, this evidence indicates, albeit implicitly, that house rental provided a source of income for a number of freedmen. The income value of rented houses is also illustrated in the case of Willy Rachel Blacket in her will she specified that her household furniture and equipment were to be sold to pay her debts and funeral expenses, but that her house was to be rented, and the income employed to maintain and educate two nieces.[99] Slaves were another form of property from which income was derived, and, as with houses, freedmen often owned more than one slave.

SLAVEOWNING

By the last few decades of the seventeenth century there were already some freedman slaveowners: twelve of the thirty-four slaves baptized in Saint Michael between 1670 and 1687 "belonged to two families of free Negroes."[100] Throughout the slave period there is no evidence that, as a group, freedmen had any compunction against owning or employing slaves, and all information leads to the conclusion that slaves were regarded by freedmen as desirable forms of property. The emphasis on slave-ownership was not restricted to those who had been born free, but also extended to former slaves who, after their manumission, often acquired their own human property. Some of the slaves owned by freedmen were

[98]Daniel McKinnen, *A Tour through the British West Indies in the Years 1802 and 1803* (London, 1804), pp. 15–16.

[99]Will of Willy Rachel Blacket January 20, 1825, RB 4/63, BDA.

[100]Richard S. Dunn, *Sugar and Slaves: The Rise of the Planter Class in the English West Indies, 1624–1713* (Chapel Hill: The University of North Carolina Press, 1972), p. 255.

their own children or spouses, whom they intended to manumit; there is every indication, however, that a majority of the freedmen's slaves did not fall into this category, and that slaveownership was regarded less as a vehicle for manumitting kin than as a fundamental property right that freedmen possessed as freemen.

The freedmen's profound attachment to the principle of slaveownership was expressed in 1803, when "upwards of three hundred" of them petitioned the Council to reject a law which would have seriously affected their right to acquire and bequeath land and slaves:

> Although we have all our lives been accustomed to the assistance of slaves, we must immediately deprive ourselves of them and perform every menial office with our own hands. . . . The greatest blessing attending upon freedom is the acquirement and enjoyment of property, and without that liberty is but an empty name. . . . Many of our children who are now grown almost to the years of maturity have from their earliest infancy been accustomed to be attended by slaves; if this bill should pass into law, when we are no more, these children cannot possess a single slave. What will then be the meaning of their condition? Surely death would be preferable to such a situation![101]

The value attached to slaveownership is also seen in the fact that, of the seventy-six non-plantation-owning freedmen for whom wills or inventories are available, fifty-seven, or 75 percent, were slaveowners. In addition, when freedmen left wills, they tended to bequeath, rather than manumit, their slaves to kinsmen, mates, or close friends. As discussed in Chapter 2, freedman wills of the late eighteenth century and the pre-emancipation decades of the nineteenth indicate that this bequeathal pattern was consistently followed. When they manumitted their slave kinsmen or mates, freedmen also attempted to provide for their material security; when practicable, this meant that slaves were held in trust for the inheritor until his or her manumission was legally effected. In general, then, although some freedmen apparently became increasingly uncomfortable with the institution of slavery, as a group, freedmen appear to have been as committed to slaveholding toward the end of the slave period as they had been in earlier years. For example, J. A. Thome and J. H. Kimball, who visited Barbados during the Apprenticeship period, intensively queried many informants about conditions that existed during slavery. Although very sympathetic to the social plight of freedmen, Thome and Kimball offered a general conclusion which other evidence corroborates:

> We regret to add, that until lately, the colored people of Barbadoes have been far in the back ground in the cause of abolition, and even now, the majority of them are either indifferent, or actually hostile to emancipa-

---

[101]"The Humble Petition of the Free Coloured People, Inhabitants of the Island," Minutes of the Barbados Council, November 1, 1803, Lucas MSS, BPL. See pp. 77–81 of the present volume.

tion. They have no fellow feeling with the slave. In fact, they have had prejudices against the Negroes no less bitter than those which the whites have exercised toward them. There are many honorable exceptions to this, as has already been shown; but such, we are assured, is the general fact.[102]

"Some of [our slaves] we have acquired by our own honest means," freedmen wrote in their 1803 petition, "and some from our parents."[103] It is difficult, however, to determine the relative importance that purchase and inheritance played during the following decades—not only in slaveholding, but also with respect to property-ownership in general.[104] Slaves, in particular, were prominently included among property bequests in freedmen's wills, and, as with whites, freedmen often divided their property among various heirs. Samuel Headley, for example, a freedman, manumitted only one of his sixteen slaves, and bequeathed the other fifteen to his relatives, including a sister, nephew, niece, and another "kinsman." Robert Collymore bequeathed his six slaves to his sisters and a niece, and his mother, Amaryllis Collymore, divided her sixty-two slaves among her seven living children and a niece—neither she nor her son manumitted any slaves in their wills.[105] Freedmen also purchased slaves, and bought them directly from their owners or at public auction. There is no evidence to establish which of these acquisition patterns was most common, but the only positive evidence that the latter occurred derives from the journal of a British military officer. One day, in 1807, he attended "a sale of Negroes. Here an elderly Negro woman and her four children, all born in the island, were exposed to sale. Two of the boys were purchased by a mulatto woman . . . and she examined the boys with all possible indelicacy. I pitied them greatly, they were to be separated from their mother and sent to

[102]Thome and Kimball, *Emancipation in the West Indies*, p. 76.

[103]"The Humble Petition of the Free Coloured People, Inhabitants of the Island," Minutes of the Barbados Council, November 1, 1803, Lucas MSS.

[104]Freedmen not only inherited from other freedmen but they also sometimes inherited from whites; most of the latter cases apparently involved freedwomen who inherited from white males as a result of a sexual relationship. Illustrations from 1832 include the following: Michael Cavan, of Middlesex county in England, left, among other property, £5,000 sterling to his "dear and faithful friend Louisa Keeling, a free woman of colour"; John Thomas Bentham, a physician of Christ Church parish, bequeathed his estate residue, after funeral and other expenses had been paid, to "Letitia Bentham, free coloured woman . . . until her four children named John Lewis Bentham, Thomas Bentham, Robert Bentham and Henry Bentham, free coloured persons . . . shall attain the age of twenty-one years," when they also were to receive a bequest; and John Rogers, a planter in Christ Church, not only directed that "a coloured girl . . . my reputed child" be purchased from her owner and manumitted but also specified that his entire estate be divided equally among "Nanny Ann Rogers, free black woman and my reputed free coloured children," of whom there were nine, all with the surname Rogers (RB 4/67, pp. 49, 60, BDA).

[105]Will of Robert Collymore, October 13, 1828, RB 4/65; will of Amaryllis Collymore, January 5, 1829, *ibid.*; and will of Samuel Headley, 1813, Wills Books, vol. 59, p. 178; all on file in BDA.

Demerara."[106] Although this is a unique reference, there is no indication that the attendance of freedmen at slave auctions was an unusual phenomenon.

However freedmen most commonly acquired their slaves (and with the exception of kinsmen and mates whom freedmen intended to manumit), freedmen and whites owned slaves for similar reasons. Slaves were employed as agricultural laborers, but, because freedmen rarely owned plantations and had relatively small quantities of agricultural land, as a group they were less dependent than whites on slave labor in agricultural enterprises. It thus appears that freedmen's slaves were largely used as house servants, shop assistants, tradesmen, and the like. Freedmen (and whites) also hired slaves for these purposes,[107] but, most important, freedman slaveowners (and white ones) also derived income from renting their slaves to private individuals or governmental bodies.

Slave labor was hired for a variety of reasons, including public works projects, such as road repair or the clearing of parochial church yards; field labor on plantations whose slave contingents were low; to perform domestic work; or to work in the skilled trades.[108] Artisans were particularly valuable for "the hire which they fetch when let out to work."[109] "There are a great many inhabitants of this island," Governor Parry reported in 1788, "whose whole income, or by much the greatest part of it, arises from the hire of their Negroes,"[110] and a six-month island resident wrote that in 1814 "some of the smaller class of slave-holders existed by hiring out their slaves. I lived near one of these [in Bridgetown], he owned four slaves, of which he let out three every day. He had a wife and several children who contrived to get through each day without performing a single turn of labor of any kind. His slaves were ill fed and scantily clad."[111] A British officer stationed in Barbados during 1806–7, knew of a white creole woman who "lets out her Negro girls, to anyone who will pay her

[106][Wyvill], "Memoirs," p. 385.

[107]See, for example, "Petition of Rebecca Bosdons, Free Coloured Woman, to John Brathwaite, President of Council," [ca. 1823–24], CO 28/95. On February 6, 1816, the following notice of a runaway slave appeared in the Barbados Mercury: "Absconded some time ago, from a free black woman called Peggy Wilson . . . to whom she was hired, a Negro girl about 19 years of age."

[108]See, for example, advertisements in the Barbados Mercury on April 19 and May 24, 1783, and February 10, 1816; and replies of Brathwaite, Parry, and Council to query 8, "Report of the Lords."

[109]Waller, Voyage in the West Indies, p. 92.

[110]Parry to Sydney, August 18, 1788, PP, 1789, vol. 26, p. 15; see also Reply of Joshua Steele to Governor Parry, 1788, ibid., p. 26.

[111][Browne], Yarn of a Yankee Privateer, p. 111. The stipendiary magistrate for Bridgetown reported in 1836: "This district is chiefly composed of non-praedials, and a great proportion of them belonging to persons in needy circumstances . . . who have been in the habit of sending them out to look for employment" ("Papers . . . in Explanation of the Measures Adopted . . . for Giving Effect to the Act for the Abolition of Slavery . . . ," pt. 4, PP, 1837, vol. 53, rept. 521-1, p. 384).

for their persons, under the denomination of washerwomen, and [becomes] very angry if they don't come home in the family way."[112] Although whites predominated among the slaveowners who hired out their slaves, available information prevents an estimate of how many, and what proportion of, freedmen and whites were economically dependent on slave hire. Yet, within both groups the number must have been consequential, for many landless slaveowners owned small groups of slaves, and freedmen were conspicuous among these owners.

On the basis of information derived from property-tax accounts in the island treasurer's office, a committee of the Barbados Council reported that in 1822 there were 5,206 slaveowners, 1,535 of whom (including 302 plantations with sugar mills) were landowners, but "the remaining 3,671 owners of slaves [had] no land at all."[113] A number of years later the island's agent wrote that freedmen comprised "the greater proportion of the 3,671."[114] Although this may be an overestimate, it certainly suggests that a considerable number of freedmen were slaveowners; and this estimate even excludes those additional freedman slaveowners who also held land for which they were taxed. As of emancipation, in August 1834, there were 5,349 slaveowners,[115] but only 2,294 (including 399 plantations with sugar mills) were landowners, the remaining 3,055 being landless.[116] The white population increased very little, if any, between 1822 and 1834, while the number of freedmen rose substantially during these years (see Table 1); since there is no indication that freedmen lessened their emphasis on slaveownership, it is reasonable to assume that the new slaveowners who appeared between 1822 and 1834 were largely freedmen. In general, then, there may have been a few hundred freedman slaveowners by the beginning of the nineteenth century, but, as the years progressed, their numbers increased considerably. In 1814 it was reported that "many were slave owners,"[117] and by emancipation the number may have approached 2,000; although this estimate is, of necessity, a very rough one, all information points to the conclusion that, as the freedman community increased in size, the number of its slaveowners increased as well.

Most freedman slaveowners held relatively few slaves. In 1833, for example, the island's agent confidently asserted that an analysis of the 1832 slave registry returns would show an increase over previous years in the number of freedmen "possessing from one to four slaves"; he also implied that many, if not most, freedmen owned fewer than five slaves.[118]

[112][Wyvill], "Memoirs," p. 386.

[113]*A Report of a Committee of the Council of Barbadoes Appointed to Inquire into the Actual Condition of the Slaves in this Island* (London, 1824), pp. 77–78, 127.

[114]Mayers to Goderich, March 2, 1833, CO 28/112.

[115]MacGregor to Glenelg, December 6, 1836, *PP*, 1837–38, vol. 48, rept. 215.

[116]"A Memorial of the Council and Assembly of Barbadoes . . . ," November 4, 1834, *ibid.*, 1835, vol. 50, rept. 278.

[117][Browne], *Yarn of a Yankee Privateer*, p. 103.

[118]Mayers to Goderich, March 2, 1833, CO 28/112.

His assumption is generally supported by statistical materials. Of fifty-seven non-plantation-slaveowners, fifty (87.7 percent) owned more than one slave, which indicates the frequency of multiple slaveownership. The small number of slaves owned is suggested by the fact that 43.9 percent owned from one to four slaves, while 22.8 percent owned from five to eight; the maximum owned by one person was twenty-five (Table 13). The average number of slaves per owner was 7.5; the mean was 5.0.

White non-plantation-owners, both with and without land, also possessed small numbers of slaves. In their estate inventories, eighty-nine such persons owned between one and twenty-five slaves (Table 13); three others possessed twenty-six, thirty-eight, and forty slaves. Eighty-one (91.4 percent) of the eighty-nine owned more than one slave, which suggests that multiple ownership among whites was roughly comparable to that of freedmen. However, 32.6 percent of the white owners held from one to four slaves, and 37.1 percent owned from five to eight; in addition, the mean number of slaves per white owner was 7 (5 for the freedmen). The figures on white and freedman slaveowners suggest that a greater percentage of the latter owned small groups of slaves, even though the average number of slaves per owner was about the same (7.6 for whites and 7.5 for freedmen).

In general, these statistics suggest a similarity in slaveownership between freedman and white property-holders who did not own plantations. But the two samples from which the statistics derive are not strictly comparable. The white sample is drawn from 1815, 1825, and 1830, and freedmen were wealthier during these years than in earlier ones. However, if a freedman sample for the same years had been used, the number of cases would have been so small as to render any comparison virtually meaning-

Table 13. Freedman and White (Nonplantation) Slaveownership

No. of Slaves per Owner	Freedman Owners		White Owners	
	No.	%	No.	%
1–4	25	43.9	29	32.6
5–8	13	22.8	33	37.1
9–12	8	14.0	12	13.5
13–16	4	7.0	7	7.9
17–20	5	8.8	4	4.5
21–25	2	3.5	4	4.5

Sources: Compiled from materials discussed in Chapter 6, note 11.

less. In addition, since whites apparently had a greater tendency than freedmen to leave wills, the white sample is probably more representative of white slaveowners than the freedman one is of freedman slaveowners. Thus, these statistics (as well as others employed) can at best be taken only as suggestions of slaveholding patterns followed by non-plantation-owning freedmen and whites.[119]

However, the figures do support other evidence that freedmen were committed to slaveownership and generally shared this commitment with whites. Landowning and landless whites together, of course, owned a greater number of slaves, but the numerical differences in slaveownership between whites and freedmen appear to have been largely a function of economic differences rather than ideological ones. Whites were, on the average, wealthier, and they virtually monopolized the larger landholdings, including plantations. The factors which curtailed the number of slaves owned by freedmen were related to economic considerations such as these rather than to moral or ethical objections to the principle of slaveownership. The freedman's commitment to slaveownership, it can also be suggested, was a powerful force which influenced his conservatism on the issue of slave emancipation and generally made him unwilling to challenge the institution upon which the Barbadian social order rested. Political considerations also influenced this conservatism, such as a reluctance to risk alienating the plantocracy in the struggle for civil rights, but, as a slaveowner himself, and because his greatest mobility and most visible successes were in the economic system, the freedman was less likely to object to slavery—an institution which most colonials perceived to be essential to the health and viability of their economic lives.

Although freedmen appear to have been as committed to slaveownership as whites were, it is difficult to assess how they treated their slaves and whether this treatment was, in general, any better or worse than the treatment received by slaves owned by whites. Evidence of the physical mistreatment of slaves by white slaveowners is considerable, but the sources simply do not provide sufficient information on freedman slaveowners. In the late eighteenth century, William Dickson, a critic of the Barbadian slave system and a defender of the freedman, nonetheless observed that "free Negroes are generally more severe, because less enlightened, owners, than white people."[120] Yet, as the years progressed and more freedmen became slaveholders, they may have come in for a disproportionate amount of criticism. An American who lived in Bridgetown for six months in 1814 observed that freedmen "had the reputation of being much more cruel to their slaves than the white proprietors. I had no means of knowing how much of this censure they deserved, but I suspect it must

---

[119]See note 11 above.
[120]Dickson, *Letters on Slavery*, p. 55.

be received with many grains of allowance, for it was a character given by whites who seemed to entertain a hostile feeling against them."[121]

It should be clear, however, that the relationship between freedman and slave was more involved than simply that between master and servant, and that both groups shared a common plight based on their racial features. The quality of their intergroup relations is discussed in Chapter 9, but, as has already been indicated, in everyday life and in a variety of institutional contexts, the two groups were often and inevitably in contact. Chapters 7 and 8 discuss two other national institutions—the religious and the educational—in which freedmen and slaves often participated together.

[121][Browne], *Yarn of a Yankee Privateer*, p. 103.

VII

THE RELIGIOUS SYSTEM: CHURCHES AND CHRISTIANITY

There is abundant evidence that Barbadian slaves, as indeed those throughout the West Indies, participated in a fundamentally African system of magico-religious beliefs and practices commonly known as Obeah. There is some suggestive evidence, in early-nineteenth-century Barbadian laws prohibiting Obeah, that freedmen participated in this system, and in a passing comment relating to these laws the island's governor implied that those who subscribed to Obeah came from "among the [more] ignorant slaves, and even free coloured people."[1] The depth and degree of freedman participation in Obeah is not known, although one might assume that slaves would not have given up such practices and beliefs immediately upon securing their freedom, despite the legal and acculturative pressures to do so.

In considering the freedman's religious life, however, this chapter confines itself to the more salient features of his participation in Protestant churches. Although the information on these groups which specifically refers to freedmen is limited, a summary account can be provided of the Church of England (the island's official church), the Methodist, and the United Brethren, or Moravian. During the period that is the focus of this book, no other Christian denominations were functioning on the island. Catholicism, important in the seventeenth century, especially among the Irish population, was virtually nonexistent in the early nineteenth; the Quaker community, which had flourished in the seventeenth century, was moribund by the late eighteenth; and groups such as the Baptists, which were important in other islands of the British West Indies, never established missions in Barbados during the slave period. Furthermore, of the Anglicans, Methodists, and Moravians, the last had the least impact on the freedman's involvement with Christianity.

---

[1]Laws of 1806 (CO 30/18, no. 262) and 1818 (CO 30/20, no. 367); Combermere to Bathurst, December 28, 1818, CO 28/87.

MORAVIANS AND METHODISTS

Moravian missionaries, the first of whom arrived in Barbados in 1765, were the earliest Protestants who came specifically to work among the island's slave population. (Anglican catechists, however, had been assigned to the slaves of the Codrington plantations—owned by the Society for the Propagation of the Gospel in Foreign Parts—since the early eighteenth century.) Largely due to their almost total concern with plantation slaves, the limited number of their mission stations, and their confinement to rural areas,[2] the Moravians had an insignificant influence on freedmen. They are rarely mentioned in United Brethren accounts of their activities,[3] and the few available statistics on the number of congregants—that is, persons baptized in the mission—also suggest the very limited participation of freedmen in the Moravian church: in 1811, out of 221 congregants, only 3 were freedmen, the remainder being slaves;[4] in 1829 30, 8 out of 628 congregants were freedmen;[5] and in 1833 all of the 981 congregants were slaves.[6] Furthermore, freedmen (and, more rarely, whites) only occasionally attended services as "hearers." One can generally conclude that even this minor participation was a by-product of work among slaves, for there is no indication that Moravians made any special effort, or showed any particular concern, to proselytize freedmen, and the few freedmen congregants may have been converted prior to their manumissions.

In 1788 the Methodists started their missionary activities in Barbados, also with the intent of working among the slaves. But their missionaries were generally disliked by the established church and often had difficulties with planters and other whites; over the years they were frequently harassed and their services were disrupted. Anti-Methodist sentiments reached peaks in 1816, when some whites accused the missionaries of complicity in the slave revolt, and especially in 1823, when a white mob destroyed the Bridgetown chapel and forced the departure of the missionary.[7] It appears that the outspoken criticisms of white Barbadians' behavior and morality, in particular, were largely responsible for the difficulties and harassment Methodist missionaries often experienced. Al-

---

[2] Their first mission was established at Sharon, in Saint Thomas parish; not until 1825 was the second one started, at Mount Tabor in Saint John parish. A third station, in Bridgetown, commenced after emancipation.

[3] *Periodical Accounts Relating to the Missions of the Church of the United Brethren, Established among the Heathen*, 13 vols. (London, 1790–1834), *passim*.

[4] *PP*, 1814–15, vol. 7, rept. 478.

[5] Compiled from *Periodical Accounts*, 12 (1831): 42–43, and *PP*, 1831–32, vol. 47, rept. 660.

[6] *Periodical Accounts*, 13 (1834): 31–32.

[7] The mob included "one person of colour, who had been educated in England. With this man the people of colour would not afterwards associate" (W. J. Shrewsbury to Goy, November 11, 1823, quoted in John V. B. Shrewsbury, *Memorials of the Rev. William J. Shrewsbury* [London, 1868], p. 143).

though the cause of such difficulties was sometimes rationalized by the plantocracy and those associated with it in terms of the Methodists' preaching to slaves, it remains that the Moravians, who preached to audiences almost entirely composed of plantation slaves, never evoked the bitterness and hostility that the Methodists received from white society. It is significant that there is no evidence that the Moravians were ever critical, publicly at least, of white behavior. Observations made by the governor in 1802 generally hold true for most of the period under discussion here: "Against [the Methodists] the planters are very much prepossessed," he wrote, but the Moravians "are usually well esteemed, their moral conduct is irreproachable *and their manners quiet and inoffensive.*"[8]

In general, then, Methodists had little success in obtaining permission to preach to plantation slaves, and, unlike the Moravians, their activities were largely confined to Bridgetown, where a large proportion of the island's freedmen was clustered. By the early 1820s, the Methodists had established a small congregation in Speightstown; it was "almost wholly composed of free persons; two-thirds of them blacks and persons of colour, the rest the white inhabitants of the place."[9] Missionaries, however, often found it difficult to travel to Speightstown, and the irregularity of their visits caused the congregation to dwindle.[10]

In Bridgetown, especially after the opening of the chapel in 1820, it was common for the missionaries to preach to audiences that numbered in the hundreds;[11] but actual membership in their congregation was relatively small, albeit racially mixed (see Table 14). Freemen of both races were primarily from the lower classes,[12] and were perhaps largely attracted by the emotional appeal of the services, the social diversion they offered, and the *relative* lack of class differences between themselves and the missionaries to whom they were exposed.[13] In addition, discriminatory practices in the Anglican church may have caused nonwhites, in particular, to attend the Methodist services.

In the mission's early years, whites formed a significant proportion, and sometimes a majority, of its membership and of those attending prayer meetings. But gradually the number of freedman and slave congregants

[8]Seaforth to Bishop of London, March 8, 1802, Seaforth Papers, 46/7/4, SRO, italics added.

[9]Shrewsbury and Nelson to Wesleyan Missionary Society, November 8, 1821, Box 1821–22, no. 102, MMSA.

[10]Nelson to Wesleyan Missionary Society, January 12, 1822, Box 1821–22, no. 205, *ibid.*

[11]Shrewsbury and Larcum to Wesleyan Missionary Society, March 28, 1820, Box 1817–20, no. 120, *ibid.*; Shrewsbury and Nelson to Wesleyan Missionary Society, November 8, 1821, Box 1821–22, no. 102, *ibid.*

[12]Gilgrass to Coke, May 25, 1810, Box 1803–13, no. 200, *ibid.*; Rayner to Taylor, December 27, 1819, Box 1817–20, no. 96, *ibid.*

[13]See Seaforth to Bishop of London, March 8, 1802, Seaforth Papers, 46/7/4; and Joseph Boromé, ed., "William Bell and His Second Visit to Barbados, 1829–1830," *JBMHS*, 30 (1962): 34.

Table 14. Methodists: Number of Members and Persons Attending Services

| Year | Members | | | | Approximate Average Number Attending Services | | | |
	Slaves	Freedmen	Whites	Total	Slaves	Freedmen	Whites	Total
1789	–	–	16	50	–	–	–	–
1793	10	7	34	51	–	–	–	–
1804	18	8	18	44	–	–	–	–
1806	–	–	20	41	–	–	–	–
1811	6	13	11	30	–	–	–	–
1824	50	25	15	90	–	–	–	–
1826	25	65	5	95	385	165	10	560
1827	25	78	5	108	385	208	17	610
1828	29	81	6	116	389	211	21	621
1829–30	32	88	9	129	392	268	26	606

Sources: 1789 (Robert H. Schomburgk, *The History of Barbados* [London, 1848], pp. 95–97); 1793 (Thomas Coke, *Extracts of the Journals of the Rev. Dr. Coke's Five Visits to America* [London, 1793], p. 178); 1804 (Box 1803–13, no. 190, MMSA); 1806 (*ibid.*, no. 194); 1811 (*PP*, 1814–15, vol. 7, rept. 478); 1824 (John V. B. Shrewsbury, *Memorials of the Rev. William J. Shrewsbury* [London, 1868], p. 159); 1826–30 (*PP*, 1831–32, vol. 47, rept. 660).

increased, and in later years freedmen comprised the largest group of members; from 1826 to 1830, for example, their annual average was close to 70 percent (Table 14). This participation was unique among church groups, and, despite the greater number of freedmen in the Church of England, they seem to have been relatively more integrated into the Methodist congregation.

There are other indications of this integration, aside from the freedman's proportional representation in the mission's membership. For example, after the destruction of the Bridgetown chapel in 1823 the Methodists continued to meet, but this time in the house of Mrs. Ann Gill, a freedwoman and a devout member of the congregation; during the next year or so she endured considerable persecution from whites, some of whom threatened to destroy her house to commemorate their destruction of the chapel in 1823.[14] Furthermore, as contrasted with the Anglicans,

[14]Warde to Bathurst, December 2, 1824, CO 28/93. For materials relating to the "trials of the Christian heroine of Barbados," see Shrewsbury, *Memorials, passim*; William Moister, *Memorials of Missionary Labours in Western Africa, the West Indies, and at the Cape of Good Hope* (London, 1866), p. 290; and *An Authentic Report of the Debate in the House of Commons, June 23, 1825, on Mr. Buxton's Motion Relative to the Demolition of the Methodist Chapel and Mission House in Barbadoes* . . . (London, 1825), pp. 36–40.

there were no formal discriminatory practices in the Methodist church services, and freedmen could assume positions of nominal responsibility within the small congregation. In 1804 McDonald Devine was the steward,[15] and, when there were no white missionaries on the island, freedmen such as Richard Beck conducted the mission's affairs and Sunday services;[16] in fact, in his novel *Peter Simple*, Frederick Marryat, who visited Barbados around 1813, provided a lengthy, albeit racist and ethnocentric, description of a Methodist service in Bridgetown and the sermon given by its "Negro" preacher.[17]

Freedmen Methodists appear to have been involved in and to have identified with their church to a high degree, and it was perhaps this very involvement which led to a greater disappointment when missionaries behaved toward them in a manner they had long been accustomed to experiencing from whites in general. In 1814 Beck complained that Methodist ministers would sometimes slight their freedmen congregants. One preacher, for example, prompted by a "coloured" boy laughing in church, threatened to expel him, and then proceeded to give a talk that "degrad[ed] the coloured people very much . . . [and] without exception they have got so hurt many will not attend."[18] The missionary later apologized for this incident, but similar ones apparently occurred with some regularity.

As suggested above, the Methodist missionaries in general held a very low opinion of the state of religion in Barbados and of the morals of its population. "Pride," wrote one in a typical assessment, is a "characteristic of this people and is consequently a powerful obstacle to truth. The Barbadians pride themselves on the idea that they are superior West Indians. This hateful passion is especially prevalent among youth, and shews itself in the vanity of dress and the assumptive airs and manners. . . . connected with this is self-righteousness. The extent to which this fatally delusive sin prevails is truly astonishing."[19] Some missionaries were more vocal than others in making their displeasures known, but their criticisms were not reserved for one segment of the population; although the "white inhabitants" were considered "extremely immoral and profane," freedmen were found to "differ but little . . . except they have more vanity and pride."[20] When depreciative moral and behavioral judgments were openly and sometimes personally directed against freedmen, some retreated from

[15]Devine to Wesleyan Missionary Society, November 2, 1804, Box 1803–13, no. 192, MMSA.

[16]Moister, *Memorials*, pp. 287–88.

[17]Frederick Marryat, *Peter Simple* (London, 1834), pp. 452–55.

[18]Beck to Thomas, July 21, 1814, Box 1814–15, no. 126, MMSA.

[19]Nelson to Wesleyan Missionary Society, January 12, 1822, Box 1821–22, no. 205, *ibid.*

[20]Shrewsbury and Nelson to Wesleyan Missionary Society, November 8, 1821, Box 1821–22, no. 102, *ibid.*; see also Shrewsbury and Larcum to Wesleyan Missionary Society, March 28, 1820, Box 1817–20, no. 120, *ibid.*

the mission and pursued their religious activities elsewhere. Thus the Methodists may have discouraged potential congregants and may inadvertently have driven some freedmen into the Anglican church. In addition, it appears the Methodists had an unintended role in stimulating what were apparently the earliest socioreligious groups organized by, and composed of, freedmen.

In an 1822 letter, the missionary in Barbados gave his reasons for the slow growth of the Methodist congregation. In discussing these reasons, he described the "Thornites":

> Several young coloured men of respectability . . . by the hearing of the word in our chapel . . . several months ago began to meet together to pray and read, etc. One of them was distinguished as their leader, a Mr. Thorne[21] from whom they have since been denominated Thornites. Soon after they first began their meetings they sent two or three of their body to Mr. Garnett, the rector of St. Michael's, for direction and desired to be under his superintendence. He gave them some advise and lent them Blair's sermons to read. They then obtained a large room as a meeting house and here their leader, Mr. T. officiated. . . . They have gone on and now, I believe, have three meeting houses each of which will contain from 100 to 150 persons. And at each of these ten or a dozen of the young men alternately officiate two or three evenings of the week. The result is that when a young man comes to [the Methodist] chapel and gets convinced of sin and concerned for his soul, he goes and joins these instead of entering our society. And as to themselves, they entertain a notion that they are eminently pious of their wise resolutions and virtuous endeavors. . . . As they still occasionally attend our preaching, the Divine spirit has convinced one or two of them of the necessity of something more than they at present experience, two or three have joined our society.[22]

Little else can be ascertained about the origin of the "Thornites" or how they were organized. It is tempting to speculate, however, that they were important social groups to the freedmen in Bridgetown because they provided an organizational context in which freedmen exercised control and direction, enjoyed self-respect, and were cushioned from the embarrassment and hostility they could encounter from white clergy and laymen. The apparently rapid success of the "Thornites," judged by the expansion of the number of their meeting houses and their seating capacities, clearly reflected a desire on the part of freedmen for an organization that was not internally dominated by whites.

Although many of the individuals who were associated with the "Thornite" groups appear to have been affiliated with the Anglican church, the

[21]See p. 166.
[22]Nelson to Wesleyan Missionary Society, January 12, 1822, Box 1821–22, no. 205, MMSA.

church offered no specialized program of religious education for freedmen as a group; thus the "Thornites" also provided opportunities that were otherwise lacking for the acquisition and discussion of religious ideology. Perhaps freedmen related their religious discussions to political or social issues since, at this period, the controversy over emancipation and their struggle for civil rights were topical subjects. In any event, their meetings would have afforded convenient opportunities for such discussions, and, in the absence of white attendants, these topics could be treated in a relatively free and uninhibited manner.

By the early 1820s, freedmen also belonged to the "Barbados Auxiliary Bible Society"[23] (a probable affiliate of the London-based Protestant interdenominational "British and Foreign Bible Society"[24]); although information is lacking as to whether there was a membership overlap or connection between it and the "Thornites," these groups came to be viewed with suspicion and as potentially dangerous vehicles of political expression. In late 1823, when tensions between freedmen and whites were particularly acute, and freedmen were advancing their claims for civil rights, whites threatened the destruction of a meeting house. A group of freedmen then informed the governor's secretary "that a considerable body of free coloured persons had assembled armed to defend their house, which they were resolved to do if attacked; and quarrels and even blows took place, as a son of [Jacob Belgrave] the most respectable free coloured person on the island . . . was beaten by a white inhabitant, which caused a very strong and unpleasant sensation."[25] Tensions were still strong in March 1824, when the all-white Saint Michael vestry cautioned that "a certain class of free coloured people have formed societies, and [might], under the mask of religion . . . project schemes dangerous to the legal establishment of the colony."[26]

Whatever secular topics were discussed at meetings of these "societies," and whatever social needs they satisfied for the freedman community, the religious organizations were not intended to replace established church groups or to provide essential ritual services, such as baptisms, marriages, and burials. For these rites freedmen largely turned to the Church of England. In fact, at an early period, one problem the Methodists had in proselytizing was their lack of a burial ground and their inability to purchase land for this purpose. Efforts in this direction were made as early as 1804,[27] but over the next ten years they yielded no positive results; moreover, the Anglican clergy refused their burial grounds to per-

[23]On August 21, 1829, a notice in the *Barbadian* announced the "Twelfth Anniversary of the Barbados Auxiliary Bible Society"; the notice was signed by the Society's secretaries, Joseph Kennedy and Charles Phipps, both of whom were freedmen.
[24]See Olivier P. Beguin, "Bible Societies," *Encyclopaedia Britannica* (Chicago, 1970).
[25]Warde to Bathurst, March 19, 1824, CO 28/93.
[26]Saint Michael Vestry Minutes, March 25, 1824, BDA.
[27]Bradnack to Wesleyan Missionary Society, July 21, 1804, Box 1803–13, no. 190, MMSA.

sons not baptized in the Church of England, and this was a source of considerable frustration to Methodist missionaries. As one of them despairingly wrote on the death of an elder congregant, "We have not a foot of land in which we can put her and she must either be buried in some private place or thrown into the sea."[28]

ANGLICANS

By the late seventeenth century, freedmen were being baptized in the Anglican church,[29] but, as a body, the church in Barbados was never particularly concerned with their proselytization. Occasionally, however, a parish rector made special efforts to baptize nonwhites. In 1729, for example, the Reverend Arthur Holt, himself a slaveowner, proudly notified the bishop of London that he had "baptized several white adults, two free Negro adults and some slaves in Christ Church," and reported that his father, the rector of Saint Joseph, had baptized "twelve Negroes, eight of them free."[30] Generally speaking, however, efforts to baptize nonwhites were sporadic, were directed toward very few people, and were often discouraged by the plantocracy.[31] Yet, over the years, small numbers were gradually brought into the church. By the late eighteenth century, although "slaves and their children [were] not in general baptized,"[32] "the greater part"[33] of freedmen were, and some of the latter, especially in Saint Michael, were regular churchgoers.[34] By the first decade or so of the nineteenth century, the number of Anglican freedmen began to rise significantly, and the rector of Saint Michael, for example, explained the higher value of his rectory as a result of increased services performed for those in Bridgetown—"some of whom marry," he noted, "and all [of whom] have their children baptized."[35] Yet, unlike the white population, there were

[28]Boothby to Smith, February 26, 1814, Box 1814–15, no. 124, *ibid.*

[29]Richard S. Dunn, *Sugar and Slaves: The Rise of the Planter Class in the English West Indies, 1624–1713* (Chapel Hill: The University of North Carolina Press, 1972), p. 255.

[30]Holt to Gordon, March 7, 1729, Fulham Papers, General Correspondance, vol. 15, pp. 266–67, LPL.

[31]See, for example, reply to query 7, "Answers to the Queries Addressed to the Clergy," 1724, *ibid.*, pp. 203–14; and Holt to Newman, February 18, 1729, Letter Books, vol. B6, no. 62, USPGA.

[32]Reply of Governor Parry to query 18, "Report of the Lords of the Committee of Council . . . ; Submitting . . . the Evidence . . . concerning the Present State of the . . . Trade in Slaves; and . . . the Effects and Consequences of this Trade, . . . in Africa and the West Indies . . . ," pt. 3, Barbados section, *PP*, 1789, vol. 26. See also replies of Brathwaite and Council of Barbados, *ibid.*; and Reply of Joshua Steele to Governor Parry, 1788, *PP*, 1789, vol. 26, p. 28.

[33]Parry to Sydney, August 18, 1788, *ibid.*, p. 18.

[34]Reply of Joshua Steele to Governor Parry, 1788, *ibid.*, p. 28; William Dickson, *Letters on Slavery, to Which Are Added Addresses to the Whites and to the Free Negroes of Barbados* (London, 1789), p. 58.

[35]Garnett to Beckwith, December 5, 1811, *PP*, 1814–15, vol. 7, rept. 478. See also "The Humble Petition of the Free Coloured People, Inhabitants of the Island," entered into the Minutes of the Barbados Council, November 1, 1803, Lucas MSS, BPL.

many unbaptized freedmen, and even in the 1820s, while the reformist movement was accelerating and serious missionizing began among the slaves, freedmen did not become the object of any special concern to the Anglican church. This lack of interest continued a tradition wherein Anglican missionaries were usually specifically instructed to deal solely with slaves and not with freemen of either racial group.[36] And when, in 1823, a local association of Anglican clergymen and some planters was formed "for the purpose of affording religious instruction to the slave population," it was understood that the association's efforts would not extend to freedmen.[37] In general, then, it appears that many of the freedmen who sought Anglican religious instruction and baptism took the initiative themselves. There is little evidence that parochial rectors made a habit of refusing such requests, but there is equally little indication that, as a group, they made any concerted effort to encourage them.[38]

However, the Anglicans attracted more freedmen than did the other Protestant denominations. This attraction was assured by the presence of the Church of England from the earliest period of the island's colonization, by its official status and financial support from the civil structure, and by the numerical superiority of its churches (one in each parish in addition to, by the 1820s and 1830s, chapels in some[39]) and clergymen—the Church of England monopolized the religious establishment of the colony, and Anglicanism was, for all intents and purposes, the state religion. For the freedman (as well as the white creole), being a Christian largely meant being an Anglican, and the island's cultural traditions thus dictated that those who would enter a church would naturally be prone to enter the Church of England. In addition, the church had a profound formal and informal influence on the island's educational institutions, an influence that was especially marked in the public educational facilities for nonwhites in the later years of the slave period.

The fact that freedmen, when they did attend or join a church, went to the Church of England is clear from all qualitative evidence, and is reflected in the figures for church attendance during 1829-30. At this time, an approximate average of 5,999 persons attended the services of the three denominations under discussion; of this number, 1,003 were freedmen, 72 percent of whom attended the Anglican services, 27 percent the Methodist, and close to 1 percent the Moravian ones (Table 15). One can assume that the percentage of church-attending freedmen who attended the Anglican church was even higher in earlier periods.

[36]See, for example, Instructions for Missionaries to the West India Islands (London, 1795), pp. 3–6.

[37]"Resolutions Passed at a General Meeting of Persons Concerned in the Government of Slaves," September 15, 1823, CO 28/92, no. 47.

[38]See, for example, replies of clergy to circular letter from Lord Bathurst, 1817, CO 28/86.

[39]The chapel on the Codrington plantations, which was specifically intended for the slaves, was also frequented on Sundays by "many of the neighboring free coloured persons" ("Treatment of Slaves in Barbadoes," Christian Remembrancer, 5 [1823]: 407).

Table 15. Approximate Average Attendance at Church Services, 1829–30

Group	Average Attendance			
	Anglican	Methodist	Moravian	Total
Freedmen	727	268	8	1,003
Slaves	1,208	392	998	2,598
Whites	2,372	26	0	2,398
Total	4,307	686	1,006	5,999

Sources: Derived from estimates given by Moravian and Methodist missionaries and Anglican parish rectors (no estimates are available for the Anglicans for the parishes of Saint John and Saint Peter) and published in *PP*, 1830–31, vol. 41, rept. 660. Anglican communicants and noncommunicants are grouped together; Moravian and Methodist congregants are grouped with "hearers"—that is, with the nonbaptized or noncommunicants.

By 1829–30 the proportion of freedmen attending the Anglican church was roughly comparable to their representation in the island's total free (white and freedman) population. That is, in 1829, 25.5 percent of the free population were freedmen (see Table 1), and, in 1829–30, 23 percent of the freemen attending Anglican services were freedmen (Table 15). The greatest percentage of freedmen participated in Anglican ritual and church services in Saint Michael, primarily in Bridgetown. Furthermore, the participation of those in Saint Michael was proportionately greater than their distribution in the island-wide freedman population. In 1829–30, 72 percent of the freedmen attending Anglican church services did so in Saint Michael,[40] but at this time the freedman population of the parish represented about 61 percent of the island's total (see Table 2).

The Saint Michael freedman's greater participation in the Anglican church can also be shown by reference to baptisms, burials, and marriages. During the second and third decades of the nineteenth century, an annual average of about 61 percent of the island's freedmen lived in Saint Michael (see Table 2), but 69 percent of the baptisms and 81 percent of the burials performed on freedmen by Anglican clergymen during a comparable period occurred in this parish (Tables 16 and 17). Similarly, 74 percent of the Anglican marriages involving freedmen from 1808 to 1820 and from 1825 to 1830 were performed in Saint Michael (Table 18). There is no reason to suspect that the percentages, or proportions, of baptisms, burials, and marriages for earlier or later years deviated to any significant degree from those cited here.

[40]Calculated from information in *PP*, 1830–31, vol. 41, rept. 660. Communicants and noncommunicants are grouped together in these percentages. The total average number of communicants attending services was 711 whites, 156 freedmen, and 71 slaves (of these 322, 100, and 32, respectively, attended services in Saint Michael).

Table 16. Anglicans: Number of Baptisms

| | Slaves | Freedmen | | Whites |
Year	All Parishes	Saint Michael	All Parishes	All Parishes
1810	–	138	236	500
1811	–	146	200	474
1812	432	145	177	462
1813	317	129	183	446
1814	362	119	148	495
1815	474	195	240	472
1816	425	182	216	535
1817	544	161	257	533
1818	467	192	265	431
1819	515	127	205	448
1820	564	175	284	450
1822	753	146	261	368
1824	–	159	240	–

Sources: 1810–11 (all groups, *PP*, 1814–15, vol. 7, rept. 478); 1812–16 (freedmen and slaves, CO 28/86; whites, *PP*, 1823, vol. 18, rept. 80); 1817–20 (all groups, *PP*, 1823, vol. 18, rept. 80); 1822 (all groups, CO 28/92); 1824 (all groups, CO 28/95). All figures are based on returns made by parish rectors; figures do not include returns on slaves for Christ Church parish from 1817 to 1820.

Table 17. Anglicans: Number of Burials

| | Slaves | Freedmen | | Whites |
Year	All Parishes	Saint Michael	All Parishes	All Parishes
1810	–	94	123	555
1811	–	99	137	564
1812	203	116	139	694
1813	116	87	111	420
1814	122	89	104	349
1815	144	105	124	411
1816	154	108	124	641
1817	203	148	181	732
1818	170	110	131	471
1819	203	130	164	503
1820	174	119	143	556
1822	145	118	139	300
1824	–	145	184	–

Sources: Same as those for Table 16.

Table 18. Anglicans: Number of Marriages

Years	Slaves All Parishes	Freedmen Saint Michael	Freedmen All Parishes	Whites All Parishes
1808–14	3	20	26	–
1815–20	1	16	25	–
1825–30	17	72	94	534

Sources: 1808–20 (*PP*, 1823, vol. 18, rept. 80; no figures were reported for Saint Joseph); 1825–30 (*ibid.*, 1831–32, vol. 47, rept. 660; no figures were reported for Saint Peter and Saint John, and the 1830 statistics go only up to the end of September). All of the above figures are based on returns made by parish rectors.

The above figures reflect the greater number of religious facilities, including schools, that were available to freedmen in Saint Michael, or Bridgetown, and they also suggest the influence of the urban environment, including its job opportunities, in encouraging acceptance of the European-derived institutions, norms, and practices to which the island's white population adhered. In addition, the figures support evidence which indicates that the freedman town dweller had greater access to European-derived models of beliefs and practices, including religious ones, and was also more inclined to conform to these models than his rural counterpart.

Yet, for much of the slave period, as noted above, the Anglican church in Barbados generally took no active role in encouraging the freedman's participation, and, until the mid-1820s and the arrival of the first bishop of Barbados (whose presence was a direct result of the reform movement in Britain[41]), it assisted little in improving his social status. In fact, the discriminatory practices he experienced outside of the church were active in the church as well; his free status, when weighed against his racial ancestry, had little influence on his acceptance or treatment in the church. He was relegated to a marginal to nonexistent role in its affairs and was continually discouraged or prohibited from assuming positions of leadership or responsibility. As late as the Apprenticeship period, "no colored student has yet been admitted within the walls of Codrington College,"[42] which by this time was educating divinity students, and throughout slavery there were no freedman ministers and there is evidence of only one catechist. In 1823, the one Anglican missionary who had been assigned (by the Incorporated Society for the Conversion and Religious Instruction and Education of Negro Slaves in the English West Indies[43]) to work among the island's plantation slaves hired a freedman assistant, Joseph Thorne.

[41]Bathurst to Warde, July 26, 1824, CO 29/30.
[42]Joseph Sturge and Thomas Harvey, *The West Indies in 1837* (London, 1838), p. 141.
[43]During the slave period, the Anglican's Church Missionary Society had stations in Jamaica, Trinidad, and Guiana, but none in Barbados. The Society's involvement in Barbados was limited to its financial support of the Colonial Charity School (see pp. 173–76).

This proved to be a wise decision and encouraged the missionary to hire more lay catechists. But, he wrote, "the employment . . . of coloured catechists would, I fear, meet with much opposition as there is considerable prejudice against them. . . . This I regret very much as I am sure that much fitter persons could be obtained from that class than from the lower order of white men."[44] By 1826 twelve catechists were assisting the missionary, but Thorne was the only freedman.

Thus Thorne appears to have been the only freedman who achieved a position of even modest responsibility within the Anglican church establishment during most, if not all, of the pre-emancipation period. Brief references to him in a handful of sources permit a reconstruction of some of the threads of his life.[45] In 1792 the dark-complexioned Thorne was born a slave on the Belle plantation in Saint Michael. Freed at the age of twenty, he educated himself "in a plain manner, and then set up business as a boot-maker in Bridgetown." Although he may have been influenced by the Methodists, he became an Anglican either before his manumission or shortly thereafter and began to return to Belle at regular intervals to preach to its slaves; by 1823, the plantation had "been attended for some time past" by him. His religious zeal and ability to effectively "address himself to the hearts and understandings" of the slaves prompted his hiring as an Anglican catechist, for which he was paid "a small sum for each estate that he visits." By the early 1820s, as discussed above, he had become a leader in the socioreligious group that was known as the "Thornites." There is no evidence, however, that at this period he assumed a leadership position in secular affairs or that he became actively, if at all, involved in the freedmen's struggle for civil rights. His name does not appear in discussions of political events involving the freedman community, and it is absent from petitions on which lists of signatories could be found. In any event, Thorne continued to work as a lay catechist, and after emancipation the bishop of Barbados appointed him a licensed catechist for Saint Michael. By 1836 he was regularly working with apprentices in Bridgetown and on five estates in the parish. The case of Thorne is exceptional, and white hostility and prejudice generally functioned to prevent more freedmen from assuming positions of responsibility or prestige within the church.

[44]King to Howley, October 20, 1823, Fulham Papers, General Correspondance, vol. 16, pp. 203-4, LPL.

[45]These biographical notes were compiled from the following sources, some of which contain additional details on Thorne's life and behavior: Nelson to Wesleyan Missionary Society, January 12, 1822 (Box 1821–22, no. 205, MMSA); King to Howley, July 1, 1823 (Fulham Papers, vol. 2, p. 640, USPGA); King to Howley, October 20, 1823 (Fulham Papers, General Correspondance, vol. 16, pp. 203–4, LPL); John B. Colthurst, "Journal as a Special Magistrate in the Islands of Barbados and St. Vincent, July 1835–August 1838," entry for June 1836, pp. 45–48, Boston Public Library; J. A. Thome and J. H. Kimball, *Emancipation in the West Indies* (New York, 1838), pp. 73–74.

Although the Barbadian clergy maintained that they "never felt the smallest repugnance to admit slaves . . . to the most solemn rites and ordinances of the Christian religion,"[46] social conventions prohibited slaves and freedmen from taking communion with whites. "Very great strictness is still observed here on the subject of distinction of colour," William Bell reported in 1830 (after an absence from the island of some twenty years), "& at a moment when it would be least & should be so observed. I mean the ministration of the Lord's Supper, when the coloured people & slaves are forbidden to approach the table with the whites!"[47] In fact, the "liberal" rector of Saint Lucy incited a political furor in 1827 by, in the words of a resolution passed by whites of the parish, "his offensive sermon . . . and his disgraceful conduct whilst administering the most Holy Sacrament of the Lord's Supper, thereby endeavoring to alienate their slaves from a sense of their duty, by inculcating doctrines of equality."[48] As far as can be ascertained, the segregating of racial groups during communion persisted throughout the slave period, and equally enduring was the confinement of nonwhites to specially defined seating areas in the churches.

The details of the seating arrangements varied with the physical layout of the church and the inclination of its pastor. For example, in 1817 one found a "gallery set apart for their accommodation," or "two pews, beside the aisle set apart for the use of . . . black persons"; in the largest of the parish churches, in Saint Michael, "8 pews [were] set apart solely for their use and benches are placed in all the aisles and galleries for them."[49] Later, as Thome and Kimball reported, "the despised color was confined to the galleries, afterwards it was admitted to the seats under the galleries, and ultimately it was allowed to extend to the body pews below the cross aisle. If perchance one of the proscribed class should ignorantly stray beyond these precincts, . . . he was instantly, if not forcibly, removed."[50] Thome and Kimball cited these seating arrangements as specific evidence for their more general observation on racial prejudice against freedmen. "Most of all," they wrote, "did this wicked prejudice delight to display itself in the churches."[51] The fact that these

[46]"Resolutions of the Clergy of Barbados," quoted in letter to the editor, *Christian Remembrancer*, 6 (1824): 22–24.

[47]Boromé, "William Bell," p. 24.

[48]*Barbadian*, April 24, 1827. One of the charges brought against the Reverend William M. Harte was that he permitted freedmen to take communion before whites, but in his defense he strongly maintained that "the consecrated elements were administered in no instance to the coloured before the whites" (*ibid.*, July 24, 1827). For more details on the case of Harte, see *ibid.*, August 7, 10, 14, 21, September 21, 25, October 9, and December 18, 1827. I am grateful to Michael J. Chandler for providing these references.

[49]Replies of clergy to circular letter from Lord Bathurst, 1817, CO 28/86; see also "Religious Establishment in Barbadoes," *Christian Remembrancer*, 5 (1823): 473.

[50]Thome and Kimball, *Emancipation in the West Indies*, p. 79.

[51]*Ibid.*

authors derived a great deal of their information from conversations with freedmen might suggest that freedmen found discrimination in the churches particularly offensive—at least more so than other contemporary sources imply or indicate.

Although it is relevant to establish the existence of a "color bar" in as important an institution as the Anglican church, it is not necessary here to assess whether its maintenance was a result of the racist proclivities of individual clergymen and/or the result of constraints imposed on them by nonclerical whites. One cannot ignore the role played by local vestries in controlling their churches, and undeniably there were Anglican clergymen who were not racists, even by the standards of the period. Yet, throughout Barbadian history, clergymen often shared the racial (and class) biases of white society. Some were creoles themselves and were active supporters of the slave system, and clergymen in general often owned slaves as domestic servants; sometimes they even owned plantations with large slave contingents.[52] For most of the slave period, Barbados's Anglican ministers generally avoided involvement in issues that could have been interpreted as relating to societal modifications in the control and treatment of slaves. It was sometimes suggested, however, that they would have been willing to press harder for the Christian instruction of slaves and to justify such ministrations as legitimate aspects of their sacred charge. But, since their salaries were fixed by legislative enactment, their dependence on the "generosity" of the plantocracy made them reluctant to risk its alienation while it perceived religious instruction of slaves to be a potential threat to the stability of the social order.[53] It is difficult to say how valid this argument was, but there is little doubt that, for most of the slave period, Anglican clergymen, as a group, were, wittingly or unwittingly, accomplices in perpetuating Barbados's system of white supremacy. Even in the later days of the slave period, most parochial rectors made little or no effort to eliminate the subordinate position of freedmen in their churches. Although freedman communicants, in particular, may not have held the rectors personally responsible for this affront, as emancipation approached they certainly appear to have found it more and more offensive.

In late 1831 a group of freedmen, in an apparently spontaneous action, directly challenged the seating arrangement in Saint Michael's Cathedral. Since the mid-1820s the vestry had nominally reserved certain parts of

[52]See, for example, Henry E. Holder, *A Short Essay on the Subject of Negro Slavery, with Particular Reference to the Island of Barbados* (London, 1788), *passim; The Report from a Select Committee of the House of Assembly, Appointed to Inquire into the Origin, Causes, and Progress, of the Late Insurrection* (Barbados, [1818]), p. 41; Griffith Hughes, *The Natural History of Barbados* (London, 1750), p. 21; William Dickson, *Mitigation of Slavery in Two Parts* (London, 1814), p. 432; Thomas to Combermere, August 4, 1817, CO 28/86; and *A Declaration of Inhabitants of Barbados, Respecting the Demolition of the Methodist Chapel* (Barbados, 1826), p. 3.

[53]See, for example, Seaforth to Bishop of London, March 8, 1802, Seaforth Papers, 46/7/4.

the galleries for freedmen, but as the number of church-attending slaves increased, they began to occupy the freedmen's pews; the vestry did not enforce its own regulations, and freedmen found themselves "lacking seats" in the reserved areas. At a Sunday afternoon service "several coloured persons," their confidence undoubtedly buttressed by the reformist trend of the period and their achievement of full legal equality about six months earlier, seated themselves in pews on the ground floor, an area that was "exclusively the property of the white population and entirely appropriated to their use."[54] The vestry instructed the church-warden, if the incident repeated itself, to "request" freedmen to return to their own area; if they refused, they were to "be turned out of the pews."[55] On the following Sunday, however, "there were two coloured persons in a pew below stairs," and after they ignored the churchwarden's directive, the beadles were summoned to eject them from the church. At that moment there was "a great roar of persons coming down below stairs which proved to be coloured persons leaving the galleries who came down, and made a stand under the organ loft."[56] The event so shocked the white community that legal proceedings were instituted against "several" freedmen. These persons, however, did not include the "well established members" of the freedman community, whose behavior in church a newspaper found "humble, inoffensive and respectful" (the others were cautioned to "remember their situation" and to "exhibit those most beautiful features of the Christian character, meekness and humility").[57] Charges against the accused were dropped only after a committee of freedmen convinced the vestry that the incident had not been premeditated, that there was no organized effort to challenge the segregation pattern, and gave its assurance that no further efforts would be made to occupy seats which were reserved for whites. The committee explained the incident by observing that, since the galleries had been so overcrowded with slaves, freedmen had been forced into areas of the church from which they were traditionally excluded; nonetheless, the vestry was notified that "there was a strong and general feeling amongst the free coloured population that accommodations below ought to be afforded to them, and a proportion of the area set apart for that purpose."[58] Although freedmen asked only for an extension of their own seating privileges, not for the elimination of racial barriers, the vestry defended the status quo by emphasizing the concept of private property, a rationalization whites commonly employed, not only in defending the slave system, but also in perpetuating distinctions among freemen: "as the pews in the area or ground floor of the

---

[54]Saint Michael Vestry Minutes, December 7, 1831, BDA.
[55]*Ibid.*
[56]*Ibid.*, December 13, 1831.
[57]Quoted in H. A. Vaughan, "Samuel Prescod: The Birth of a Hero," *New World Quarterly*, 3 (1966): 57–58.
[58]Saint Michael Vestry Minutes, December 19, 1831, and January 2, 1832, BDA.

church, have been from the first erection of them set apart for the accommodation of, and belong to, the white inhabitants, they do not consider themselves authorized to interfere with the rights of property, and therefore cannot sanction the occupation by them of these seats."[59] By the Apprenticeship period, nonwhites were allowed to sit on the ground floor in the cathedral and in Saint Mary's, the other major church in Bridgetown; in both cases, however, "distinctions of color [were] still kept up," and nonwhites were confined to special areas.[60]

The events that took place in Saint Michael's Cathedral in 1831 reflected a reaction by freedmen to their subordinate and circumscribed status and the related effort to distinguish their position from that of the slaves. In confining freedmen to galleries in the cathedral and compelling them to share these areas with slaves, whites not only forced freedman and slave to worship together, but, in effect, made no distinction between the two. It can be assumed that freedmen, especially those who were free-born, educated, and wealthy, considered this to be another belittlement of their free status. Yet, they apparently tolerated these circumstances as long as they, in turn, had the option of segregating themselves from slaves. It is significant that, when freedmen notified the vestry of their concerns, they did not request seating among whites, but rather sought places which would be reserved for them, and from which slaves would be excluded. They thus implicitly expressed a long-standing theme in their efforts to elevate their free status, a theme which involved drawing a line between themselves and the slaves. That is, to whatever extent the freedman was compelled to share the restrictions of the slave, his free status was diminished; and, conversely, to whatever extent he was able to enjoy privileges not obtainable by slaves and held by whites, his free status was maximized. With respect to Christianity, as Governor Parry perceptively wrote in 1788, freedmen "consider the being enrolled amongst Christians, and being buried in a church-yard, as privileges conveying a certain rank; a rank which the principal slaves are sometimes ambitious of obtaining."[61]

[59]*Ibid.*, January 2, 1832.

[60]Sturge and Harvey, *The West Indies in 1837*, p. 144. However, Saint Paul's Church in Bridgetown, Thome and Kimball discovered in 1837, was "emphatically a free church. Distinctions of color are nowhere recognized. There is the most complete intermingling of colors throughout the house. . . . There is probably no clergyman in the island who has secured so perfectly the affections of" freedmen as the curate of Saint Paul's (*Emancipation in the West Indies*, p. 71). Although they did not have a chance to meet the bishop of Barbados, from conversations with the "intelligent and well-disposed classes of colored people," Thome and Kimball learned that, "while in some of his political measures, as a member of the council, he has benefited the colored population, his general influence has been unfavorable to their moral and spiritual welfare. He has discountenanced and defeated several attempts made by [some of] his rectors and curates to abolish the odious distinctions of color in their churches" (*ibid.*, p. 70).

[61]Parry to Sydney, August 18, 1788, *PP*, 1789, vol. 26, p. 18. Despite the implication in Parry's comment, it may have been that the graves of baptized freedmen were confined to certain areas of the churchyards, or that in a number of cases freedmen could not be buried in the churchyards at all. As late as 1823 in Antigua, for example, freedmen were buried in

Despite the discrimination freedmen experienced in the Anglican church, they strove to become Christians, not only because of the spiritual benefits they were encouraged to perceive in Christianity, but also because baptism and Christianity helped to differentiate them from the majority of slaves, who were not Christians (and who required the permission of their masters to undergo religious instruction and baptism). Equally important, if not more so, was the fact that Christianity brought the freedman closer to the orbit of white culture, and this *was the culture of freemen.* Thus, when a freedman became a Christian, his self-image as a freeman was reinforced. One might also assume that his status as a Christian helped to stimulate his reluctance to accept the subordinate position in which he was kept by other Christians—that is, by white freemen. In fact, freedmen used their Christianity as an argument to legitimize their claims to civil rights, "claims which we conceive ourselves justly entitled to," as they wrote in one of their petitions, "as British, Christian, faithful and loyal subjects."[62] The importance of Christianity as a presumption in the definition of free status was strengthened when the first of the ameliorative laws extended the right of legal testimony to baptized freedmen; acquisition of this right, in turn, added further weight to their supposition that as Christians they should enjoy civil rights. In effect, then, the acceptance of Christianity was associated with the practical benefit of a civil right which freedmen considered of paramount importance to the security of their persons and property; baptism was thus implicitly linked to protection of their economic interests.

The economic implications of baptism were also manifest in church-related charity schools that were established for poor freedmen (and slaves) by the end of the second decade of the nineteenth century. Baptism was a precondition for entrance into these schools. As Christians, the children of poor freedmen were able to acquire a limited education which facilitated access to jobs that favored persons who adhered to the values that white and creole society stressed for the lower classes; accommodation to these values was not only implied in seeking access to the schools but was also reinforced in the schools. The schools were another example of an institutional context in which freedmen and slaves jointly participated, and in which their shared phenotypic characteristics were of more significance for white society than their status differences.

---

places apart from whites and could not be buried in the same churchyards (Elsa V. Goveia, *Slave Society in the British Leeward Islands at the End of the Eighteenth Century* [New Haven: Yale University Press, 1965], pp. 214–15); however, concrete evidence is lacking on the practice followed in Barbados.

[62]"We . . . the Undersigned Free Coloured Inhabitants of this Island," July 15, 1830, petition entered into the Minutes of the House of Assembly, July 20, 1830, and printed in *Barbadian*, April 22, 1831. See also, for example, petitions of 1803 (entered into the Minutes of the Barbados Council, November 1, 1803, Lucas MSS) and 1811 (entered into the Minutes of the House of Assembly, February 19, 1811, BDA).

VIII

THE EDUCATIONAL SYSTEM: SCHOOLS AND LITERACY

When, in the late 1780s, Governor Parry noted that freedmen were "frequently taught to write and read," he may have overstated the case;[1] but his observation indicates that freedmen had taken advantage of certain educational opportunities long before the establishment of public (that is, non-fee-paying) schools for nonwhites late in the slave period. Until some fifteen years before emancipation, however, the source materials contain virtually no information on the educational facilities available to freedmen, although it can be assumed that their literacy skills were acquired through the occasional efforts of clergymen in the course of Christian education, by informal and formal individual tutoring, and in private schools. The children of freedmen were barred from private schools attended by white children, but undoubtedly white and freedman teachers in the late eighteenth and early nineteenth centuries were hired to give tutorial lessons and/or operated small private schools for freedmen. Such teachers or schools provided educational services, for example, to the children of a freedwoman whom the Reverend Robert Nicholls had known in the late eighteenth century; he described her as "very industrious in the care of her family, and in raising poultry to sell, with the profits of which she paid the expenses of her children's schooling."[2] In addition, the existence of educational facilities for freedmen at an early date is indicated in the 1772 will of a plantation-owner who manumitted a slave child and stipulated that

---

[1]Reply of Governor Parry to query 19, "Report of the Lords of the Committee of Council . . . ; Submitting . . . the Evidence . . . concerning the Present State of the . . . Trade in Slaves; and . . . the Effects and Consequences of this Trade, . . . in Africa and the West Indies . . . ," pt. 3, Barbados section, *PP*, 1789, vol. 26. The fifty-eight freedman signatories (who presumably represented somewhat of an elitist group) to what was apparently the earliest petition calling for amelioration in the freedmen's status, included fifteen persons who could not write their names and who signed with their "marks." See "The Humble Memorial and Remonstrance of the Free Coloured People . . . ," October 14, 1799, Minutes of the Barbados Council, October 15, 1799, Lucas MSS, BPL.

[2]Testimony of Reverend Robert Nicholls, *PP*, 1790, vol. 30, p. 333.

he "be put to school and decently clothed."[3] It is not known how many freedmen were teachers, but in the late eighteenth century William Dickson reported what must have been the highly unusual case of "a black teacher who is employed by several white families in Bridgetown [who] writes a variety of hands very elegantly. . . . he teaches English and arithmetic."[4] In 1803, a member of the Barbados Council argued that a bill limiting the freedmen's property holdings would impose a special hardship on their children, who "have had good educations."[5] Moreover, it may have been that by the late eighteenth and early nineteenth centuries a few freedmen had been educated abroad (as was the case in later years), a pattern they shared with wealthier whites, who often sent their children to private schools in Britain.

However the freedman acquired his literacy skills throughout most of the slave period, there were no public schools for him until 1818. In that year the Colonial Charity School was established in Bridgetown under the patronage of Governor Combermere "for the education in reading, writing, and arithmetic, of such free and slave children of the coloured and black population" who for financial reasons "and other local impediments" were unable to acquire these skills except through "public charity."[6] The stimulus for the school came from a British army officer who, while stationed on the island, began teaching nonwhite children and eventually succeeded in acquiring "the assistance of others in his work of charity."[7] By 1818, "legal provision" had been made "for the instruction of . . . the very lowest class of white people only" (supported by the parochial taxes levied on all races).[8] Although the Colonial Charity School was specifically created for the children of poor nonwhites, it was also the island's first "public school for people of colour"[9] and "the first institution of its kind in the West Indies."[10]

The Colonial Charity School was a daily school for boys and girls between the ages of five and twelve, but older children were sometimes accepted; in order to qualify for admission, however, all were required to have been baptized in the Anglican church. Admission was controlled by a

[3]Will of Francis Ford, April 29, 1772, quoted in *The Barbadian Diary of Gen. Robert Haynes, 1787-1836*, ed. E. M. W. Cracknell (Medstead, Hampshire, 1934), pp. 59-60.

[4]William Dickson, *Letters on Slavery, to Which Are Added Addresses to the Whites and to the Free Negroes of Barbados* (London, 1789), p. 75.

[5]Minutes of the Barbados Council, November 1, 1803, Lucas MSS.

[6]*Proposed Institution of a Colonial Charity School. On the System of Dr. Bell. Under the Patronage of His Excellency the Governor. Barbados, 16th November, 1818* [Bridgetown, 1818], p. 1.

[7]Edward Eliot, *Christianity and Slavery; in a Course of Lectures Preached at the Cathedral and Parish Church of St. Michael, Barbados* (London, 1833), pp. 47-49.

[8]Combermere to Bishop of London, 1818, Fulham Papers, vol. 2, p. 753, USPGA.

[9]Harris to Secretary of Church Missionary Society, August 10, 1825, Mission Books, vol. 1, pp. 451-52, CMSA.

[10]Eliot, *Christianity and Slavery*, pp. 47-49.

governing committee which included (or was entirely comprised of) freedmen, and which attempted to maintain an enrollment evenly divided between freed and slave children.[11]

A distinctive feature of the school was its use of the monitorial system, a way of organizing instruction which was popular in England at this time for educating the poor. The organization of the system in Barbados appears to have followed the English model. The schoolroom was divided into small units or "benches"; each of these was the responsibility of a monitor, who was usually one of the older and brighter children. The teacher instructed only the monitors, who in turn taught the children in their units.[12] In general, Barnard's assessment of the monitorial system in England can in all probability readily be applied to Barbados:

> The subject-matter was carefully graded, but it was very elementary. The whole technique was mechanical; there was no opportunity for the asking of questions nor, of course, for the development of individuality. In fact, the system was one of mass production in education. . . . it substituted machinery for personality and forced facts into the pupils' memory in a purely mechanical way. Yet up to a point it worked. The children did learn something; they were taught to be quiet and orderly; and above all the system was cheap.[13]

One by-product of the monitorial system for the Barbados nonwhite community was the creation of a group of informal teachers among the pupils themselves. As Charles Phipps, a freedman and the school's only teacher for the first few years of its existence, proudly wrote, they "are actually employed in teaching their parents, [other] grown people, and other children."[14]

Another feature of the English system which was followed in Barbados was "religious education in strict and undeviating conformity with the principles of the established Episcopal church." A very heavy emphasis was thus placed on sectarian instruction, bible studies, and church attendance—in fact, pupils were required to attend church on Sundays and holidays.[15] The course of study appears to have lasted three months, and there

[11]For details on the organization, aims, and progress of the Colonial Charity School, see *Proposed Institution, passim*; manuscript materials in CMSA; and Jerome S. Handler, *A Guide to Source Materials for the Study of Barbados History, 1627–1834* (Carbondale: Southern Illinois University Press, 1971), p. 137. Henry Nelson Coleridge implied that by 1825, at least, the governing committee was entirely composed of freedmen (*Six Months in the West Indies in 1825* [London, 1826], p. 51).

[12]See H. C. Barnard, *A History of English Education from 1760* (London, 1961), pp. 52–57; and S. J. Curtis, *History of Education in Great Britain* (London, 1967), pp. 206–9.

[13]Barnard, *History of English Education*, p. 54.

[14]Phipps to Secretary of Church Missionary Society, [1821], Mission Books, vol. 1, pp. 110–11, CMSA. Phipps ultimately became one of the secretaries of the governing committee and taught at the school until at least August, 1831—and perhaps longer.

[15]*Proposed Institution*, p. 1; "Rules and Regulations of the Colonial Charity School," 1825, Mission Books, vol. 1, pp. 453–54, CMSA.

was no shortage of applicants.[16] Shortly after the first year of operation, enrollment jumped considerably, and pupils filled most, if not all, of the available places. By the end of the first four or five years, 47 freedmen and 44 slave children had been graduated.[17] Despite the enrollment during these years (Table 19), however, these graduation figures suggest that quite a few students did not finish the course of studies.

Table 19. Colonial Charity School Enrollment

Year	Freedmen	Slaves	Total
1819	57	32	89
1820	73	64	137
1821	86	76	162
1823	74	86	160
1825	77	81	158
1830	132	169	301
1833	113	109	222

Sources: 1819 (Robert H. Schomburgk, The History of Barbados [London, 1848]. p. 105); 1820, 1821, 1823, and 1825 (Mission Books, vol. 1, pp. 34, 101, 376, 455, CMSA); 1830 (PP, 1831–32, vol. 47, rept. 660); 1833 (Incorporated Society for the Conversion . . . , Annual Report, 1833, pp. 50–51; the drop in 1833 enrollment was probably caused by the increased availability of other charity or public schools).

From its inception the Colonial Charity School was, as the governor related, "supported by the voluntary contributions of the coloured people themselves, in which they have been assisted by a few liberal minded and charitable white people"; yet, he added, "it is fair to state that many of the [white] community . . . still view this institution . . . with a jealous eye."[18] Through public subscriptions enough funds were raised to erect an 87-by-23-foot schoolroom (which, during the 1820s, was also used to hold public meetings for discussion of issues relating to the struggle for civil rights),[19] but these subscriptions were insufficient to keep the school out of financial difficulties. The teacher's salary was paid by the Church Missionary Society, an Anglican organization with headquarters in London. Without such assistance, wrote Thomas Harris, the freedman secretary of the governing committee, "the school would inevitably go to ground for want of

[16]See, for example, Harris to Secretary of Church Missionary Society, August 27, 1822 and April 12, 1825, Mission Books, vol. 1, pp. 151, 413, CMSA; and Phipps to Secretary of Church Missionary Society, [1821], and July 1825, ibid., pp. 110–11, 455.

[17]Phipps to Secretary of Church Missionary Society, October 1823, ibid., p. 376.

[18]Combermere to Bishop of London, 1818, Fulham Papers, vol. 2, pp. 753–54, USPGA.

[19]Located on Mason-Hall Street, this building (and the one for girls later added adjacent to it) was destroyed during a massive hurricane of 1831.

funds to support the master."[20] Over the next few years the school continued to have financial problems and considerable difficulty in increasing the number of its subscribers. There was certainly insufficient white support, and one wonders to what extent wealthier freedmen maintained their contributions.

After the arrival, in 1825, of the first bishop of Barbados, William Coleridge, the school's financial state improved. One of Coleridge's charges was to increase the facilities for the religious instruction of the slaves, and he rapidly gave the school his moral and financial support (from a special fund provided by the bishop of London), became president of its governing board, and enlisted more white patrons. Not long after his arrival, a separate school for girls was established, and within a few years total enrollment in the Colonial Charity School (whose name had been changed to the National School for Coloured Children) doubled (Table 19). By the early 1830s about 90 pupils were graduating every year or so, with many of the boys going into the skilled trades, and the girls "into business" or finding work as domestics.[21] As of 1830, eleven years after it started enrolling pupils, the boys' school alone had graduated about 300 children,[22] most of whom (as did graduates of the girls' school) came from families of "the lowest order of the free coloured and of the domestic and mechanic slaves in Bridgetown and its immediate vicinity."[23] During this period, however, other free schools were operating for nonwhites in Saint Michael and other parishes.

"At the commencement of the year 1825," Bishop Coleridge reported, "the number of schools in Barbados in connection with the church (and there were few if any others) for the religious instruction of the poor, were six for white children, one for coloured, and one on Codrington College property for slaves";[24] by the end of the year there were nine schools for whites and six for freedmen and slaves,[25] the bishop himself having been instrumental in founding, under the monitorial system, the additional schools for nonwhites.[26] The majority of these were in Saint Michael and were "scattered about in the part of the town principally inhabited by the coloured people, who are by these means more readily induced to send their children."[27] Over the next few years the number of public schools

[20]Harris to Secretary of Church Missionary Society, February 15, 1821, Mission Books, vol. 1, p. 101, CMSA.

[21]"Report of the Society for the Education of the Coloured Poor," *Christian Remembrancer*, 15 (1833): 53–55.

[22]Joseph Boromé, ed., "William Bell and His Second Visit to Barbados, 1829–1830," *JBMHS*, 30 (1962): 30–31.

[23]Coleridge, *Six Months*, p. 52.

[24]Quoted in Robert H. Schomburgk, *The History of Barbados* (London, 1848), p. 106.

[25]*PP*, 1826–27, vol. 15, rept. 159.

[26]Harris to Secretary of Church Missionary Society, August 10, 1825, Mission Books, vol. 1, pp. 451–52, CMSA.

[27]Coleridge, *Six Months*, pp. 51–52.

increased still further. In 1829–30 there were about seventeen for whites and eleven for freedmen and slaves (Table 20),[28] although the combined island-wide population of nonwhites was almost six times that of whites. By 1833, the number of schools for freedmen and slaves had increased to fourteen, and these were located in eight of the eleven parishes.[29] These developments in educational facilities for nonwhites, as noted, cannot be divorced from the influence of religious, particularly Anglican, organizations which in turn were influenced by the emancipation movement in Great Britain. Thus, although local clerical and nonclerical whites, as well as wealthier freedmen, played some role in their development, the early and major forces stemmed directly or indirectly from outside the society.

Not until the mid-1820s and early 1830s, then, were there a variety of schools which freedmen and slaves attended and in which they were taught, *to one degree or another*, literacy skills. The remainder of this chapter focuses on this period and discusses four kinds of schools: Public daily, private, Sunday, and plantation.

Public daily schools required no fees and included several types which can be identified by their mode of financing and the racial group to which they catered; for present purposes, however, they can be considered under two major categories, the parochial school and the charity school. Parochial schools were largely supported by taxes levied by the parish vestries (sometimes supplemented by private contributions or endowments) and had originally been founded solely for the instruction of poor whites. As far as can be ascertained, no parochial schools accepted freedmen during the slave period. By 1829–30, poor whites in all parishes had access to a parochial school, while the eleven charity schools for freedmen and slaves[30] were distributed in only six of the parishes, four of the schools being located in Saint Michael (Table 20). Charity schools, whose basic

[28]It is difficult to be precise on these and other figures mentioned below. Unless otherwise noted, all subsequent information on schools during the period 1829–30 has been compiled from the often fragmentary data provided by parish rectors and published in *PP*, 1831–32, vol. 47, rept. 660, and Incorporated Society for the Conversion and Religious Instruction and Education of the Negro Slaves in the British West India Islands, *Annual Report, 1828* (London, 1829), and *Annual Report, 1833* (London, 1834).

[29]Incorporated Society for the Conversion . . . , *Annual Report, 1833*, pp. 48–65.

[30]There were also a handful of charity schools for poor whites. For example, the Central School was founded in Bridgetown in 1819 and was organized along the same lines as the Colonial Charity School. Also in Bridgetown, Harrison's Free School (later renamed Harrison College), which was opened in the eighteenth century, had elements of both a "charity" and a fee-paying system, as did Codrington College in Saint John, for which the Society for the Propagation of the Gospel had a "duty under Christopher Codrington's will to spend his endowment on the education of the white people of the island, not on Negro instruction" (J. Harry Bennett, *Bondsmen and Bishops: Slavery and Apprenticeship on the Codrington Plantations of Barbados, 1710–1838*, University of California Publications in History, vol. 62 [Berkeley and Los Angeles, 1958], p. 86). In 1829–30, Saint Joseph's parish had the "Charity School for White Girls, supported by voluntary subscriptions."

Table 20. Public Daily Schools, *ca.* 1829–30

| | Number and Type | | | Enrollment | | |
| | Slave-Freedman | White | | | | |
Parish	Charity	Parochial	Charity	Slaves	Freedmen	Whites
Saint Andrew	0	1	0	0	0	30
Christ Church	1	1	0	43	24	24
Saint George	0	2	0	0	0	30
Saint James	1	1	0	18	23	41
Saint John	2	1	1	49	73	56
Saint Joseph	0	2	1	0	0	28
Saint Lucy	0	1	0	0	0	30
Saint Michael	4	2	2	285	223	221
Saint Peter	1	1	0	20	23	36
Saint Philip	2	1	—	100	70	200
Saint Thomas	0	0	0	0	0	0
Total	11	13	4	515	436	696

Sources: *PP*, 1831–32, vol. 47, rept. 660; Incorporated Society for the Conversion . . . , *Annual Report, 1828*, and *Annual Report, 1833*. The parochial school for whites was not operating in Saint Thomas. Children from that parish attended the Saint James school, and the vestry of each parish contributed one-half of the finances for the school's maintenance.

educational features were the same as those of the Colonial Charity School, were financed by donations from freedmen (who, by 1827, had formed the Society for the Education of the Coloured Poor, and Other Charitable Relief[31]) and some "liberal" whites, but usually depended to a considerable degree on a fund controlled by the bishop of Barbados.

In all cases freedmen and slaves attended the same schools, and, as indicated above, these were kept distinct from the white ones. There were no racially mixed public schools, and there is no evidence that the white establishment ever considered integrating the schools racially; the parochial vestries reserved their schools for whites, and the efforts made by the Anglican church to increase educational facilities involved providing more schools for "poor" children of *each* racial group, and not schools for "poor" children in general, regardless of race.

Racial distinctions were also maintained among the teachers. In 1829–30 the public schools had approximately thirty-five paid teachers, most of

[31]See "Fourth Annual Report [for 1830] of the Society for the Education of the Coloured Poor, and for Other Charitable Relief," *Barbadian*, March 22, 1831. In the same year, the "Ladies' Branch Association for the Education of Female Children of the Coloured Poor on the Principles of the Established Church of England" was formed and worked in support of the Colonial Charity School for girls in Bridgetown (*ibid.*).

whom were males and seven of whom were freedmen.[32] Although some of the white teachers taught nonwhite children, freedman teachers taught only nonwhites; that is, in the public schools, white children were taught only by white teachers. In addition, differential salaries were paid teachers of each racial group. Public school salaries were generally paid on an annual basis and appeared to be comparable in a number of cases. The actual pay scale, however, was related to the race of the teacher and the race of the children he taught. Thus, freedman teachers who taught nonwhite children were paid approximately £1 sterling per annum per child, while white teachers who taught nonwhite pupils received an average of £2 sterling. When they taught white children, white teachers (sometimes the same as those who taught nonwhites) received an approximate average stipend of £3.5 sterling per child per annum. The differential pay scale reflected the fact that white students in public schools were being taught under lower student-teacher ratios than nonwhites. In 1829–30 there was an approximate average of from seventy to eighty nonwhite pupils per teacher, while the comparable average for white pupils was about twenty-five to thirty per teacher. However, the lower pay scale was also a manifestation of the discriminatory practices to which freedmen were exposed, and it served as another reminder of the barriers white society created to perpetuate its own superiority. Not only did freedman teachers not teach white children, but white teachers were paid less for teaching nonwhite ones, a dual statement by the white establishment of the lesser value of both the freedman teachers and the pupils they taught.

Racial distinctions had some, but a minor, effect on the public school curriculum. As a result of the dominant influence of the Anglican church, there was, as noted above, a heavy emphasis on sectarian studies. In all white schools, pupils were taught arithmetic, reading, and writing. At first the nonwhite schools established by Bishop Coleridge in 1825 omitted these subjects, "a point certainly not of any vital importance, and wisely conceded to prejudices which will in due time melt away."[33] These subjects were gradually introduced, however, and by the early 1830s reading, writing, and arithmetic were taught in all Anglican-supported schools, and in some the girls received sewing instruction as well. The charity schools, especially the National School for Coloured Children, encouraged pupils to enter the skilled trades or domestic services; although even minimal literacy skills were probably an asset in such occupations, what was probably more important in job acquisition was the implicit acknowledgment by the upper socioeconomic levels of the society that graduates from the

[32]The freedman teachers were John R. Lynch (Christ Church), James W. Drake (Saint James), Charles Phipps (Saint Michael), and four others, presumably all men, for whom last names are reported: Sealey, Nurse, Young, and Braithwaite (Saint Philip). See n. 28 for the sources on which this paragraph is based.

[33]Coleridge, *Six Months*, pp. 51–52.

schools adhered to values and norms that were considered appropriate for persons from the lower classes. That is, in terms of the educational goals of the schools, it is well to bear in mind, as Barnard noted for England, that "the educational ideal of the time was the training of the poor to an honest and industrious poverty which knew its place and was duly appreciative of any favours received."[34]

Private, or fee-paying, schools also educated freedmen, but it is difficult to ascertain the number of such schools, their availability to non-whites, and the number of nonwhites in attendance. These difficulties reflect incomplete information in the sources, which, in itself, is largely the result of the often temporary nature of the schools and wide fluctuations in their numbers from year to year.[35] However, some indication of freedman attendance and participation in private schools can be gained by citing a few specific cases. In 1827, in the parish of Saint Peter, at least thirteen freedman children received private educations, while twenty-two attended the charity school. In the same year, Saint Lucy had two private schools for freed children; each school had about ten pupils, and freedmen were the owners-teachers.[36] In Saint Andrew there were no public schools for non-whites in 1829–30, and the parochial school's white teacher was hired to give private lessons to three freedman children.[37] Additional cases derive from 1833: in Saint Joseph there were "in daily attendance at private schools" sixteen freedman children and twenty-three slave children, "the expense of whose education is defrayed by their parents"; in Saint Michael, where the bulk of freedmen were educated, 503 nonwhite children attended charity schools, but 1,613 attended private ones—how many of these were freedmen and how many were slaves is not mentioned in the source.[38]

The racial distinctions that were maintained in the public schools appear to have generally operated within the private ones as well. There is evidence of only two racially integrated private schools during the period 1829–33, although there may have been a few more; in 1829–30 a private school in Saint George was attended by twelve whites, eight slaves, and four freedmen, and in 1833 at a school in Saint Thomas "a few slaves, among some whites and free-coloured children," were taught by a widow and her daughter, who were given "a small stipend from the funds placed at his Lordship's disposal for such purpose."[39] The latter school was par-

[34]Barnard, *History of English Education*, p. 52; see also Coleridge, *Six Months*, p. 51.

[35]In the mid-1840s Schomburgk also found, with respect to private schools, that "their number and character cannot be ascertained with any accuracy" (*History of Barbados*, p. 106).

[36]Incorporated Society for the Conversion . . . , *Annual Report, 1827* (London, 1828), pp. 82, 83.

[37]*PP*, 1831–32, vol. 47, rept. 660.

[38]Incorporated Society for the Conversion . . . , *Annual Report, 1833*, app., pp. 50, 58.

[39]*Ibid.*, p. 57.

tially a charity one, and in both schools the white pupils presumably came from the lower classes.

With the exception of the Colonial Charity School, established in 1818, freedmen did not have access to public schools until the mid-1820s; thus, throughout most of the slave period they derived their literacy skills from private schools or individual tutoring. After the establishment of public schools, however, it is more difficult to assess the relative importance of private and charity schools in the acquisition of literacy skills. There are no island-wide enrollment figures for the private schools, and, although there are figures for charity school enrollment in 1829-30, there are no statistics on the total number of children in the island's freedman population at this time. Even so, private schools, especially in Saint Michael, were probably more important than the paucity of literary and statistical evidence suggests. For example, in 1833, as noted above, 2,116 nonwhite children were enrolled in Saint Michael's schools, but 76 percent of them were enrolled in private schools. Although the statistics do not provide a distinction between freedmen and slaves, a majority of the pupils were undoubtedly the children of freedmen—one can make this assumption because freedman parents had greater financial resources than slave parents, and because many slaveowners refused to incur expenses in the education of their slaves.

In general, then, although private schools must have been important for the education of freedmen, there is very little information on them and conjecture must, of necessity, take the place of concrete evidence. Many private schools for nonwhites, as well as whites, were probably rather small. It is not known if all of them met on a daily basis, and tutors may have accepted a few pupils with whom they met only occasionally. The curriculum seems to have been similar to that in the public schools, although some private tutors may have exposed freedman children to the classics and other subjects not included in the public curriculum.

In addition to their being educated in private schools on the island, some freedmen, of both sexes, attended schools in Britain. Samuel Prescod, a forceful and articulate leader in the freedmen's struggle for civil rights in the 1830s, and his wife "were both liberally educated in England,"[40] and in 1828 Nathaniel Roach, a friend of Prescod, returned from England, where he had been educated and had lived for twelve years; Roach later opened his own school in Bridgetown.[41] In 1837, London Bourne, one of Bridgetown's wealthiest merchants, sent his "promising son of eleven" to Edinburgh, "where he [was] to remain until he . . . received the honors of

---

[40] H. A. Vaughan writes that in Prescod's early life "he had little formal schooling," and suggests that he went to England to secure legal training shortly before emancipation ("Samuel Prescod: The Birth of a Hero," *New World Quarterly*, 3 [1966]: 56, 59).

[41] *Ibid.*, p. 59.

Scotland's far famed university."[42] The white mob that destroyed Bridge-town's Methodist chapel in 1823 even included "one person of colour, who had been educated in England" (and whose actions isolated him from the rest of the freedman community).[43] In general, freedman parents who could afford to send their children abroad for an education appear to have made considerable efforts to do so,[44] but there is no information on how many of these efforts were realized, and it must be assumed that this type of education was a luxury that relatively few could afford.

Sunday schools established by church groups for Christian education also provided reading instruction for some freedmen and a number of slaves. Methodist missionaries may have occasionally taught reading, but it is likely that such instruction was systematically started in their Sunday schools just prior to emancipation.[45] Although the Anglican and Moravian schools were established primarily for slaves, freedmen were not pro-hibited from attending, and it is also possible that some recently manu-mitted slaves had learned how to read at Sunday schools while they were still enslaved. During the 1820s and 1830s the Moravian Sunday schools (and evening schools) taught reading as an intrinsic feature of their pro-gram of religious instruction. In addition, the missionaries conducted classes at least once a week on various plantations near their two mission stations. As discussed in Chapter 7, Moravian activities were largely con-fined to slaves, but they occasionally included some freedmen.

By 1829–30 the Anglican church had Sunday schools for slaves and freedmen in all of the parishes; generally speaking, however, these schools had been made available to them only within the few preceding years. The average island-wide attendance around this time was approximately 380 nonwhites;[46] a minority of these, perhaps 50 or 60, appear to have been freedmen, most of whom attended in Bridgetown. Instruction at Anglican Sunday schools was generally oral. Reading was taught at about half the schools, but only to a minority of those attending. Only in Saint James and Saint Michael was reading a regular feature of the instructional pro-

---

[42]J. A. Thome and J. H. Kimball, *Emancipation in the West Indies* (New York, 1838), p. 75.

[43]W. J. Shrewsbury to Goy, November 11, 1823, quoted in John V. B. Shrewsbury, *Memorials of the Rev. William J. Shrewsbury* (London, 1868), p. 143.

[44]Thome and Kimball, *Emancipation in the West Indies*, p. 76.

[45]The Methodist public school in Bridgetown that Joseph Sturge and Thomas Harvey visited in 1837 "was commenced some years ago, by a colored man, who was a cabinet maker, in humble circumstances. He observed a number of children, accustomed to play in the street before his door, and conceived the idea of occupying their time and attention more profitably by teaching them to read. He succeeded, and his scholars soon became so numer-ous, that he was compelled to seek other means of having them instructed. His efforts re-sulted in the establishment of the present school, which is held in a small, dilapidated build-ing, crowded with about one hundred and fifty children" (*The West Indies in 1837* [London, 1838], p. 148).

[46]Incorporated Society for the Conversion . . . , *Annual Report, 1828*, app., pp. 9–12.

gram, and none of the schools taught writing. In 1829–30, the Saint Michael Sunday school was attended by 139 slaves, 30 freedmen, and 8 whites, and was taught by a freedman, a Mr. Lewalling; most, if not all, teachers in the other parishes were whites. By 1833, when the number of Anglican Sunday schools had increased to thirteen or fifteen, reading (but not writing) was regularly taught in the majority of them.[47]

It should be emphasized that the white establishment generally considered literacy instruction to be a means to Christian education, and its value was not viewed as extending beyond that goal. The rather rapid acceptance of reading in Anglican Sunday schools between 1829–30 and 1833 reflected not only its utility in religious instruction but also wider changes in Barbadian society, including a recognition of the value of literacy in the conversion of slaves. The establishment of plantation schools was a related manifestation of these changes.

Plantation schools were financed by owners and provided religious, and sometimes reading, instruction, primarily to slave children. These schools are discussed here because, as with Sunday schools, it is likely that they were the sources of literacy skills for slaves manumitted in the few years prior to general emancipation (a period when the number of manumissions increased), and some freedmen, such as the children of "militia tenants," may have attended these schools.

Plantation schools did not exist to any significant extent until the late 1820s. Their establishment was closely linked to the wider issue of missionary activities among slaves, and particularly to the use of reading in Christian education. Planters were generally reluctant to accept slave conversion as a general principle, but by the early nineteenth century, as the catechist on the Codrington plantations reported, "the opinion seems [to be] gaining ground that the religious instruction of young Negroes to a certain point will make them not only better Christians but even more profitable slaves than the present race."[48] This opinion grew slowly, but planters were even more hesitant about accepting reading instruction as a feature of the Christianizing process. "The planters urge," Governor Seaforth wrote in 1802, "that such instruction could be of no avail to a race of men doomed to . . . slavery, that extending their means of information could only awaken them to a keener sense of their situation which would of course render them more unhappy in themselves and more dangerous to their masters."[49]

Seaforth's opinion was undoubtedly confirmed for many planters in 1816, when literate slaves (and some freedmen) were accused of provoking an insurrection, and the leadership role of these slaves was apparently not

[47]*Ibid., 1833*, app., pp. 48–65.
[48]Moody to Bishop of Durham, July 16, 1803, Fulham Papers, vol. 2, p. 539, USPGA.
[49]Seaforth to Bishop of London, March 8, 1802, Seaforth Papers, 46/7/4, SRO.

forgotten during the early 1820s, when whites fearfully anticipated another slave revolt.[50] Coincidentally, during the latter period of political tension, Anglicans made efforts to organize missionary activities among the slaves, and these efforts, in turn, once again raised the question of reading instruction in Christian education. Although the Anglican church had long recognized that reading was one of the best devices for teaching Christianity to slave children,[51] when a group of parochial rectors and other whites gathered in 1823 to form "an association . . . for the purpose of affording religious instruction to the slave population," it was pointedly resolved that instruction should be oral.[52] Governor Henry Warde, a "liberal" on the slavery issue, also had grave apprehensions about the potential role of literate slaves. In a confidential letter to a friend he expressed not only his personal anxieties but also the sentiments of many slaveowners:

> It would require very little to move the black population to play a second St. Domingo scene. . . . Many, in their kind wishes to convert [the slaves] . . . to Christianity would have them all taught to read & write. Whenever this takes place (as they will probably read more of Carlisle than of their Bible), I conceive that the fate of the white population is decided. To cause a mass of mankind who have so long been in perfect ignorance should not be enlightened too suddenly. In my opinion they would not become better men but worse by reading unless you could ensure their not reading improper publications.[53]

In general, then, for many years the Christian education that existed on plantations was conducted orally. Reading instruction came to be accepted only by little more than a handful of the plantocracy in the late 1820s and early 1830s, when the view was more generally accepted that "the Negroes converted to Christianity are by far the most honest, *tractable*, and moral of their colour";[54] this general sentiment was shared by some freedmen, who, for example, in the Belgrave address of 1823, noted that Christianity would teach the slaves "to be contented and happy with their present highly improved position."[55]

---

[50]See, for example, Minutes of the Barbados Council, March 22, 1826, CO 31/50.

[51]See, for example, *Instructions for Missionaries to the West India Islands* (London, 1795), pp. 9–10. A chaplain on the Codrington plantations raised the issue of reading in religious instruction as early as 1746, but the Society for the Propagation of the Gospel did nothing about it; instruction on the plantations was oral until 1795, when reading was introduced into the program for the religious education of slave children (Bennett, *Bondsmen and Bishops*, pp. 84, 88, 106–9).

[52]"Resolutions Passed at a General Meeting of Persons Concerned in the Government of Slaves," September 15, 1823, CO 28/92, no. 47.

[53]Warde to Clinton, October 10, 1821, Rhodes House Library, Oxford University.

[54]Seaforth to Bishop of London, March 8, 1802, Seaforth Papers, 46/7/4, italics added.

[55]See pp. 91–93.

In 1828 there were at least some plantations in all of the parishes (but a definite minority in each) where religious instruction was given to slaves on a regular basis. Instructors were usually missionaries or Anglican catechists, sometimes plantation managers or overseers (or members of their families), or a white servant, and, occasionally, paid tutors.[56] Although literate plantation slaves often voluntarily taught reading to the illiterate ones,[57] reading instruction was rarely given by whites at the plantation schools; as the rector of Saint James admitted in 1829, a "difficulty . . . [was] met with to induce proprietors to allow instruction in reading the scriptures to their young slaves."[58] By 1833, however, when slaves were regularly receiving Christian education on many plantations, approximately 50 of the island's approximately 400 plantations[59] conducted daily schools, and many of the 50 included reading as part of their educational programs.[60]

By the early years of apprenticeship there were more plantation schools and "few or no estates where there are not some among the Negro population who can read."[61] Some apprentices, however, were reluctant to send their children to plantation schools, for "fear that by so doing their children will become bound to the estate."[62] Instead, they sent them to public schools, if any were located in the vicinity of their homes, or, on occasion, to small private schools. In a number of parishes, and especially in Saint Michael, public educational facilities increased as a result of the stimulus provided by various church groups and assistance from the British government. Teachers were black and "colored," the schools were well attended, and frequently "the accommodation [was] not nearly equal to the wants of the people";[63] in addition, many children who could not go to school

[56]By 1833 the number of hired tutors appears to have increased. Most were white; there is concrete evidence for only two paid freedman teachers, but there may have been more (Incorporated Society for the Conversion . . . , *Annual Report, 1833*, app., p. 55; *PP*, 1831–32, vol. 47, rept. 660).

[57]See replies to query 19, "Returns to Questions Addressed to the Clergy of . . . Barbados . . . up to December 31, 1828," Incorporated Society for the Conversion . . . , *Annual Report, 1828*, app.

[58]Boromé, "William Bell," p. 26.

[59]*PP*, 1835, vol. 50, rept. 278, p. 83.

[60]Incorporated Society for the Conversion . . . , *Annual Report, 1833*, app., pp. 48–65.

[61]Governor Lionel Smith, quoted in Sturge and Harvey, *The West Indies in 1837*, app., p. xxxii.

[62]"Papers . . . in Explanation of the Measures Adopted . . . for Giving Effect to the Act for the Abolition of Slavery . . . ," pt. 4, *PP*, 1837, vol. 53, rept. 521-1, p. 403.

[63]*Ibid.*, p. 401. During a conversation with the bishop of Barbados, Sturge and Harvey learned that the church-supported schools were experiencing difficulties with black and "colored" teachers, not because of "the want of qualification" on their part, but because of "their preference for more lucrative employments" (*The West Indies in 1837*, p. 135), presumably in the growing number of private schools for freed and apprenticed children. "Some of the most popular instructors," Thome and Kimball observed, "are colored men and ladies and one of these ranks high as a teacher of the ancient and modern languages" (*Emancipation in the West Indies*, pp. 75–76).

"receive[d] instruction from other children, and improve[d] themselves by attending the Sunday schools."[64] Thus, the stress on literacy or education, already clearly evident in the slave period, became especially strong during the Apprenticeship period and was commensurate with the increase in educational facilities for nonwhites. "There is a desire," reported one stipendiary magistrate, "for educating their children amongst the apprentices"; another, more critical of this "desire," observed that apprenticed "parents entertain the fanciful idea of rearing their offspring for employments to which nature has not assigned them, for in no instance will they entertain the idea of agriculture as a pursuit."[65]

Plantation field labor was the hallmark of slave status; to the extent to which one could remove himself, or his children, from this labor, he was removed from the classic and most degraded position of the slave. Education and literacy became desirable goals when and if they permitted or reinforced occupational mobility, such as entrance into the skilled trades or domestic services. Even given the limited opportunities of a monocrop plantation society and its relative lack of occupational diversity, this mobility was perceived as potentially facilitated by possession of minimal literacy skills, and equally, if not more, important, by accommodation to the European-type values and norms implied within the Christian-oriented education that slaves received. That is, those who manifested the least African or African-like cultural attributes were, in effect, rewarded and had greater chances to escape from the more oppressive aspects of the slave regimen—the system itself reinforced those who acculturated to the European-type creole patterns of Barbadian society.

Literacy and religious education, then, could assist the slave in elevating himself from the lowest echelons of the slave hierarchy, and, in a similar fashion, these attributes helped the freedman distinguish himself from the mass of the slaves, who were largely illiterate and to whom literacy was consciously denied during most of the slave period. Long before the appearance of public schools, freedmen attempted, in one way or another, to acquire an education, however limited it may have been in many cases. And, as with Christianity, education—aside from whatever implications it had for nonagricultural occupational opportunities, especially in the urban areas—contributed to a maximization of the freedman's status by reinforcing the distinction between himself and the slave.

It must be stressed, however, that the education received by poor freedmen in non-fee-paying schools toward the end of the slave period largely involved the rote learning of religious and scriptural subjects. The white establishment, which was primarily responsible for the introduction of

---

[64]Sturge and Harvey, *The West Indies in 1837*, p. 135.
[65]"Papers . . . in Explanation of the Measures adopted . . . for Giving Effect to the Act for the Abolition of Slavery . . . ," pp. 393, 414.

charity, Sunday, and plantation schools, was not concerned with producing an intellectually aware and well-educated population of poorer freedmen and slaves, anymore than it was interested in having a lower-class white population that would challenge its own class privileges. Although reading and writing were part of the Colonial Charity School's curriculum from the school's inception in 1818, literacy skills were primarily taught as devices to facilitate Christian education; even so, these subjects were not at first introduced in the new charity schools established by the bishop of Barbados in 1825, and were not common in Anglican Sunday schools until shortly before emancipation. The educational system emphasized religious, not secular, subjects and stressed the Christian and class values that best served the white establishment—submissiveness and obedience to authority, acquiescence and acceptance of secular society, a concern with rewards in the afterlife, and so forth. The definition of education was very narrow, and, by emphasizing conservative religious values, the educational system thus favored accommodation to the social order and protection of the interests of the upper classes; it was an educational system that was concerned with producing a lower-class population that, as Barnard observed for England, "knew its place."[66] In Barbados, however, the situation was compounded by the factor of racial ancestry, and, to the extent that racial characteristics were associated with class status, the church-dominated or church-influenced schools helped perpetuate the linkage between class and race.

Thus, as with other West Indian societies during the slave period, Barbados was "not in any sense an educated one."[67] The majority of slaves were excluded from educational facilities, there were many illiterate whites and freedmen, and, for those who were referred to as "educated," education by and large meant possession of basic literacy skills and an awareness of scriptural precepts. Even by local standards for the period, relatively few freemen of either racial group were considered well-educated, but some freedmen had opportunities to acquire educations which surpassed most of their peers and many in the white population.

Despite the "restrictions under which they [had] formerly labored," freedmen wrote in an 1834 petition, they had "among them individuals fitted by education and gentlemanly habits, if not by equal wealth, to be entitled to participate with their white fellow subjects in . . . posts of honor or emolument."[68] The white society was extremely reluctant to allow freedmen into such positions, but it did not doubt that the freedman community included well-educated people. Such freedmen were among

[66]Barnard, *History of English Education*, p. 52.
[67]Shirley C. Gordon, *A Century of West Indian Education* (London, 1963), p. 18.
[68]"Address of the Free Coloured and Free Black Inhabitants of Bridgetown" to the Council and Assembly, April 2, 1834, CO 28/113.

those who provided leadership for their community in political and social affairs, and most of them were apparently freeborn and came from wealthy families.[69] There were others, however, who had been born slaves and who, by their diligence and native abilities, became well educated and created a life style commensurate with this education. Joseph Thorne, for example, the Anglican catechist, was born a slave; as a young man he educated himself "in a plain manner" and earned his living as a shoemaker. When Thome and Kimball made his acquaintance and visited his home in 1837, they were

> struck with the scientific appearance of Mr. Thorne's parlor. On one side was a large library of religious, historical, and literary works, the selection of which displayed no small taste and judgement. On the opposite side of the room was a fine cabinet of minerals and shells. In one corner stood a number of curious relics of the aboriginal Caribs, such as bows and arrows, etc., together with interesting fossil remains. On the tops of the book-cases and mineral stand, were birds of rare species, procured from the South American Continent. The centre table was ornamented with shells, specimens of petrifications, and elegantly bound books. The remainder of the furniture of the room was costly and elegant.[70]

"That so many of the colored people should have obtained wealth and education," Thome and Kimball concluded in general from their visit to Barbados, "is a matter of astonishment, when we consider the numerous discouragements with which they have ever been doomed to struggle."[71] And, indeed, one need go no further than a reading of the freedmen's petitions during the struggle for civil rights to acknowledge not only educational achievements but also intellectual abilities. In fact, Barbados was certainly no exception to the general rule that, in societies controlled by whites and based on their own notions of racial supremacy, the subordinated racial groups were able to achieve intellectually, despite their limited opportunities and the restrictions placed on their mobility, and these achievements increased as their opportunities expanded.

In the late 1820s and early 1830s many of the poorer freedmen who attended charity schools with slaves had probably been slaves themselves or the children of slaves. At this period, as discussed earlier, the number of manumissions was increasing, and the manumitted slaves swelled the ranks of lower-class freedmen. Since education was a valued goal and many could not afford private schools, freedmen had no choice but to enter the charity schools to which nonwhites, regardless of group status,

---

[69]See, for example, I. W. [J. W.] Orderson, *Spare Minutes at the Pier; or, a Short Discussion on the Equality of Rights That May Be Granted to the Free Coloured Inhabitants of this Island* (Barbados, 1831), pp. 5–6.

[70]Thome and Kimball, *Emancipation in the West Indies*, p. 73.

[71]*Ibid.*, p. 76.

were confined. In these cases lower-class freedmen probably felt that status distinctions between themselves and the slaves were temporarily irrelevant and/or offset by the pragmatic benefits that could be derived from the educational system. The freedman community itself was financially unable to create a network of freedman charity schools (nor is there any suggestion it ever attempted to do so); the schools required financial support from white groups, within and without the island, and these groups were primarily interested in the religious education of slaves, not freedmen. There is no indication that the Anglican church, for example, was sympathetic to the support of charity schools that were solely for freedmen, and without its support these schools could not have been maintained. Wealthier freedmen, however, supported the charity schools, such as the National School for Coloured Children; in addition, they formed societies for the "education of the coloured poor." This support suggests that wealthier freedmen shared the attitudes and values of whites at comparable socioeconomic levels, felt that such charitable endeavors were an expected concomitant of their own class position, and consciously or unconsciously also viewed the schools as devices for supporting class distinctions between themselves and poorer freedmen, especially the recently manumitted slaves.[72]

Thus, not only was Barbadian society racially divided, but, as has already been alluded to and discussed in earlier chapters, each racial group of freemen was internally stratified by criteria such as birth, property and wealth, and education. The educational system supported and reflected these class and racial divisions, by the segregation of facilities, the duality of the private and public school systems, and a curriculum in the public schools which stressed accommodation to the status quo. Class distinctions, in turn, had important implications not only for the nature of the freedman community, in particular, but also for its place in the Barbadian social order.

[72]See, for example, Orderson, *Spare Minutes*, p. 12.

IX

FREEDMEN IN THE BARBADIAN SOCIAL ORDER

THE STATUS OF FREEDMEN AND WHITE RACISM

Non-Barbadian whites, usually British visitors or temporary residents, who commented on the island's social order often stressed the fundamental importance of race as a determinant of social position and the castelike status of the freedman. J. A. Waller, for example, observed that, for the white creole, "no property, however considerable, can ever raise a man or woman of colour, not even when combined with education, to the proper rank of a human being."[1] J. Sturge and T. Harvey noted how white creole ideology involved "the belief that the blacks are by nature of an inferior race, and born to servile condition; and the spirit of caste cherished between the white, mixed, and black races."[2] S. Hodgson, who was in Barbados during the mid-1830s, also observed, but in particularly strong language, the effects of white racism on the maintenance of distinctions between freedman and white:

> Woe, woe, to the unhappy wretch, if among his ancestry can be numbered one in whose veins flowed some of the African blood; never can he hope to pass the barrier between him and these illustrious gentry! Let him be possessed of fortune, of polished manners, of spotless reputation; let him have travelled through Europe, have received and profited by an enlightened education, all these advantages will avail him nothing; hourly will he be taunted with what these European savages denominate his Negro blood, and for ever will society be barred against him.[3]

In comparing the depths of racism and hostility in Barbados with that in other West Indian colonies, it was not unusual for outsiders to stress, as did Sturge and Harvey, that "prejudice against color is stronger in Barbadoes than in any other colony," and they often attributed this prejudice to

[1]John A. Waller, *A Voyage in the West Indies* (London, 1820), p. 95.
[2]Joseph Sturge and Thomas Harvey, *The West Indies in 1837* (London, 1838), pp. 141–42.
[3]Studholme Hodgson, *Truths from the West Indies* (London, 1838), p. 59.

190

the existence in Barbados of a relatively large and old white creole popula-tion.[4] The racism of Barbadian whites was manifest in a number of areas of social life and was reflected in the laws they passed. Although a British parliamentary commission in 1823 found that the slave society was "un-deniably undergoing a beneficial change" and that many of the laws were "antiquated" and "disregarded," the laws did "retain a certain effi-cacy. . . . They draw an impassable line; they raise an insurmountable bar-rier between the white and the black and coloured population; they record an immeasurable distance; they attest an unexampled degradation."[5]

In her characterization of the Leeward Islands, Elsa Goveia effectively summarized some basic principles which are equally applicable to the slave society of Barbados:

> The West Indian whites in the plantation colonies had come to regard their racial identity and exclusiveness as the bulwark of their power and privileges; and they used their control of the colonial society to ensure that no Negro, slave or free, should be able to regard himself as the equal of a white, however poor or humble his origins or station might be. Thus . . . racial inequality and subordination . . . [were] the funda-mental principles of economic, political, and social organization. The slave society . . . was integrated on the basis of a hierarchy of racial groupings linked to differences of civil and political status and of eco-nomic and social opportunity. A heavy emphasis on racial particularism characterized the entire social order.[6]

During the period focused on in this study, the legal and social system of Barbados was consciously oriented toward the preservation of white supremacy and confined freedmen to a subordinate position. They were prevented from gaining the civil rights and social privileges which were the concomitants of the status of white freemen. The freedman group was internally differentiated; some individuals' property, education, wealth, and personal talents surpassed that of many whites, and many freedmen shared the norms, values, and life style of the white population. These fac-tors, however, did not substantially alter the freedman's position in the social hierarchy. A freedman could never be considered white, and

---

[4]Sturge and Harvey, *The West Indies in 1837*, pp. 141–42. For examples of other observa-tions on the castelike position of freedmen and the racial prejudice of creole whites, see Smith to Stanley, May 23, 1833, and July 23, 1833, CO 28/111; Warde to Horton, January 20, 1827, CO 28/100; [Benjamin Browne], *The Yarn of a Yankee Privateer*, ed. Nathaniel Hawthorne (New York, 1926), pp. 103–4; J. A. Thome and J. H. Kimball, *Emancipation in the West Indies* (New York, 1838), p. 79; "Notes on Slavery, Made During a Recent Visit to Barbadoes," *Negro's Friend*, no. 18 (London, [1830]), p. 10; and William Dickson, *Letters on Slavery, to Which Are Added Addresses to the Whites and to the Free Negroes of Barbados* (London, 1789), pp. 57–58.

[5]"First Report of the Commission of Inquiry into the Administration of Civil and Criminal Justice in the West Indies," *PP*, 1825, vol. 15, rept. 517, p. 15.

[6]Elsa V. Goveia, *Slave Society in the British Leeward Islands at the End of the Eight-eenth Century* (New Haven: Yale University Press, 1965), p. 312.

phenotypic differences among freedmen did not result in legal distinctions in their status. Unlike Jamaica, no one in Barbados of known or perceived Negroid ancestry, regardless of generational distance, could achieve a position of legal equality with whites; moreover, the Barbados legislature, in contrast to the Jamaican one, did not pass private acts granting certain categories of freedmen special privileges exempting them from the disabling acts under which the freedman group as a whole suffered.[7] Nor did phenotypic differences among Barbadian freedmen have a significant moderating effect upon the way in which freedmen were socially treated and regarded by whites. Samuel Prescod, for example, an English visitor reported, "has no distinguishing marks of Negro complexion, and in England he would be esteemed a gentleman, whilst in Barbadoes he is in some degree despised as a coloured man."[8] In general, then, the free population in Barbados was rigidly stratified on the basis of racial ancestry into superordinate and subordinate groups. The subordinate position of the freedman was determined by the dominant white group, which defined this position by Negroid ancestry; anyone with this ancestry, regardless of how phenotypically Caucasoid he appeared, and despite the personal attributes he possessed, was permanently bound within the subordinate group.

These societal features gave the appearance of a racially defined caste-like system, but the freedman's status was not clearly established, by virtue of the fact that he was neither slave nor entirely free—that is, he was not entitled to the rights and privileges whites accorded to themselves. This fact implies that the freedman occupied an intermediate status between free and slave, and, if one were to delineate the absence or presence of sociolegal rights and privileges on a continuum and place slaves at one end and whites at the other, freedmen would undeniably fall somewhere between the two extremes. There was, however, no legally defined intermediate status for the freedman that might have correlated with such a hypothetical continuum. The absence of this definition provided a wider latitude for varying interpretations of what the freedman's position in the society ideally should be, and it contributed to the essential instability and ambiguity of that position.

As a freeman, the freedman was a British subject and could theoretically lay claim to the legal rights held by white freemen; moreover, he shared with whites the obligations of citizenship, such as payment of taxes and service in the militia. Freedmen apparently neither doubted nor questioned their status as British subjects, nor was this status challenged by the

---

[7]See, for example, Edward Brathwaite, *The Development of Creole Society in Jamaica, 1770–1820* (London: Oxford University Press, 1971), pp. 171–72; Douglas Hall, "Jamaica," in *Neither Slave Nor Free: The Freedman of African Descent in the Slave Societies of the New World*, ed. David W. Cohen and Jack P. Greene (Baltimore: The Johns Hopkins University Press, 1972), pp. 196, 199–201.

[8]William Lloyd, *Letters from the West Indies during a visit in the Autumn of 1836 and the Spring of 1837* (London, [1837]), p. 17; see also Thome and Kimball, *Emancipation in the West Indies*, pp. 74–75.

Crown or uniformly denied by white colonial society. When, for example, a House of Assembly bill seriously threatened the freedman's property rights at the beginning of the nineteenth century, one Council member found the bill unconstitutional because it denied "free subjects . . . those rights and privileges legally and constitutionally incident to freedom"; another member doubted if the Crown would approve a colonial law that "destroy[ed] the rights of free subjects in their property already acquired."[9] The freedmen's status as "free subjects" was fundamental to the way in which they viewed their position in Barbadian society, and it provided the major moral underpinning of the reformist appeals they directed to legislative bodies. Their self-image as British subjects was a positive one which, in their minds, legitimized their claims to civil rights. "We His Majesty's dutiful and loyal subjects," freedmen wrote in what was perhaps their earliest petition calling for a change in their legal status, "declare our unfeigned and inviolable attachment by principle and affection to our King and Constitution."[10] In 1823, they again petitioned: "There are certain parts of our Colonial Code which exempts us from participating with our white brethren in certain privileges and to which, as British subjects, we humbly conceive we have a claim."[11] Seven years later their requests for civil rights were, they emphasized, "claims which we conceive ourselves justly entitled to as British, Christian, faithful and loyal subjects."[12]

The absence of a legally defined position of intermediacy and the contradiction between their status as free British subjects, on the one hand, and the circumscription of that status by racial qualifiers associated with Negroid ancestry, on the other, resulted in the essential instability and ambiguity of the freedmen's position in the social system. The freedmen's struggle for civil rights can largely be viewed as a collective effort to resolve this ambiguity by maximizing their free status; they did not aim to establish a clearly defined position of permanent legal intermediacy between whites and slaves.

Freedmen were profoundly aware of their indefinite and subordinate status and were not reconciled to the limitations on their freedom. "Our words are inadequate to express," they wrote in 1799, "the due sense we have of our subordinate state," but "however humble our situation and condition may be," as freemen they felt themselves entitled to "the protection of the laws."[13] Most freedmen evidently shared a desire for such protection and the right of testimony. For a period of time, however, some

[9]Minutes of the Barbados Council, November 1, 1803, Lucas MSS, BPL.

[10]"The Humble Memorial and Remonstrance of the Free Coloured People . . . ," October 14, 1799, Minutes of the Barbados Council, October 15, 1799, ibid.

[11]"The Humble Address of the Undersigned Free Coloured Inhabitants . . . ," December 17, 1823, printed in Barbadian, February 25, 1824.

[12]"We . . . the Undersigned Free Coloured Inhabitants . . . ," July 15, 1830, printed in ibid., April 22, 1831.

[13]"The Humble Memorial and Remonstrance of the Free Coloured People . . . ," October 14, 1799, Minutes of the Barbados Council, October 15, 1799, Lucas MSS.

appeared (as a matter of political expediency or genuine conviction) to rest satisfied with limited rights that served their most immediate interests and functioned to clearly distinguish them from the slaves. The group which in 1817 thanked the legislature for granting the right of testimony emphasized that this right "was all we wished for, having . . . obtained that we are perfectly satisfied and contented"; "where slavery exists," the group acknowledged, "there must necessarily be a distinction between the white and free coloured inhabitants, and . . . there are privileges which the latter do not expect to enjoy."[14] Although some of these men later participated in actions which contradicted these views, the freedman community in general appears always to have had political divisions between conservative and progressive elements; however, these divisions increasingly came to hinge on disagreements over strategies and means by which to achieve complete civil equality with whites, rather than on disagreements over the desirability of this goal.

In any event, as the freedman community grew larger, became more organized, and achieved greater economic success, and as reformist pressures from Britain increased, the civil rights movement became less equivocal on the nature of rights sought and less hesitant in expressing the pace at which these rights should be achieved. Those freedmen who publicly expressed an acceptance of permanent sociolegal distinctions between white and freed became noticeably fewer; those, such as Samuel Prescod, who most forcefully challenged these distinctions and articulated a progressive concern with status maximization became leaders and were able to rally the greatest support from within the freedman community.

In the early phases of the civil rights struggle, freedmen concentrated on the security of their property and persons and the right of testimony, but as time went on they sought removal of other legal disabilities and the lessening of discrimination in various areas of social life. Ultimately their goals were defined not only in legal but also in social terms as they sought a level of parity with whites. In what was perhaps their final petition during the period of slavery, they expressed in no uncertain terms that it was "impossible for them to rest satisfied until they . . . [were] placed on an equal footing with the present class of freeholders [that is, whites] in all respects"[15]—a public expression of status aspirations which would have been unthinkable a few decades earlier.

The subordinate position of the freedman was expressed in a wide variety of discriminatory practices, some of which derived their strength from the legal code and others from the force of social conventions

---

[14]"To the Honorable John Beckles, Speaker of the House of Assembly and the Rest of the Honorable and Worshipful Members," March 4, 1817, CO 28/86. See also "The Humble Petition of the Free Coloured People, Inhabitants of the Island," entered into the Minutes of the Barbados Council, November 1, 1803, Lucas MSS.

[15]"Address of the Free Colored and Free Black Inhabitants of Bridgetown to the Council and Assembly," April 2, 1834, CO 28/113.

based on the premise of white supremacy. Although the "brown privilege bill" of 1831 formally eliminated social prerequisites to the definition of a freeholder and extended to freedmen the political rights of voting and holding elective office—thus removing the final legal constraints on their free status—the legislature wrote the bill in such a way that it implicitly discriminated against freedmen. In general, the withdrawal of legal disabilities in the twilight of the slave period did not fundamentally alter the social status of freedmen, and they continued to experience the racial discrimination that white colonial society had consciously nurtured throughout Barbadian history. "As far as legislative enactments could remove the unnatural and impolitic distinctions between us and our white fellow-subjects," freedmen wrote in 1833, "those distinctions have been removed. . . . [However,] the distinctions are, in reality, still kept up; and are now rendered, in consequence of that enactment [the "brown privilege bill"], more obviously invidious, and more galling to those whose prejudice they operate."[16]

The catalog of "unnatural and impolitic distinctions" was sizable, but not unusual for a society internally dominated and controlled by a white population imbued with an ideology of racial supremacy. Freedmen were excluded from positions of leadership, responsibility, and prestige in the Anglican church, an institution to which they were heavily committed; there were no freedman ministers throughout the slave period, and there is evidence of only one lay catechist. In addition, freedmen (as well as slaves) were prevented from taking communion at the same time as whites, and nonwhites were confined to special seating areas within the churches. Freedmen were neither encouraged to attend, nor admitted to, Codrington College, owned by the Church of England's Society for the Propagation of the Gospel.[17] Public schools and the vast majority of private schools were racially segregated, and racial distinctions were maintained among the teachers with respect to the pupils they taught and the salaries they received. Whites and freedmen were taxed by the parish vestries, but freedmen could not serve on these vestries, and the indigent among them could neither attend the publicly financed parochial schools nor receive pensions or other forms of relief provided by vestries from tax funds, as did the white poor.[18] Freedmen were obliged to serve in the militia, but were

[16]"The Humble Loyal Address of His Majesty's Free Coloured and Free Black Subjects . . . ," May 6, 1833, printed in *Barbadian*, May 15, 1833.

[17]Between 1830 and 1900, 390 divinity students were educated at Codrington College, but only 10 percent were nonwhite, and all of them attended the college in the post-Apprenticeship period (see Jean Bullen and Helen E. Livingstone, "Of the State and Advancement of the College," in *Codrington Chronicle: An Experiment in Anglican Altruism on a Barbados Plantation, 1710–1834*, ed. Frank J. Klingberg, University of California Publications in History, vol. 37 [Berkeley and Los Angeles: University of California Press, 1949], p. 121).

[18]See, for example, *PP*, 1826, vol. 28, rept. 353; Combermere to Bathurst, January 18, 1819, CO 28/88; and Edward Eliot, *Christianity and Slavery; in a Course of Lectures*

denied commissions and other important leadership positions within it; the militia units themselves were segregated, and freedmen were formed into their own companies led by white officers.

In the early nineteenth century the legislature attempted to curtail severely the freedmen's property rights, and the social conventions based on racism prevented freedmen from acquiring good agricultural land of consequential acreage; with few exceptions, wealthier freedmen were unable to become plantation owners. Freedman "merchants of wealth were shut out of the merchants' exchange" in Bridgetown, and "colored gentlemen were not allowed to become members of literary associations, nor subscribers to town libraries."[19] There is suggestive evidence that whites reserved certain residential areas in the towns for their own use, and segregation was maintained in the Bridgetown jail.[20] From 1721 to 1830 most freedmen were legally prohibited from testifying in proceedings involving whites, although the testimony of whites could be used against freedmen. There is no indication—and it is highly unlikely—that freedmen served on juries prior to their legal debarment from doing so in 1721, and from that year until 1831 they could neither vote nor hold elective office; not until 1843 did Samuel Prescod take his seat as the first "colored" member in the House of Assembly's over two-hundred-year-old history, and it is doubtful that he would have been elected had it not been for the black and "colored" vote in the Bridgetown constituency from which he ran for office.

Eligible freedmen of wealth and education were also debarred from prestigious appointive positions in the civil-political structure and could not become justices of the peace or magistrates. Attaining positions such as magistracies became an important political issue to freedmen after they achieved legal equality in 1831, and they viewed their inability to gain these appointments as a symbol of their subordinate status; only in 1836, after considerable struggle, were two of their body appointed to magistracies.[21] "Parents, however wealthy," Thome and Kimball reported, "had no inducement to educate their sons for the learned professions, since no force of talent nor extent of acquirement could hope to break down the granite walls and iron bars which prejudice had erected round the pulpit, the bar, and the bench."[22]

Preached at the Cathedral and Parish Church of St. Michael, Barbados (London, 1833), pp. 225–26.

[19]Thome and Kimball, *Emancipation in the West Indies*, p. 79.

[20]"Humble Petition of the Debtors in the Prison," April 16, 1830, CO 28/106; see also Minutes of the House of Assembly, March 20, 1821, CO 31/49.

[21]Sturge and Harvey, *The West Indies in 1837*, app., p. xxxiv. Thome and Kimball reported that in 1837 one of the stipendiary magistrates was a "Mr. Galloway . . . a colored gentleman, highly respected for his talents" (*Emancipation in the West Indies*, p. 66). In actual fact, "Galloway" may have been Joseph Garraway, a stipendiary magistrate who assumed office in November 1836 (see "Papers . . . in Explanation of the Measures Adopted . . . for Giving Effect to the Act for the Abolition of Slavery . . . ," pt. 4, *PP*, 1837, vol. 53, rept. 521-1, p. 403).

[22]Thome and Kimball, *Emancipation in the West Indies*, p. 76.

When addressing freedmen, whites would generally eschew forms of address such as Mr., Mrs., or Miss. G. Pinckard, for example, observed how "the title Mrs. seems to be reserved, solely, for the ladies from Europe, and the white creoles, and to form a distinction between them and the women of colour of all classes and description—none of whom, of whatever shade or degree, are dignified by this appelation."[23] Baptismal, burial, and marriage records designated the racial affiliation of the freedman.[24] Illustrating how "every opportunity was maliciously seized to taunt the colored people with their complexion," Thome and Kimball related the case of "a gentleman of the highest worth," who "stated that several years ago he applied to the proper office for a license to be married. The license was accordingly made out and handed to him. It was expressed in the following insulting style: 'T— H—, F.M., is licensed to marry H— L—, F.C.W.' The initials F.M. stood for *free mulatto*, and F.C.W. for *free colored woman*! The gentleman took out his knife and cut out the initials; and was then threatened with a prosecution for forging his license!"[25]

Freedmen were urged to maintain "a respectful deference to the whites [as an] . . . indispensable duty";[26] they were expected to "know their place" and not to step out of the confines into which white society chose to keep them. Reactions to violations of customary social taboos ranged from the physical to the verbal. As a young man, Samuel Prescod was "summarily ejected" from the House of Assembly while simply listening to the proceedings; "this show of interest on his part was regarded as an act of presumption."[27] When, in 1833, Thomas J. Cummins, a wealthy and prominent member of the freedman community, applied for an appointive position for which he was qualified, but which had been traditionally reserved for whites, he was personally insulted for his audacity.

Yet, when freedmen acquiesced, or appeared to acquiesce, to their subordinate social position and assumed the role of compliance and accommodation expected by whites, their behavior could be met with public approbation—an approbation which reiterated the values and demeanor that whites found supportive of the status quo and appropriate for those who belonged to a subordinate group. In 1808 the death of John Straker Thomas, a relatively wealthy carpenter, claimed the notice of a local newspaper because of "the uniform unassuming tenor of his life, which af-

[23]George Pinckard, *Notes on the West Indies*, 2 vols. (London, 1806), 1:249; see also R. R. Madden, *A Twelve Months' Residence in the West Indies during the Transition from Slavery to Apprenticeship*, 2 vols. (London, 1835), 1: 24.

[24]See Parish Registers, BDA.

[25]Thome and Kimball, *Emancipation in the West Indies*, p. 79, italics in the original. The freedman was undoubtedly Thomas Harris, a wealthy and prominent member of the freedman community with whom Thome and Kimball had some lengthy conversations (*ibid.*, pp. 72–73).

[26]Dickson, *Letters on Slavery*, p. 174.

[27]H. A. Vaughan, "Samuel Prescod: The Birth of a Hero," *New World Quarterly*, 3 (1966): 56.

forded an example of humility and industry to that class of society in which he was placed, as they would do well to follow and imitate."[28] In 1831, when some freedmen challenged the restrictive seating arrangements in the Saint Michael Cathedral, they were publicly informed to "remember their situation" and to "exhibit those most beautiful features of the Christian character, meekness and humility"; those who did not participate in these events were found properly "humble, inoffensive and respectful."[29] The right of testimony was extended in 1817 to a portion of the freedman community, which included the "most respectable of that class," whose behavior the plantocracy judged "highly meritorious" during the 1816 slave revolt.[30] And the House of Assembly considered the 1823 Belgrave address as "loyal and dutiful" because it "exhibited the grateful appreciation of the protection enjoyed by the Free Coloured Body"; in fact, the House expressed its "most pleasurable feeling" that the signatories were led by Jacob Belgrave, the wealthy plantation-owner, "a person whose fidelity and attachment to the local interests of the community, so justly entitle him to the favorable consideration of this House."[31]

Belgrave was viewed as a "very intelligent man . . . of the highest respectability of character,"[32] but, regardless of how "respectable," "enlightened," or wealthy whites may have judged individuals such as Belgrave, or other freedmen of his class, to be, this did not prevent the maintenance and perpetuation of a rigid social distance or generally challenge the view that the freedman group should remain in a position of subordinacy. White creoles, particularly those of the middle and upper classes, avoided contacts and relations with freedmen which might imply social equality. "Social intercourse," as Thome and Kimball reported, "was utterly interdicted. To visit the houses [of wealthy and educated freedmen] . . . and especially to sit down at their tables, would have been a loss of caste."[33] Waller made similar observations, based on his year's residence in 1807–8, and also recounted how he "was once severely reprehended by a lady at Bridgetown, for having been seen walking in the street with a surgeon of a frigate who happened to be a man of colour, though brought up in England, and educated at the University of Edinburgh."[34] A Method-

---

[28]Quoted in E. G. Sinckler, "Births, Deaths, and Marriages from the *Barbados Mercury* and *Bridgetown Gazette*, 1805 to 1818," in *Caribbeana*, ed. V. L. Oliver, 6 vols. (London, 1910–20), 2: 42.

[29]Quoted in Vaughan, "Samuel Prescod," pp. 57–58.

[30]*The Report from a Select Committee of the House of Assembly, Appointed to Inquire into the Origin, Causes, and Progress of the Late Insurrection* (Barbados, [1818]), p. 11.

[31]Resolutions passed by the House of Assembly, February 18, 1824, printed in *Barbadian*, February 25, 1824.

[32]Carrington to Horton, July 10, 1825, CO 28/96.

[33]Thome and Kimball, *Emancipation in the West Indies*, p. 79; see also "Notes on Slavery," p. 10.

[34]Waller, *Voyage in the West Indies*, p. 95.

ist missionary reported that he "once knew a young lady to say she wished not to go to heaven if people of colour are there."[35]

However, as in other New World slave societies, sexual relationships between white males and freedwomen (and slaves) were exempt from the system that socially separated members of the two groups. Waller discovered that white creole males "cohabit with people of colour at a very early age"; creole females, he added, "have been accustomed to witness incontinency in almost all their acquaintence[s] of the other sex, and frequently in their fathers and brothers, who openly keep their mulatto mistresses."[36] Freedwomen "from the highest as well as the lowest families" participated in the system of concubinage.[37] "I was told," a temporary resident in 1814 reported, "that many colored parents educated their female children for this special purpose,"[38] and in 1806 a British army officer personally knew "a free mulatto woman who . . . has three daughters considered beauties who she, for a round sum, trafficks away to Europeans as housekeepers; or, as she chooses to call it, by marrying them off for a certain time."[39] Years later, Thome and Kimball learned that "in many cases" young freedwomen "who have been sent to England to receive education, have, after accomplishing themselves in all the graces of womanhood, returned to the island to become the concubines of white men. . . . Colored ladies have been taught to believe that it was more honorable, and quite as virtuous, to be the kept mistresses of *white gentlemen*, than the lawfully wedded wives of *colored men*."[40] Freedwomen who became involved in these sexual relationships "were actually proud of their position in society, and considered themselves as many degrees above those who were obliged to labor."[41]

There is no doubt that white creole males, who were not particularly noted for either their premarital chastity or their postmarital fidelity, were active participants in the system of sexual liaisons with freedwomen (and slaves), despite the large number of white females in the island's population (see Table 4). One cannot discount, however, the importance of foreign-born whites, who also sought out nonwhite women for the domestic and sexual services they could provide. "Young merchants and others who

[35]Nelson to Wesleyan Missionary Society, January 12, 1822, Box 1821–22, no. 205, MMSA.

[36]Waller, *Voyage in the West Indies*, pp. 19, 20. See also Joseph D. Husbands, *An Answer to the Charge of Immorality against the Inhabitants of Barbadoes* (Cooperstown, N.Y., 1831), p. 8 and *passim*; Minutes of the House of Assembly, March 15, 1744, BDA; and Dickson, *Letters on Slavery*, pp. 92–93.

[37]Thome and Kimball, *Emancipation in the West Indies*, p. 76.

[38][Browne], *Yarn of a Yankee Privateer*, p. 104.

[39][Major Richard A. Wyvill], "Memoirs of an Old Officer," [1814], p. 383, Manuscript Division, Library of Congress, Washington, D.C.

[40]Thome and Kimball, *Emancipation in the West Indies*, p. 76, italics in the original.

[41][Browne], *Yarn of a Yankee Privateer*, p. 104; see also Husbands, *Answer*, p. 18.

were unmarried, on first going to the island, regularly engaged colored females to live with them as housekeepers and mistresses, and it was not unusual for a man to have more than one";[42] by the late eighteenth century, British military officers and enlisted men who were stationed in Barbados, as well as sailors whose ships stopped at the island, also were important elements in the system of interracial sexual relationships.

The social conventions of Barbados neither condemned nor inhibited these sexual relationships, and, for whatever reasons white creole and noncreole males encouraged concubinage and white females condoned or were indifferent to it,[43] freedwomen evidently perceived it as a device for social mobility and material security. Just as the slave mistress of a white man could sometimes achieve freedom for herself and her children, and acquire material rewards or removal from the more onerous aspects of slavery, such as field labor, so a freedwoman could materially benefit from a sexual alliance with a white man. He could provide her with decent clothes, a house and furnishings, and other goods and property such as land, a horse and carriage, and even slaves. She might also benefit from his will, and her children, who might have been his children as well, could obtain advantages such as an education on the island or abroad, or their manumissions if they were still enslaved. If the freedwoman's white sexual partner was particularly wealthy and well placed in the social hierarchy, she might achieve some degree of permanency and stability in her material security, or derive sufficient advantages from the relationship to permit her material independence after the relationship was terminated. Her sexual partner could even protect her from some of the more humiliating experiences to which her status exposed her; for example, if her freedom was challenged, he could testify on her behalf in legal proceedings.

In sum, the slave society compelled freedwomen to assume social and economic roles that were governed by the restrictions imposed on their racial ancestry. For freedwomen who wanted material advantages and security, but who at the same time desired an escape from the more menial economic and occupational pursuits to which they were confined, sexual liaisons with white men were a major device through which this escape could be sought. With the abolition of slavery, there is evidence that freedwomen increasingly rejected their roles as the concubines of white men;[44] during the slave period, however, the approval that freedwomen seem to have received from their peers when such sexual liaisons

[42]Thome and Kimball, *Emancipation in the West Indies*, p. 79; see also Waller, *Voyage in the West Indies*, pp. 20–21.

[43]Waller suggested that white women were indifferent toward the system of concubinage because they essentially regarded nonwhite women as a "distinct species" and not subject to the same standards of evaluation as themselves; "it would excite," he remarked, "much more surprise in a Creole lady, that a man should be without one of these mistresses, than that he should have one" (*Voyage in the West Indies*, p. 20).

[44]Thome and Kimball, *Emancipation in the West Indies*, p. 79.

were achieved in effect acknowledged the success of persons who were able to maximize their self-interests by strategically locating themselves in the social system.

Although interracial sexual relationships, especially those which were more than ephemeral and involved cohabitation, could reach levels of genuine shared affection, these relationships remained fundamentally relationships between individuals from superordinate and subordinate groups, and could not elevate the freedwoman to a position of social equality with whites. "Let their connexions be what they may," Barbadian-born Joseph Husbands wrote, "they are never permitted to be the associates of the white females of Barbadoes," and, regardless of the emotional intensity or temporal duration of the relationship, "a matrimonial contract between a white man and a coloured female is never dreamt of by either."[45] There is one known case of a state-recognized church marriage between black and white, but this took place in the seventeenth century and was considered highly unusual for the period; all indications are that in later years concubinage did not result in such marriages, as it occasionally did in Jamaica.[46] In Barbados these marriages were not prevented by law, as was the case in most of the American South,[47] but in Barbados, where the line between freedman and white was more rigidly drawn than in Jamaica, legal prohibitions against marriage were unnecessary; the force of social convention was sufficient to maintain the essential distinctions between free groups and to prevent the social relationships which symbolically and in fact might have challenged these distinctions.

FREEDMEN AND SLAVES

The social distance between whites and freedmen ultimately derived from the racism of whites and their refusal and reluctance to grant freedmen full freedom and equality of opportunity. There was, however, a social gap—of a different, more ambiguous, and not as rigid kind—between freedmen and slaves. Whatever social and psychological factors operated to support "that jealousy which seems naturally to exist between the free

[45]Husbands, *Answer*, p. 18.

[46]From a careful search of the seventeenth-century parish register of Saint Michael, Richard S. Dunn concluded that "the most intriguing early entry . . . is a marriage celebrated on December 4, 1685, between 'Peter Perkins, a negro, and Jane Long, a white woman' " (*Sugar and Slaves: The Rise of the Planter Class in the English West Indies, 1624–1713* [Chapel Hill: The University of North Carolina Press, 1972], pp. 255–56). Dunn emphasizes the uniqueness of this event, and there is presently no evidence that marriages of this kind occurred in later periods. Although this study could not accomplish it, an intensive and systematic search of surviving parish registers in the Barbados Department of Archives would permit a more definitive statement. On interracial marriages in Jamaica, see Brathwaite, *Creole Society*, pp. 188–89.

[47]Eugene Genovese, "The Slave States of North America," in *Neither Slave Nor Free*, ed. Cohen and Greene, p. 262.

coloured people and the slaves,"[48] freedmen often emphasized their "higher rank in society than the slaves"[49] by attempting to maintain this gap. Although this gap could not be as easily preserved as the distance between freedmen and whites, interest in maintaining it was reflected in the freedman's concern with stressing the sociolegal differences between himself and the slave. That is, for many freedmen the process of maximizing their free status involved not only direct efforts to remove the disabilities associated with Negroid ancestry, but also the complementary process of distinguishing their status from that of the slaves.

The concern with distinguishing themselves from the slaves is reflected in the freedmen's various efforts to alter their legal status, wherein they consistently placed highest priority on the right of legal testimony. The 1721 law which prohibited anyone of Negroid ancestry from testifying in proceedings involving whites eliminated a civil right which freedmen had theoretically enjoyed up to that time, and thus reduced their free status. This law still allowed the testimony of freedmen against slaves, but one passed in 1739 further reduced the freedman's status by explicitly permitting slave testimony against him. From the freedman's perspective, this change again reinforced his inferior position in the social order and placed him on a comparable footing with the slave. Furthermore, by prohibiting the freedman's testimony against whites, the legal code thrust him more forcefully into the position of the slave, for, as in the case of the slave, it was very difficult to avail himself of legal redress and protection against those very abuses of power to which his subordinate social position and racial ancestry already exposed him. Lacking the privilege of legal testimony, freedmen wrote in 1811, "manifestly tends to brand their condition with infamy and contempt,"[50] epithets which they felt were applicable to slavery, not freedom. The right to testify assumed greater importance as freedmen were subjected to physical assaults by lower-class whites and as they expanded their participation in commercial activities and increased their acquisition of wealth and property. This right was necessary, however, for reasons other than personal security and the protection of property and economic interests; it was also vital to the definition of freedom, and consequently to the distinction between free and slave statuses.

With each real or threatened restriction to their freedom, freedmen saw themselves pushed into the position of the slave, a process which they viewed with acute sensitivity and alarm. In the late eighteenth century, for example, when they complained of their lack of protection in the law, they emphasized "if a white man may murder a Free Coloured Man, and escape

---

[48] Minutes of the Barbados Council, November 1, 1803, Lucas MSS.
[49] Dickson, *Letters on Slavery*, p. 174.
[50] "The Memorial of the Free People of Colour," October 7, 1811, CO 28/80.

the punishment of such laws, then we have no security for our lives, and we are in a much worse condition than our slaves";[51] when threatened with a loss of property rights in the early nineteenth century, they anxiously wrote that, if this threat were to materialize into law, "as well might we be reduced to a state of slavery for the greatest blessing attending upon freedom is the acquirement and enjoyment of property, and without that liberty is but an empty name."[52] As a general rule, then, to the extent that freedmen were compelled to share the restrictions of the slave, they saw their free status diminished; and, conversely, as they were able to obtain privileges withheld from slaves and reserved for whites, their free status was maximized. It can be suggested that it was often as vital to their practical interests and self-image for freedmen to emphasize the social, cultural, and legal attributes by which they differed from slaves as it was to stress the attributes they shared with whites.

As "free subjects," the right to own and bequeath property, including slaves, was an important attribute which freedmen shared with whites, and one which affected their perspectives on slavery and their relationship to slaves. An indeterminable number and proportion of freedmen's slaves were kinsmen, mates, or spouses, whom they intended to manumit, but many of the slaves that freedmen owned did not fall into these categories. In general the evidence points to the conclusion that many freedmen regarded slaves as a legitimate and desirable form of property and had a significant ideological commitment to the principle of slaveownership. Perhaps the strongest expression of this commitment was made in 1803, when "upwards of three hundred" freedmen protested legislative threats to their rights of slaveownership and bequeathal: "Many of our children who are now grown almost to the years of maturity have from their earliest infancy been accustomed to be attended by slaves; if this bill should pass into law, when we are no more, these children cannot possess a single slave. What will then be the meaning of their condition? *Surely death would be preferable to such a situation.*"[53] As the years progressed, and more and more manumitted slaves joined the ranks of the freedmen, it is hard to believe that such strong sentiments could have typified the freedman community as a whole. Nevertheless, as Thome and Kimball reported, despite "many honorable exceptions," freedmen lacked a "fellow feeling with the slave"; "until lately" they "have been far in the back ground in the cause of abolition, and even now [1837], the majority of them are either indifferent, or actually hostile to emancipation."[54] As their wealth

[51]"The Humble Memorial and Remonstrance of the Free Coloured People . . . ," October 14, 1799, Minutes of the Barbados Council, October 15, 1799, Lucas MSS.

[52]"The Humble Petition of the Free Coloured People . . . ," entered into the Minutes of the Barbados Council, November 1, 1803, *ibid.*

[53]*Ibid.*, italics added.

[54]Thome and Kimball, *Emancipation in the West Indies*, p. 76.

and property, including slaves, increased, and as they became more successful in the economic system, more freedmen appear to have perceived
that they had materially benefited from the established order; since an
intrinsic feature of the established order was slavery, the maintenance of
which slaveholders generally regarded as vital to the social and economic
well-being of the colony, by challenging the slave system many freedmen
apparently felt that they would, in effect, have been challenging their own
self-interests. In any event, despite the involvement of a handful of freedmen in the 1816 slave revolt, there is no evidence of a widespread desire
for such fundamental changes in the social order as would have been involved in the ending of slavery.

The apparent conservatism of freedmen on the issue of slavery, however, went beyond what they probably defined as their economic and material self-interests; it also involved wider political considerations in their
struggle for civil rights. In 1823, for example, some of the more conservative elements in the freedman community who signed the Belgrave address
publicly aligned themselves with the plantocracy by criticizing the British
emancipation movement for meddling in colonial affairs and by defending
the proposition that the condition and treatment of slaves had significantly
improved over that of earlier years. Although some freedmen felt the latter
to be an exaggerated assessment, the majority dissenting view held that
the Belgrave address should not have taken an explicit position in the
emancipation controversy and that freedmen in general were well advised
to avoid public involvement in political issues relating to slavery. That is,
although there was a general consensus on the legitimacy of trying to remove legal disabilities against them, freedmen were divided in opinion on
the best strategy for achieving their goals. Because they were concerned
with maximizing their status, and because this maximization called for the
attainment of rights and privileges available to and controlled by whites,
freedmen would have been risking total alienation from the plantocracy
had they attacked the slave issue. Some freedmen, such as the Belgrave
group, obviously felt that they had a better chance for extension of their
civil rights by publicly approving the plantocracy's stance (and, indeed,
they may have genuinely agreed with this position). Others, however, including those who had misgivings about slavery, focused on the liberalizing changes being sought as the emancipation movement in Britain increased its influence on colonial policy, and saw their interests best served
by maintaining "strict neutrality"; they emphasized their loyalty to the
Crown and "the interests of our country," but by taking no public position
they believed they risked neither offending nor supporting the plantocracy
or its British critics.[55]

[55]See pp. 92–97.

With rare exceptions, then, freedmen did not align themselves with the slaves politically, and in general they were publicly silent or negative on the subject of slave emancipation. This stance appears to have been related to various factors (though individuals probably placed differing emphasis on each) ranging from genuine antipathy and hostility to slaves, plus a vested interest in slaveownership, to political vulnerability and strategies for attaining civil rights. However, the relationship between freedmen and slaves involved more dimensions than those which derived from property-ownership or sociopolitical considerations relating to status maximization; yet, limited direct evidence makes it difficult to explore in detail and with assurance what must have been a complex and especially ambivalent relationship for many freedmen.

The line between freedmen and slaves was not as rigidly and clearly drawn as that between freedmen and whites, and it was a social fact that "the slave of today might possibly become the free coloured man of tomorrow."[56] Moreover, the social cleavage between freedman and slave was bridged by a series of cross-cutting social and psychological ties which *may* have mitigated some of the more divisive factors between the two groups.

There was, wrote a House of Assembly committee, a "nearer approximation" between freedmen and slaves than between slaves and whites, "arising frequently from original connection or previous acquaintance."[57] Many freedmen owed their free status to manumission rather than to birth. One might assume, especially in the case of adults, that the psychological and social break with slave status could not have been made easily, and that the social ties formed in the slave community could not have been broken readily—or perhaps even desired in a number of cases. Emancipated slaves retained friends in their former peer group, and a consequential number of freedmen had relatives, including parents and children, in slavery; there were also many freedmen whose only slaves were their own kinsmen and mates. Sexual contacts between freedmen and slaves appear to have been common, and an indeterminable number of liaisons involved cohabitation and the maintenance of a domestic unit or household; furthermore, during the later years of the slave period, state-recognized church marriages occasionally took place between members of the two groups.[58] Whether they owned their kinsmen or mates, or whether these slaves were owned by others, freedmen attempted to manumit persons with whom they were in relationships of close sentimentality. The efforts to manumit these

[56]Vaughan, "Samuel Prescod," p. 57.
[57]*Report from a Select Committee*, p. 11.
[58]See, for example, *PP*, 1831–32, vol. 47, rept. 660; and replies to query 15, "Returns to Questions Addressed to the Clergy of . . . Barbados . . . up to December 31, 1828," in Incorporated Society for the Conversion and Religious Instruction and Education of the Negro Slaves in the British West India Islands, *Annual Report, 1828* (London, 1829), app.

persons reflect one of the stronger ties that existed between the freed and slave communities, and it can be conjectured that the emotional bond between freedmen and their enslaved mates, spouses, and kinsmen must have transcended in some way the differences resulting from the status groups to which they belonged.

Freedmen and slaves interacted on a common basis in the internal marketing system, often as trading partners; there was not only illicit trade in goods which slaves stole from their masters' properties, but freedman hawkers were often dependent on slave producers for the goods they sold. There is some evidence that freedmen, most probably recently emancipated slaves, participated in various areas of slave social life, such as weekend dances, the magico-religious system of Obeah, funerals, and in various other leisure-time activities such as gambling and drinking. Literate freedmen sometimes gathered with slaves to read newspapers to them and to discuss political and social events of common interest. The children of poor freedmen and slaves attended the same public schools, and members of both groups attended Anglican and Methodist churches; in the latter church and in the schools there is no indication that relationships were marked by intergroup conflicts or that freedmen refused to participate in these institutions because of the presence of slaves. By the 1820s, hundreds of freedmen and slaves attended services together in the Methodist church; no formal distinctions were maintained among the groups during services, and attendance and participation of both groups increased over the years.

In many cases it may well have been, as Goveia has written of the Leewards, that, "instead of strengthening the relationship between the free people of colour and the Negro slaves, their common origin served only to embitter it."[59] Yet, both freedman and slave groups included "colored" as well as black members, and the racial ties between freedmen, as a group, and slaves were greater than those between freedmen and whites. By virtue of their racial ancestry, all freedmen could not have adhered to the type of racist ideology by which whites viewed nonwhites in general, regardless of their phenotypic characteristics. Furthermore, whatever their phenotypic characteristics, most freedmen could neither hide nor deny the Negroid ancestry they shared with slaves; in an island society as small as Barbados, passing for white would have been extremely difficult. Their racial ancestry made freedmen less free, but it also involved them in a common plight with slaves; both groups shared, to varying degrees, a degraded status that was defined, controlled, and perpetuated by a white group to which neither freedmen nor slaves could gain access. This crucial

---

[59]Goveia, *Slave Society*, p. 223. Freedmen "have had prejudices against the Negroes," wrote Thome and Kimball, "no less bitter than those which the whites have exercised toward them" (*Emancipation in the West Indies*, p. 76).

social fact may help to explain the ambivalence, as well as hostility, that many freedmen apparently felt for slaves, but it is hard to believe that in a number of cases it did not function to reduce the freedman's antipathy and make him sympathetically question his position vis-à-vis the slave group.

In the controversy surrounding the 1823 Belgrave address, some of the freedmen involved in the counteraddress explicitly denied an assertion of the Belgrave group that the treatment of slaves had improved over the years. Although this was not a major point of contention within the dissident group, the fact that the issue of slave treatment was raised at all— during a very tense period in the island's history—suggests that some freedmen were concerned about the slave issue and were critical of those who categorically defended the slave system. This concern was incidental to the freedmen's drive for civil rights and, of course, did not materialize into joint action with the slaves, but obviously some persons within the freedman community—perhaps the "many honorable exceptions" referred to by Thome and Kimball—were not "indifferent" or "hostile" to the slaves and the issue of their emancipation.[60]

The fact that the freedmen of Barbados, like those in other New World slave societies, generally "resisted opportunities to form a common racial front with the slaves"[61] does not necessarily mean that, as a group, freedmen perceived no commonality with slaves. Moreover, the potential for this commonality was recognized by the plantocracy during, for example, deliberations over a bill concerning freedmen's property rights ("if we reduce the free coloured people to a level with the slaves," a member of the Council proclaimed, "they must unite with them, and will take every occasion of promoting and encouraging a revolt"[62]), and in the effect the 1816 slave revolt had on passage of the first law ameliorating the freedman's status. The fact that this law, granting the right of testimony, was formally justified as a reward to freedmen for their "greatest attachment and fidelity to the white inhabitants"[63] only underscored and reflected white concern with the possibility of a political alliance between freedmen and slaves—a political alliance which was considered probable during the first few decades of the nineteenth century and which, in fact, had been realized (albeit on a minor scale) when a few freedmen were involved in planning and encouraging the revolt.

Although the relationship between freedmen and slaves was often ambiguous and appears to have been frequently marked by tension and conflict, the cross-cutting ties between them, the fact that membership in the

[60]Thome and Kimball, *Emancipation in the West Indies*, p. 76.

[61]Cohen and Greene, "Introduction," in *Neither Slave Nor Free*, ed. Cohen and Greene, p. 15.

[62]Minutes of the Barbados Council, November 1, 1803, Lucas MSS.

[63]"An Act Allowing the Testimony of Free Negroes and Free People of Colour To Be Taken in All Cases," February 5, 1817, copy in CO 28/86.

freedman group was not closed and that both groups experienced a broadly similar oppression at the hands of white society, may have had some positive influence on their intergroup relations. Freedmen as a group wanted their free status maximized and strengthened, and for many this involved drawing a line between themselves and the slaves; yet, the emotional, social, and racial bonds to the slave group must have exerted counterpressures which made it difficult for many freedmen to resolve with clarity and certainty their relationship to the slaves and to remain totally indifferent to the issue of slavery. The evidence suggests that the freedman group was not uniform in its attitudes and behavior toward slaves. It appears that freedmen who were psychologically and socially closest to the slaves had been slaves until their adult years (and had been fairly recently manumitted) and/or recognized and maintained close kinship ties with the slave community. It is difficult, however, to detail the ways in which the relationship between freed and slave groups varied with the sociocultural characteristics of individual freedmen, or how a freedman's class position correlated with or conditioned specific attitudes and behavior toward the slave. The freedman group was not homogeneous, and its heterogeneity was reflected not only in the nature of its links to the slave group but as well in intragroup relations and in the way in which its community was organized.

THE FREEDMAN COMMUNITY: STRATIFICATION AND CULTURE

In the early nineteenth century, Waller observed that "a great diversity prevails" among Barbadian freedmen, and he implicitly drew attention to a variety of sociocultural and economic attributes by which freedmen were distinguished from one another.[64] The plantocracy also saw and acknowledged for various purposes internal differences in the freedman community. Its perception was reflected in the choice of freedmen—considered among "the most respectable of that class"—to testify before a committee of the Assembly which investigated the 1816 slave revolt,[65] and in the first of the laws which gave freedmen the right of legal testimony, a law which qualified those who were freeborn (or who had *not* been recently manumitted) and baptized. This group included the "well established members" of the freedman community. In considering his vote on this bill, one member of the Assembly made a clear distinction between "the enlightened class of the free people of colour" and the "vulgar class"; he expressed his willingness to extend the right of testimony to the former, "who ought to

---

[64] Waller, *Voyage in the West Indies*, p. 95.
[65] *Report from a Select Committee*, pp. 38–41.

know the obligations of an oath," but not to the latter.[66] Arguing for the extension of legal-political (but not social) equality to freedmen, Orderson, a white creole, distinguished between "free-born subjects," who, in his estimation, merited such equality with whites, and "emancipated slaves," who might ultimately merit it, but only after a period of years had elapsed since their manumission.[67] Although, in making his primary distinction, Orderson focused on the mode of acquiring free status each mode implied an associated set of behavioral attributes and values. "Free-born subjects," he noted, have "advantages of early education, progressive habits of order and moral conduct, a just appreciation of the necessary restraints on the liberty of the subject, and a temperate exercise of the rights they derive from the laws.[68] The "emancipated slaves," however, and especially the "more recently manumitted," are

> a heterogeneous mass, daily augmenting, and in general thrown upon the community without any of those restraints which moral habits, religious instruction, or ameliorated manners might give as security for their peaceful and orderly behaviour. . . . [They possess] all the disorderly passions incident to ignorance and sturdy insolence, place no value upon their newly-acquired power . . . their minds being inflated with strange ideas of importance, too often become irritable and restless, until they provoke a collision with some of the white inhabitants, or the more respectable of their own class.[69]

Orderson further emphasized that "a feeling corresponding with this distinction has ever prevailed among the more respectable classes of the Free people, who have invariably kept themselves aloof from those whose less moral conduct place[s] them in a lower estimation of society."[70]

Freedmen were differentiated by characteristics such as free or slave birth, phenotype, wealth and property, occupation, education and literacy, baptism and church membership; there were also distinctions between urban and rural dwellers and differences in general life style and values. A number of these factors were operative in stratifying the freedman community, and those relating to economic position, such as wealth and property, were especially important in producing class distinctions within it. It is apparent that wealth, education, "gentlemanly habits," and a Euro-creole life style were important for high rank and prestige, and that freedmen employed a combination of these variables in defining the elite of

[66] Journal of the Assembly of Barbados, October 8, 1817, CO 31/47.
[67] I. W. [J. W.] Orderson, *Spare Minutes at the Pier; or, a Short Discussion of the Equality of Rights That May Be Granted to the Free Coloured Inhabitants of This Island* (Barbados, 1831), *passim.*
[68] *Ibid.,* pp. 5–6.
[69] *Ibid.,* p. 9.
[70] *Ibid.,* p. 12.

their community. Freedmen undoubtedly used additional criteria to draw distinctions among themselves, and it may have been that different socio-economic strata placed differing emphasis upon the same variables in forming social alliances. Although class distinctions were recognized by both whites and freedmen, the nature of the evidence makes it difficult to discuss in detail the social strata, their relative sociocultural distinctiveness, and the meaning that the differences between strata had for the freedmen themselves.

Factors associated with economic position and assimilation to Euro-creole culture were clearly of importance in the freedman's ranking system, but the role played by phenotype and free birth is more speculative. Whites and freedmen perceived "colored" and black as the two major phenotypic groupings among freedmen, but the evidence does not suggest that membership in one group or the other was the basis for social or political alliances, that these phenotypic differences produced social cleavages, or that phenotype, in and of itself, offered particular advantages for leadership positions in the freedman community. Both black and "colored" freedmen jointly participated in the petition campaigns and civil rights struggle, and "colored" freedmen, for example, did not request rights from which their black peers would be excluded or direct their appeals along phenotypic lines; in addition, there is concrete evidence that political and social leadership derived from both phenotypic groups. Although "colored" persons apparently predominated in leadership positions and in the composition of the freedman elite, it is not certain whether this was a consequence of their numerical superiority in the freedman population as a whole or a result of phenotypic criteria employed by freedmen in according rank and prestige. "Colored" males tended to be wealthier than black ones, and class position in general implied a set of attributes, such as education and a Euro-creole life style, to which importance was attached; that is, the phenotype of a person may have counted less in the way in which freedmen viewed themselves than other sociocultural and economic attributes that were often, but not necessarily and inevitably, associated with this phenotype.

In general it might be conjectured that, if white society had distributed sociolegal privileges in terms of phenotypic distinctions, freedmen would have responded by utilizing phenotype as a significant criterion in ranking themselves. Yet, all freedmen were relegated to the same position of subordinacy; Caucasoid characteristics brought no selective advantage in terms of legal rights or the ultimate possibility of being defined as white. This discussion does not mean to imply that phenotype was irrelevant to freedmen or that they attached no aesthetic or psychological value to Caucasoid characteristics; indeed, such characteristics may have had more social relevance than is indicated by the available sources. Caucasoid characteristics apparently facilitated sexual liaisons with whites, figured in the manumission process, and may have affected entrée into certain occupational categories or economic pursuits; "advantages" such as these were probably reflected in the freedman's value system and perception of phenotypic differences. In any event, when whites alluded to or defined the significant differences among freedmen, they drew attention to behavior, values, and attitudes, as summed up in the distinction between the "vulgar class" and the "enlightened class" or "respectable classes," and there is no strong indication that either they or freedmen explicitly and consistently linked these attributes to particular phenotypic categories.

Recently emancipated slaves were often included in the "vulgar class" of freedmen, but this class included freeborn persons as well. Although slave birth or generational distance from slavery may have had some significance in the way in which freedmen socially aligned and ranked themselves, slave birth per se does not appear to have attached a permanent stigma. It did not categorically prevent freedmen from achieving economic success, valued sociocultural attributes (such as baptism or education), or a general life style associated with high rank. Thomas Harris, London Bourne, and Joseph Thorne, for example, were prominent members of the freedman community during Thome and Kimball's visit in 1837, and all three were born slaves.[71] What seems to have been of major importance in drawing distinctions between recently emancipated slaves, in particular, and others was not slave birth per se, but rather the degree of assimilation to Euro-creole culture and to the life style and value system involved in this culture; participation in and assimilation to Euro-creole culture was no more determined by, or inevitably associated with, slave birth than it was with phenotypic characteristics.

During the pre-emancipation decades of the nineteenth century, the middle and upper strata of freedmen were largely composed of "colored" persons, many of whom were probably freeborn, owned property, such as land, houses, and slaves, and who by island standards were considered educated. Among them were an occasional plantation-owner and some wealthy merchants, but most persons in these strata were shopkeepers or workers in the skilled trades; they lived in Bridgetown, were baptized and were members of the Anglican church, and shared a Euro-creole life style. The upper stratum, in particular, consciously emphasized its differences from recently emancipated slaves and lower-class freedmen in general, and was sensitive to maintaining class distinctions. Although the upper stratum was numerically small (some indication of its size is suggested by the fact that even in 1833 only 75 males—about 7 percent of the total electorate—were able to meet the property qualifications for enfranchise-

---

[71]Thome and Kimball, *Emancipation in the West Indies*, pp. 72–75.

ment), it was joined with a larger middle stratum to form the "respectable classes" (defined by wider sociocultural criteria), which were most involved in the struggle for civil rights.

Class differences were apparent by the early nineteenth century, and throughout the remainder of the slave period they appear to have produced some social cleavages within the freedman community. These cleavages, however, were partially transcended and mitigated by the development of a relatively broadly based group consciousness. The roots of this common consciousness were a shared oppression and a commitment to reducing or eliminating the legal and social disabilities associated with Negroid ancestry. Freedmen did not challenge the notion of a class society, nor did they deny that the upper stratum should enjoy privileges commensurate with its rank. When, for example, freedmen appealed for parity with whites, they did not assume they were all legitimately entitled to vote, achieve elective office, or hold civil-administrative positions of "honor and profit"—neither enfranchisement nor prestigious positions were available to whites of all socioeconomic levels. It was important, however, that qualified individuals among them gain access to positions in the social order reserved for whites of comparable qualifications. When freedmen of wealth, education, and "gentlemanly habits" could achieve positions traditionally reserved for whites, their "exaltation . . . must indirectly tend to the exaltation of our whole body."[72] If their elite could break through the racial barriers to mobility, race as a determinant of social position would be weakened; this sentiment cross-cut class differences and helped to produce a measure of political unity in the freedman community. Freedmen accepted the concept of a hierarchically organized society if distinctions among all freemen were based on the set of social and economic criteria which whites employed in drawing distinctions among themselves.

Urban males of the middle and upper strata were the most visible in the petition campaigns and civil rights struggle and were the most active in the formal groupings organized within the freedman community. However, many adults—especially, but not solely, in the impoverished lower classes—never signed a petition or participated only minimally, if at all, in the civil rights struggle. Although it is assumed that such persons shared many of the broader aspirations for justice and the elimination of discrimination of those who were most involved in the civil rights movement, little can be said about them; their presence must be kept in mind, however, when generalizing about the freedman community and its internal organization.

Freedmen of the lower classes were socially distinguishable from those in the "respectable classes" in a manner that was analagous to the divi-

---

[72]"The Humble Loyal Address of His Majesty's Free Coloured and Free Black Subjects . . . ," May 6, 1833, printed in *Barbadian*, May 15, 1833.

sions that existed in the white community, and to some extent they participated in the social and cultural life of the slaves. The evidence for social
groupings and life style among freedmen, however, largely pertains to
those from the middle-to-upper strata. This evidence is limited in detail,
but it is clear that the freedman community developed a set of institutional
arrangements which met its own needs and in which its members participated on a relatively exclusive basis. That is, despite the freedmen's varying degrees of participation in white-controlled national institutions, the
social distance from whites, enforced by racism and discrimination, resulted in a variety of groupings and organized activities which often paralleled those of white society.

By the beginning of the nineteenth century, freedmen had "their balls,
routs, and assemblies [and] they have established places of public rendezvous for cock-fighting and other species of gaming."[73] The "quality balls,"
or "dignity balls," sponsored by tavern proprietresses and other freedwomen, "to which only white men were admitted," may have been of one
type.[74] There is some indication, however, that similar dances were also
organized solely for the freedman community. A visitor in 1831 reported
the participation of both freedmen and freedwomen and did not suggest
the presence of white males: "The 'quality balls' of the coloured people are
well worth visiting. The brown beaux and belles are gaily dressed—kid
gloves, silk stockings, 'tight continuations,' and quizzing glasses, are seen
on the gentlemen; whilst the ladies sport feathers, silks, book-muslin,
tinsel turbans, bustles, and satin slippers."[75] At any rate, social events
which did not imply ultimate sexual relationships between the races reflected the racial divisions of Barbadian society, and exclusive dances of
one kind or another formed an aspect of the social life of the freedman
community, just as they did in white society.[76]

Organizations such as the "Thornites" and the "Bible Society" met
religious and social needs which could not be fulfilled within white-dom-
inated institutions.[77] As in the white community, freedmen held public
meetings which served as forums for expressing grievances and drafting
petitions and addresses to legislative bodies. They also formed committees
and elected leaders to represent their interests and to conduct their public

[73][John Poyer], *A Letter Addressed to His Excellency . . . Francis Lord Seaforth, by a
Barbadian* (Bridgetown, 1801), p. 23.

[74][Browne], *Yarn of a Yankee Privateer*, p. 104.

[75]Captain J. E. Alexander, *Transatlantic Sketches, Comprising Visits to the Most Interesting Scenes in North and South America and the West Indies*, 2 vols. (London, 1833),
1: 159.

[76]For a characterization of the balls and dances given by whites in the late eighteenth
century, see J. W. [I. W.] Orderson's novel *Creoleana: Or, Social and Domestic Scenes and
Incidents in Barbados in Days of Yore* (London, 1842), pp. 60–63.

[77]See pp. 159–60.

meetings; as was apparent in the controversy surrounding the 1823 Belgrave address, freedmen attached considerable importance to the concept of elected leadership.[78]

Freedmen also organized groups for the support of their own poor. They raised funds for the construction and maintenance of the Colonial Charity School and served on its governing committee, and by 1820 a small group had formed the "Samaritan Charitable Society," which had its own meeting hall in Bridgetown.[79] In 1827 some of "the more opulent" freedmen organized the "Society for the Education of the Coloured Poor, and Other Charitable Relief," which, among other activities, devoted itself to feeding, providing medical care for, and burying the freedmen indigent. The Society was largely supported by annual subscriptions raised from within the freedman community, although this income was later supplemented by an annual grant of £50 from the Saint Michael vestry. Since the parish provided no facilities for freedmen, as it did for whites, this grant was increased in 1831 to assist the Society in erecting "The Free Coloured Hospital," an asylum to house the "sick and diseased"; during the same year, the Society planned to construct an orphanage, if the necessary funds could be raised.[80]

In 1805, freedmen were "forming a company to act plays," with their first production scheduled to be "The Fair Penitent,"[81] a tragedy which had achieved success on the London stage in 1703, and whose popularity in England had endured throughout the eighteenth century.[82] Although some authorities reacted suspiciously to the formation of a theatrical group ("You can be no stranger to the mischief," Governor Seaforth wrote the chief magistrate, "that is cooked under such pretences"[83]), it is not known whether they frustrated the group's formation at this time. It is known, however, that by 1828 the amateur theatrical group, called The Lyceum, was functioning in Bridgetown and that Samuel Prescod was its manager.[84] Not only did freedmen participate in the casting, direction, and organization of productions, but they also sought and depended on support

[78]See pp. 93–94.

[79]"Address from the Samaritan Charitable Society to King George IV," March 20, 1820, CO 28/89.

[80]"Fourth Annual Report [1830] of the Society for the Education of the Coloured Poor, and for Other Charitable Relief," *Barbadian*, March 22, 1831; Minutes of the Saint Michael Vestry, March 25, 1827, March 25, 1830, and March 25, 1831, BDA.

[81]Seaforth to Oughterson, January 7, 1805, Seaforth Papers, 46/7/11, SRO. Theatrical groups in the white community appear to have had a longer history, but it was not until 1812 that a theater was erected in Bridgetown (Robert H. Schomburgk, *The History of Barbados* [London, 1848], pp. 250–51).

[82]Malcolm Goldstein, ed., *The Fair Penitent, by Nicholas Rowe* (Lincoln: University of Nebraska Press, 1969), pp. xiii–xvi.

[83]Seaforth to Oughterson, January 7, 1805, Seaforth Papers, 46/7/11.

[84]Vaughan, "Samuel Prescod," p. 57.

from their community to insure the success and continuation of the group's operations.[85]

In their social groupings and organized activities, freedmen, like whites, made clear distinctions between the roles of men and women. There were freedwomen whose standard of living and property holdings were comparable to those of many males, but males provided the leadership in community affairs, and women apparently were neither expected nor allowed to participate in activities that could be defined as political. Although women may have attended political meetings, there is no indication that they were active participants, and freedwomen's names are conspicuously absent from the group petitions submitted to legislative bodies and from the committees organized and elected to lead the civil rights struggle. Freedman charitable, religious, and social organizations were primarily male organizations, although in the later years of the slave period freedwomen of the upper strata occasionally formed societies of their own, such as the "Ladies Branch Association for the Education of the Female Children of the Coloured Poor,"[86] which paralleled the men's associations and which also found their analogues in the white community.

The cultural similarities between the middle-to-upper strata of freedmen and creole whites were apparent in a variety of areas of life (especially during the nineteenth century). There was, for example, a shared emphasis on baptism and membership in the Church of England, and private schooling, especially in Britain, was a valued goal. Both groups held highly positive views on British royalty and identified with the institutions of the "mother country." Whites and freedmen supported a class system which involved the maintenance of clear distinctions between the upper and lower classes. Children of both racial groups were "accustomed to be attended by slaves from their earliest infancy,"[87] and all age groups depended on slaves as domestic servants and to perform a wide variety of menial chores. "Gentlemanly habits" and property were fundamental criteria for social prestige, there was a shared ideological commitment to the concept of private property, patterns of property bequeathal were similar, and to some extent both groups acknowledged that high rank and class position involved responsibility in charitable activities. In addition to a wide variety of values and norms, the sources also convey the impression of many similarities in other aspects of cultural life, such as speech patterns, diet and food preferences, recreational habits, home-visiting patterns, dress fashions, and life style.[88]

[85]Notice in *Barbadian*, February 16, 1830.
[86]*Ibid.*, March 22, 1831.
[87]Minutes of the Barbados Council, November 1, 1803, Lucas MSS.
[88]See, for example, Thome and Kimball, *Emancipation in the West Indies*, pp. 72–76; Waller, *Voyage in the West Indies, passim*; [Wyvill], "Memoirs," p. 382; [Browne], *Yarn of a*

By the pre-emancipation decades of the nineteenth century the cultural attributes that the "respectable classes" of freedmen shared with whites formed part of a creole culture which, as Goveia has written of the Leewards, "was no more wholly European than the culture of the slaves was wholly African."[89] Visitors to Barbados often alluded to this Euro-creole culture when they described the island's white population. Sturge and Harvey, for example, found that Barbados contained "a numerous middle class, and a body of native resident proprietors, who have found it possible to forget that England is 'home;' and who glory in the title of 'Barbadians.' They possess a real nationality, with characteristics, neither English, Irish, nor Scotch."[90] Freedmen, who were a creole population *par excellence*, also possessed "a real nationality" which was distinctively Barbadian but at the same time heavily Europeanized in contrast to the Afro-creole culture of many of the island's slaves.[91] Not only did many freedmen aspire to the form and content of Euro-creole culture, *which was the culture of freemen*, but in actual fact the middle and upper socioeconomic strata participated in a value and normative system which in many crucial respects paralleled that of white creoles; furthermore, the cultural attributes shared by white creoles and freedmen seem to have correlated more with class position than with racial identity or status group membership.

Since leaders in the freedman community were members of the "respectable classes," the very nature of the civil rights struggle, including its organization, goals, and strategies, reflected the identification with Euro-creole values and norms. Freedmen were neither submissive nor rebellious, and through constitutional reform they peacefully sought the conventional rights and privileges associated with the status of "free subjects" in a colonial society. The sharing of, and identification with, a variety of socio-

---

Yankee Privateer, pp. 103–4, 107–12; Shrewsbury and Larcum to Wesleyan Missionary Society, March 28, 1820, Box 1817–20, no. 120, MMSA; and Joseph Boromé, ed., "William Bell and His Second Visit to Barbados, 1829–1830," *JBMHS*, 30 (1962): 23.

[89]Goveia, *Slave Society*, p. 248; see also Brathwaite, *Creole Society*, pp. xiii–xv, 296–305, and *passim*.

[90]Sturge and Harvey, *The West Indies in 1837*, pp. 152, 154–55. Allusions to, or descriptions of, creole cultural characteristics are given in a variety of sources. See, for example, [Browne], *Yarn of a Yankee Privateer*, pp. 107–12 and *passim*; Orderson, *Creoleana, passim*; Pinckard, *Notes on the West Indies*, 1: *passim*, 2: *passim*; Thome and Kimball, *Emancipation in the West Indies*, pp. 76–80; Waller, *Voyage in the West Indies*, pp. 1–28, 88–96; and [Wyvill], "Memoirs," *passim*. See also the accounts of travellers and temporary island residents during the late-eighteenth-century and pre-emancipation decades of the nineteenth listed in Jerome S. Handler, *A Guide to Source Materials for the Study of Barbados History, 1627–1834* (Carbondale: Southern Illinois University Press, 1971), *passim*.

[91]The terms Euro-creole and Afro-creole are taken from Brathwaite, *Creole Society*, pp. 296–305, 309. Aspects of the African and Afro-creole component of Barbadian slave culture are discussed in Jerome S. Handler and Charlotte Frisbie, "Aspects of Slave Life in Barbados: Music and Its Cultural Context," *Caribbean Studies*, 9 (1972): 5–46.

cultural attributes, values, and norms with whites, as well as an importance attached to differentiation from the slaves, characterized many freedmen, and these characteristics, combined with economic mobility and increased property holdings (including slaves), helped to account for the freedmen's essential social and political conservatism. Although they strove to eliminate their second-class citizenship, freedmen did so by attempting to moderate those aspects of the society which thwarted their desire for status maximization; they did not challenge the racially based slave system which had given rise to their subordinate status in the first place. Despite their reactions to the particulars of white racism, they adhered to an ideology of class privilege and private property and were not oriented toward a fundamental restructuring of the island's social system or its economic foundations; moreover, they accepted the premises of colonial authority and were interested in maintaining the links which bound the island to Great Britain.

Relative to earlier periods, the trend in the nineteenth century was a progressive one, and neither external forces nor insular conditions compelled freedmen to define their plight of subordinacy in terms of desperation. Although the struggle for civil rights was arduous and frustrating, after 1804, when efforts to curtail the freedmen's property rights were dropped, social change moved toward the removal of disabilities, not the addition of repressive legislation. With growing economic mobility and material gains, freedmen who were assimilated to Euro-creole culture increasingly rejected their subordinate social and legal status. They were given cause for optimism by changes that occurred in colonial policy as a result of the impact of the emancipation movement and the weakening economic and political influence of West Indian interests in the "mother country." The links with Great Britain had a significant effect on the later phases of the freedmen's struggle for civil rights and gave impetus to that struggle and its goals. Despite white resistance to slave emancipation and the extension of civil rights, freedmen derived both moral and practical support from the reform pressures in Britain. Their limited requests for protection under the law and the right of legal testimony, which had emerged in the early nineteenth century, ultimately evolved into demands for parity with their "white fellow-subjects," and by the end of the slave period many freedmen were not content with legal equality; they were also pressing for social privileges commensurate with class position and disassociated from racial ancestry.

If insular and external conditions and events had been different in the nineteenth century, and if legal and economic oppression against freedmen had intensified, perhaps they would have taken a more radical position and viewed rebellion, as well as political alliances with the slaves, as strategies for achieving desired changes. But the nature of political and economic conditions, as well as their ideological proclivities, did not force freedmen to question whether civil rights could be obtained by means other than legally constituted ones. Being a politically circumscribed minority which lacked the power to effectively challenge the dominant white group, freedmen depended on support from the colonial power, and colonialism, in effect, became a positive force in helping freedmen to achieve political equality; one can only speculate on how long it would have taken for freedmen to achieve civil rights and for slaves to be emancipated had these decisions rested entirely in the hands of local whites.[92] The strategies that freedmen employed in attempting to alter their group status reflected these realities of minority and colonial status, as well as the creole values and norms they shared with white society. Despite their efforts, however, and despite the benefits they derived as by-products of the movement for slave emancipation, by 1834 freedmen were still the victims of a social order in which racial ancestry was a crucial determinant of social position. Although they finally achieved legal parity with whites, the racism of white society continued to relegate them to a subordinate and often ambiguously defined status. As long as the slave society persisted, freedmen were neither slave nor truly free; they were, in the 1802 phraseology of Governor Seaforth, "an unappropriated people."[93]

[92]See Goveia, *Slave Society*, pp. 334–35.
[93]Seaforth to Hobart, June 6, 1802, Seaforth Papers, 46/7/7.

INDEX

THE JOHNS HOPKINS UNIVERSITY PRESS

This book was composed in Press Roman text and Melior display type by Jones Composition Company, Inc. from a design by Alan Tyson. It was printed on 60-lb. Sebago regular finish stock and bound in Fictionette natural finish cloth by Universal Lithographers, Inc.

Library of Congress Cataloging in Publication Data

Handler, Jerome S.
    The unappropriated people.

    Includes bibliographical references.
    1. Freedmen.   2. Slavery in Barbados.   I. Title.
HT1105.B3H35   301.44'93'0972981   73-18489
ISBN 0-8018-1565-7